Commerce on Early
American Waterways

D1528672

Commerce on Early American Waterways

The Transport of Goods by Arks, Rafts and Log Drives

EARL E. BROWN

McFarland & Company, Inc., Publishers
Jefferson, North Carolina, and London

Library of Congress Cataloguing-in-Publication Data

Brown, Earl E., 1932–
    Commerce on early American waterways : the transport of
goods by arks, rafts and log drives / Earl E. Brown.
       p.   cm.
    Includes bibliographical references and index.

    ISBN 978-0-7864-4742-8
    softcover : 50# alkaline paper ∞

    1. Waterways— United States— History —18th century.
    2. Waterways— United States— History —19th century.
    I. Title.
    HE627.B76   2010
    386'.1097309033 — dc22   2010006113

British Library cataloguing data are available

On the cover: Log driver's ark, 1898 (courtesy of the Clearfield
County Historical Society, Clearfield, Pennsylvania); background
©2010 Clipart.com

Manufactured in the United States of America

McFarland & Company, Inc., Publishers
  Box 611, Jefferson, North Carolina 28640
    www.mcfarlandpub.com

Table of Contents

Acknowledgments

After assembling this work, I feel more like an editor than an author, for many people contributed to what lies within. A great deal is owed to both George A. Scott, editor emeritus of the *Clearfield Progress* in Clearfield, Pennsylvania, and Professor Sam King at the Penn State Center in DuBois, Pennsylvania, for providing the basic research to start this project. I am grateful to Virginia Wright of the Painted Post Historical Society in New York. After a year of searching she found Schuyler S. Strong's eleven articles published in the *Bath Plaindealer*, from March to May of 1887, of his voyage down the Susquehanna in 1838. And of course to Mr. Schuyler S. Strong, *Esq.*, for writing his journal.

Thanks are also due to William Langdon, who took the time to write his diary for the year 1855, giving us a timetable of events in the life of a raftsman who felled the trees and ran two rafts to market; to Jim Campbell of the Snyder County Historical Society in Pennsylvania for finding Jacob G. Shively's *Navigation on Penns Creek* and for collecting all the information in 1963; and to O. Lynn Frank of Clearfield, Pennsylvania, for his knowledge of the West Branch of the Susquehanna River and the construction of rafts. He never failed to answer my questions.

I am also grateful to those who fostered my interest in this topic. My father, Homer E. Brown, first took me over to the river to see the last raft in 1938 as it tied up at Selinsgrove, Pennsylvania. My mother, Daisy Miller Brown, told me local history stories from the time I was young. My father-in-law, J. Bruce Meyer, and mother-in-law, Mary Stamm Meyer, nourished my interest in the West Branch of the Susquehanna River rafting and logging.

Gweneth and Warren Fox of the Clearfield Historical Society in Pennsylvania are owed thanks for carrying on George Scott's fine tradition of providing support to researchers. Finally, to my wife, Ruth Anne Meyer Brown, who served as my motivator, cheerleader and most importantly my editor, thank you very much.

Preface

Personnel working in dangerous or adventurous occupations are seldom recognized as doing anything extraordinary in their lives. They usually accept their jobs with tolerance and good humor. Only after industrial revolution improvements made their jobs safer, or obsolete, did authors and film makers pick up their tales and make them the leading characters of their stories. So it was with the jack-tars, the sailors of wind jamming sailing ships. It wasn't until authors like C. S. Forester came along with his Horatio Hornblower series that their profession was celebrated. Authors such as Louis L'Amour and hundreds of movie makers raised the common cowboy to a western icon.

The men, however, who ran rafts and arks or drove logs down colonial and early American rivers have all but been forgotten. At best, the watermen, arksmen, raftsmen and log drivers are only remembered on special occasions once a year at local festivals, and then most of the time only the role the local heroes played, not how their work fit into the overall process of making our nation great.

This book brings the hazardous occupations of watermen, arksmen, raftsmen, woodhicks (Allegheny and Appalachian Mountain lumberjacks) and log drivers to life. It presents the what, where, why, when and how of their careers.

Soon after the pioneers moved into the frontier, they began to produce more than they could consume, while at the same time the coastal communities outgrew their food and wood supply. How the early settlers manufactured spars, square timbers and boards from the abundant trees, and then transported them and their excess farm products to the coastal markets is the subject of this book. Forms of transportation are discussed in the order in which they evolved. The introduction to each chapter will specify the methods of transportation used, when it began and about when it ended, as well as the occupational specialty needed to perform the tasks.

Early pioneers used rivers and streams for transporting heavy goods (Chapter 1). In 1791 a fearless miller opened the Susquehanna Watershed to the Chesapeake Bay and the Baltimore market (Chapter 2). The Penns Creek is but one tributary of the Susquehanna River that prospered as a result of its access to the Baltimore market. Flour was the oil of its day, bringing money to all who could export it (Chapter 3). Ark and raft traffic increased from 1792 until the early 1800s (Chapter 4).

The vast primeval forest, which covered the Allegheny and Appalachian

1

Mountains in central and western Pennsylvania and lower New York State, provided spars for shipbuilding, and square timbers for building bridges, wharfs, large buildings and ship hulls. Port Deposit, Maryland, became the market for all lumber products.

New York watermen ran board rafts to market through many hazardous points (Chapters 5 and 6). A West Branch (Susquehanna) diarist tells us how he spent the winter of 1854-55 in the woods felling trees, and when the spring freshet came, ran the spar rafts to market. Women made trips to market on rafts, and Paul Bunyan's legend was born in Cherry Tree Joe (Chapters 7 and 8).

After the canals and railroads connected Williamsport, Pennsylvania, with markets throughout our country, woodhicks cut and then drove logs out of the mountains and down the rivers to a boom to supply the 35 sawmills with lumber (Chapters 9 and 10). In the early 1800s, the west side of the Allegheny Mountains supplied lumber products all along the Ohio and Mississippi Rivers to New Orleans (Chapter 11). The appendix details how watermen, arksmen and raftsmen constructed and ran their respective vessels, and the glossary gives a list of colorful terms used by the men involved.

Introduction: The Use of Rivers and Streams to Transport Heavy Loads to Market

The techniques of moving heavy loads down stream to markets was developed in Europe and brought to the New World by the early settlers. The Swedes, Norwegians, Germans and French all built rafts to bring lumber from their forests to down stream markets. Today travelers along the Rhine River in Europe can see medieval castles. These castles were built by wealthy landowners who collected tolls from river traffic passing their part of the river. The early settlers in this country continued the practice.

The lower Delaware Valley was first settled by the Swedes, and by 1547 the governor, John Printz, reported that he had built a mill at a place called Mölndal (on Cobb's Creek near present day Philadelphia). Later in 1658 some Dutch settlers petitioned for permission to build a mill at Turtle Falls on the Delaware River. This was granted on condition that they would not charge a higher toll for river traffic to pass through their dam than was charged by the company's mill at Mölndal. From this we know that streams in the colonies were used to transport goods as early as 1547 (Kuhlmann 21).

The Appalachian Mountains— which run from southeastern Canada through New England and the Mid-Atlantic states into the South — possessed a vast virgin forest of white pine and hardwoods. Initially this forest needed to be cleared for farm land and trees were burned. Then settlers along the Penobscot River in Maine and the Hudson and Delaware Rivers began to realize there was a market for the lumber down stream. Pike's *Tall Trees, Tough Men* gives an excellent history of lumbering in Maine. Since the Penobscot is only about 100 miles long, spars, square timbers and saw logs were usually floated down to Penobscot Bay without rafting them. Maine became the source of spars for the British shipbuilders, since England was running out of tall pine trees.

The Hudson River also provided transportation from its forests to New York City markets. John Patchin learned the lumbering business along the shores of Lake George in Upstate New York (near Ticonderoga). In the early 1830s when timber became scarce, he moved to the West Branch of the Susquehanna River in Clearfield County, Pennsylvania (*Caldwell's* 24). Mr. Patchin is given credit for bringing the technology to construct square timber and spar rafts to make the over 300 mile trip down the Susquehanna to the Chesapeake Bay. Having already established his market in New York City, he would have the rafts piled three or four on top of each other (called floats) and towed through the Chesapeake and Delaware Canal to the Delaware Bay and up the inland waterway to the city by steamboat.

In 1746 the first rafts were used to move lumber down the Delaware River to market in Philadelphia, Pennsylvania (Dunaway 290). These rafts were most likely board rafts, made from boards 16 feet long, sawed by water driven sawmills using an up and down saw (called a muley saw).

In 1769 the frontiersmen along the Juniata River partitioned the Pennsylvania Assembly to improve the navigation on the river since it was essential to building their economy. On March 9, 1771, they passed a law making the Susquehanna River and several of its tributaries common or public highways. The tributaries named were the Juniata, Conestoga, Bald Eagle, Machanoy, Penns Creek, Swatara, Connedoguinet and Kiskiminets (Livingood 7). The next day they passed a similar public highway law for the Delaware River and its tributaries. This "Public Highway Law" reversed the laws established by the Swedes in 1547 and the Dutch in 1658 when they allowed the collection of tolls for passing through their dams.

When William Penn took over the colony in 1681, he drew up a set of laws by which his "holy experiment" would be governed (Dunaway 42). He promised the immigrants religious, political and economic freedom. To allow this type of taxation would hinder the colony's fledgling economy.

Similar public highway laws were adopted by New York and Maryland. Pennsylvania passed a public highway law for the Allegheny and Clarion Rivers in the western part of the state. This colonial law protected the rights of the arksmen, raftsmen and log drivers to use the rivers up until the early 1900s. River traffic could not be impeded in either direction.

By 1789 rafts were seen on the Susquehanna River at Harrisburg, Pennsylvania (Livingood 29). Two years later in 1791, Michael Cryder constructed the first known ark anywhere in the New World. He ran his ark down the Juniata River with a load of flour to the Susquehanna River, through its dangerous Conewago Falls, and then through the equally treacherous Susquehanna Gorge to the Chesapeake Bay. From there he took his flour to Baltimore to be exported to the worldwide flour markets. This opened the river to raft traffic that found its way to Port Deposit, Maryland, and then on to the markets along the eastern seaboard.

Shively (15) stated that in the mid–1820s enough cargo was being shipped out of Penns Creek to require over 400 arks annually. This was occurring on almost all of the Susquehanna's tributaries. Arks remained a popular form of transportation until the railroads replaced them in the 1850s. The rivers and creeks in the Susquehanna Watershed are too shallow to support steamboat traffic, whereas the Mississippi watershed saw its first steamboat in 1811 and by

1834 had 1,200 boats to carry cargo on the river. Therefore arks were never as numerous.

The West Branch of the Susquehanna River's immeasurable virgin forest wasn't exploited until after 1840, when the lumbering operations in Maine, Canada and along the Hudson River had begun to subside. Lumbermen from these areas migrated to Pennsylvania for work, bringing their skills with them.

The skills needed to be a raft pilot, a master spar maker, and how to manufacture sticks and other necessities were passed from one generation to the next with no written record. Only when the lumber began to run out in the late 1800s did some of the "lumber barons" begin to document their work. Also, the introduction of narrow gauge railroads and steam driven sawmills changed lumbering. Waterways were no longer needed to move lumber.

Many woodhicks (Pennsylvania lumberjacks) lived into the mid–1900s when a renewed interest in lumbering produced many first-person accounts. Some of the lumber men, interviewed by Samuel King in their old age, had left Pennsylvania in their younger years to get work in West Virginia, the Carolinas, Louisiana, Minnesota and even the Northwest, taking their skills with them. Local historical societies in the Susquehanna Watershed proved to be a rich source of information on just how these men accomplished their work. A search of the Library of Congress and other major libraries revealed no information how different tasks were achieved.

The Susquehanna Watershed acted like a funnel for information on rafts and log drives when men migrated there from the Penobscot, Hudson and Delaware River Valleys to the Susquehanna Watershed, and then onto other major lumbering areas throughout the United States.

In the year prior to this research a museum docent on the Mississippi Watershed had read about arks being used on their river, but could not find information about what they looked like or how they were constructed. A lady from Houston, Texas, had a picture of her grandfather standing on a square timber raft in Pennsylvania holding a tool. She wanted to know what it was and how it was used. The research for this book answered their questions. Also, a man from California furnished a picture of one of the greatest storytellers on the West Branch of the Susquehanna river (his uncle).

The arksmen, raftsmen and log drivers who worked the Susquehanna Watershed now have descendants living all over the United States.

1

Early Colonial America

This chapter provides the history of the use of rivers and streams in the Colonies for moving heavy loads from the very beginning until 1791, when the Susquehanna River in Pennsylvania was opened to the Chesapeake Bay, providing export markets to lower New York State and central Pennsylvania. The first mention of the use of waterways for transportation was in 1658 when some Dutch settlers petitioned for permission to build a mill at Turtle Falls on the Delaware River (Kuhlmann 19). This was granted on condition that they would not charge a higher toll than was charged by the company's mill at Mölndal.

The Beginning

Early colonists moving inland in the early 1700s had no highways, railroads or other means of conveyance to move their household goods and tools. The only mode of transportation to and from the frontier was by pack animals, or by using canoes on the rivers and creeks like we use highways today. Birchbark canoes were ideal for traveling since they were light and easy to portage around falls and riffles, but if heavy objects were carried in them, they broke. The Indians taught the colonists how to make dugout canoes to transport heavier loads, such as mill stones to grind wheat into flour. Most of the time millwrights could manufacture everything to build a mill from the forest, except the five to seven foot diameter mill stones which weighed three tons or more. These had to be taken upstream by a large boat, as did the iron used in the mill's gears and straps.

Once established, the frontiersmen wanted to sell their surplus products. The only way to market with a large load, however, was downstream in dugout canoes and later Durham type boats, sometimes called keel boats or flat boats, again using the rivers and creeks as highways. Lumber from their forests was also brought down these highways to market in the form of rafts or logs.

Rafts, Durham Boats and Conestoga Wagons

Three innovations to move heavy loads appeared in the late 1740s that contributed significantly in the development of the future United States. They were the raft, the Durham boat and the Conestoga wagon.

Rafts were not used to carry boards or timber down the river, they were the end product itself. However, sometimes people did load small amounts of shingles or valuable lumber on top to take to market. It was the Germans, French and Swedes who brought this technology to the colonies. As towns near the mouths of rivers grew and the land around them was cleared of trees, the upriver pioneers saw a way to make money. They dammed small mountain streams to drive water sawmills, which was an improvement over a sawpit to make boards. When water mills were not available, a large log was placed on two teasels over a pit in the ground. While one man stood on the log, another man got into the pit and they sawed boards from the log.

After water mills were developed, when the mountain streams provided the water, the pioneers sawed board. In the winter they made board rafts while waiting for the spring freshets. Once the ice went out in the spring the rafts-men rushed to complete their rafts and float them down the streams and rivers to market. The upper reaches of the Delaware River were very shallow and rocky, and only during freshets was the river navigable.

Four years after the first rafts were seen on the Delaware River, the Durham Iron Furnace, near Easton on the Delaware River, built sharp pointed, sixty foot long boats decked at both the stern and bow (Dunaway 290). These boats were later built along the Susquehanna River. They were eight feet wide and two feet deep, and when laden with 15 tons, drew only 20 inches. Five men manned the boat — a steersman, plus four men who managed the two sails or pushed the boat with poles. To pole the boat a pair of men standing near the bow put their poles on the river bottom and pushed the boat by walking to the stern on the gunwales. While the first pair returned to the bow, the second pair walked to the stern on the gunwales pushing the boat. The two pairs alternated to pro-pel the boat. This is the type of boat that General George Washington used to cross the Delaware River in 1776.

Perhaps the biggest impact on the economy was the Conestoga wagon, which was popular by 1750. They originated among the Germans in Lancaster County, Pennsylvania, about 25 years earlier (Dunaway 295–296). Lancaster County borders the eastern shore of the Susquehanna River and is southeast of Harrisburg. The Conestoga wagon was the tractor-trailer of the colonial era and was used extensively during the French and Indian War. They became the principal means of moving country products to market. Their wheels were six to ten inches wide to carry the heavy wagons over unpaved roads and were usually drawn by six horses. Additionally, the wheels of these wagons were made with spokes and had a large diameter, making them easier to pull. The Conestoga Wagons were built in all sizes, like trucks of today, and could carry up to three tons. The driver rode on a horse or on a seat on the side of the wagon.

Philadelphia

From the day Philadelphia was laid out in 1683, it was the commercial center of the New World, exporting products from the Delaware River Valley to the West Indies, especially wheat, with most of the import-export businesses and ships owned by the Quakers (Livingood 6). The settlers along the Delaware, Schuylkill and Lehigh Rivers brought their products to the city by dugout canoes. The city was prospering to such an extent from exporting the local wheat, flour and other farm products to the West Indies that they had little time to consider the Susquehanna Valley trade (Dunaway 125). The Susquehanna Valley settlers had to send their excess products, if they had any, to Philadelphia, because in 1704 Maryland had passed a law banning import of staples from Pennsylvania (Livingood 4).

Philadelphia passed the first export laws in1700, with shippers required to put their brand mark on each cast of flour. In 1722 when Jamaica complained of the deterioration of Pennsylvania flour, the Pennsylvania Laws of 1724–25 established a system of inspection to guarantee that buyers were not defrauded in quantity and quality (Kuhlmann 21).

In 1754, at the outbreak of the French and Indian War, the Pennsylvania Assembly had 36 members, of whom 26 were Quakers. They dominated the assembly even though Quakers only made up about one fifth of the state's population. For 75 years they had run the state, dictating its laws.

Baltimore and the Susquehanna Valley

Baltimore, founded in 1729 at the upper end of the Chesapeake Bay, two hundred miles from the Atlantic Ocean, was located on a deep inlet of the Patapsco River (Livingood 5). The port's warm waters made the harbor practically ice free. Another feature which facilitated Baltimore's growth was its location on a fall line, where water provided power for watermills. Most important was Baltimore's location in the center of a vast hinterland in the Piedmont, suitable for growing wheat.

Before the French and Indian War the new settlers in the valley often didn't produce enough for survival, so they had to buy from the more established settlers in the valley, leaving very little for export (Livingood 6).

The French and Indian War

The French and Indian War from 1754 to 1763 brought about an arrested period in the development of the Susquehanna Valley, since most of the pioneers had to leave the valley for their families' safety (Dunaway 119–137). When the war broke out in 1754, few settlers had moved west of the Allegheny Mountains and the frontier ran along the Cumberland Valley to the Susquehanna,

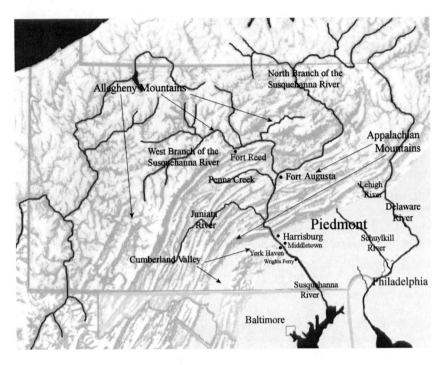

The Susquehanna Valley after the French and Indian War.

and up the Susquehanna to the confluences. Several families had settled along the Juniata River and Penns Creek, but few people lived along the North and West Branches, and none in New York State along the North Branch and its tributaries.

The Quakers Lose Control of the Pennsylvania Assembly

According to their religion the Quakers could not make preparations for war or vote money for supplies or men during war. During previous wars the Quakers did provide money to the British government by voting "to feed the hungry and clothe the naked," or as "a gift to the Queen." Therefore, before the French and Indian War they had formed no militia or built no forts, leaving the frontier completely undefended. When the governor of Pennsylvania declared war on the Indians and placed a price on their scalps, the Quakers began retiring from the Pennsylvania Assembly. By 1756, they were replaced with men who supported the war, but still had the same mindset that all of the Susquehanna River trade would and should be exported through Philadelphia (Dunaway 125).

Baltimore

Before the end of the French and Indian War in 1761, Joseph Ellicott, a Quaker from Philadelphia, moved to Baltimore to establish his mills and eventually help make the city the flour exporting capital of the New World (Kuhlmann 28). Annapolis port records showed that as early as 1756 to 1766 it was exporting annually nearly 10,000 barrels of flour, besides shipbread and unground wheat, with 70 percent going to Barbados in the West Indies. From there wheat was carried to the French and Spanish islands (Kuhlmann 29). Piedmont wheat contained only about 14 percent moisture, much lower than European wheat, where wet weather conditions produced a wheat with a much higher moisture content. The American flour's low moisture content made it last longer, while European flour often fermented during the long voyage to the Caribbean (Sharrer 15).

The Pennsylvania Assembly was slow to recognize that the products from west of the Susquehanna and the Cumberland Valley were being taken by shorter roads to Baltimore. Baltimoreans were politically, racially and religiously more like the Pennsylvania settlers than the wealthy Philadelphia merchants, and they were closer and gave higher prices. Roads or turnpikes constructed from Baltimore to the Pennsylvania state border facilitated the movement of wheat, flour and other farm products to Baltimore. Economic conditions evidently contributed to Maryland's no import law of 1704 being repealed, and Pennsylvania goods were welcome in Baltimore.

Between 1750 and 1770, eight turnpikes were built from Baltimore into lower Pennsylvania. Wheat, a product Philadelphia exported, was being taken to Baltimore, where flour became one of their major exports to the West Indies (Livingood 5).

Between the Wars

In 1769 the land owners along the Juniata River petitioned the assembly to improve the river, pointing out that if they didn't, all their products would be exported through Maryland. The Juniata River was needed to move products to Middletown, where they were transported to Philadelphia. The Pennsylvania Assembly on March 9, 1771, feeling pressure from the frontiersmen to do something for them in return for their taxes, and mindful of the Scots-Irish march on their city just five years earlier to protest the lack of support during the war, passed a law making the Susquehanna River and several of its tributaries common or public highways (Livingood 7).

This cost the assembly no money, but showed the frontiersmen the government had not forgotten them. The tributaries named were the Juniata, Conestoga, Bald Eagle, Machanoy, Penns Creek (to a point twenty miles upstream from its mouth), Swatara, Connedoguinet and Kiskiminets. With the passage of this law these rivers and streams so named could not be blocked by dams, nor could anyone establish toll gates, as the wealthy landowners had done on the rivers in Europe. If a miller wanted to build a dam for his mill, he had to provide a chute and sometimes a lock in his dam for watercraft to pass up and down the stream unhindered. However, since the assembly had not had a complete change of heart, it stated that no money should be spent on the river below Wrights Ferry (Livingood 7). This was to keep Maryland from benefiting. At the time the Susquehanna River below Wrights Ferry was considered unnavigable. In 1772, the Delaware River area was exporting over 250,000 barrels of flour and 38,000 casks of bread (Kulhmann 21).

The Revolutionary War 1775–1783

Pennsylvania

The settlers withdrew to Fort Augusta at the confluence of the North and West Branches of the Susquehanna River to wait out the war until 1783. Revolutionary soldiers who had fought in lower New York State were impressed with the area of the Chemung Valley, and after the war in 1787 immigrants flocked to the valley in large numbers.

By the time the Revolutionary War started in 1776, settlers in the area west and south of the confluence of the Susquehanna River had pushed far enough westward that there was no penetration of British and Indian forces. However, they did man the forts built during the French and Indian War.

Flour barrels were made of seasoned material with staves 27 inches long and ends 16.5 inches in diameter. The barrel had to have 10 hoops around the cask. Barrel size varied slightly from state to state, but all contained 196 pounds of flour (courtesy Colvin Run Mill, Fairfax County Park Authority, Great Falls, Virginia).

Baltimore

Before the war all colonial ports were shipping flour and other products to established markets in the Caribbean. However, business was halted when the British blockaded the entrances of Boston, New York, Philadelphia and the Chesapeake Bay.

Baltimore had a secret weapon, the clipper ship, which was light, fast and could sail into the wind at about 45 degrees off the direction the wind was coming from. This was the smaller two masted clipper ship, not the later and larger three, four and five masted ships that went around Cape Horn to California. The slow, heavy British Man of War could only sail at ninety degrees off the wind direction. With ships this cumbersome, the British didn't venture up the Chesapeake Bay to confront Baltimore or Annapolis.

A barrel of flour could be purchased in Baltimore for four Spanish dollars and sold in Havana, Cuba, for $36.00 (Kulhmenn 39). Therefore, there was no shortage of clipper ship captains and crews who were eager to slip by the upwind side of the British Man of Wars sailing across the mouth of the Chesapeake Bay. The American dollar, always considered equivalent to the Spanish dollar, was designed to contain the same amount of silver as the Spanish dollar in 1821 (Weatherford 119).

This unique situation filled the gristmill and ship owners' coffers in Baltimore during the seven years of the American Revolution. Many entrepreneurs owned both gristmills and ships.

After the Revolutionary War

Pennsylvania

After the war, settlers rushed up the West Branch as far as Fort William Reed, a blockhouse at Lock Haven, to clear the fertile valleys of trees and start farms again. Above Fort Reed on the West Branch little farmland was available and the Iroquois Indians called this the "Endless Mountains." This area would have to wait for settlements.

The Pennsylvania Assembly passed a law in 1781 establishing the standard weight of a full flour cask at 196 pounds. If the standard size barrel weighed more than 196 pounds, the flour had absorbed too much moisture and the inspector rejected the barrel. All flour made for shipping out of state was inspected for "due fineness, with no mixture of coarse or unmerchantable flour." The wagon transporting the flour must have a "good and sufficient covering." The inspectors bored into the cask to test the flour before branding the cask with the state coat of arms (Kulhmann 21).

By 1786, Lancaster had 18 flour mills within 10 miles and Middletown became a collection point for the wheat trade along the Susquehanna River with 160,000 to 180,000 bushels collected annually (4,800 to 5,400 tons). The wheat was taken to the Lancaster mills for grinding and then shipped to Philadelphia (Kulhmann 22). The Piedmont east of the Susquehanna River produced a lot of wheat which was ground into flour and shipped to Philadelphia.

On May 10, 1776, the Second Continental Congress suggested that each state form a new government. This is exactly what the people of Pennsylvania needed to overthrow the old government. In June each of the eleven counties and the city of Philadelphia had eight members in the new assembly, and by September of that year Benjamin Franklin was elected president of Pennsylvania. Representation had come to the frontier; however, all the members were new to the government process and were not adept at keeping the Susquehanna Valley trade only in Pennsylvania (Dunaway 209–215).

Middletown, York Haven and Columbia

Middletown, Pennsylvania, was laid out in 1755 along the eastern shore of the Susquehanna River about 10 miles below Harris' Ferry (Harrisburg) (Livingood 29). Its strategic location placed it halfway between Philadelphia and Carlisle, at the northern end of the fertile Cumberland Valley, and just above the Susquehanna River's unnavigable Conewago Falls, so that all river traffic coming down the river would have to stop there. The first commercial raft with boards and scantling (a timber of slight width and thickness, used as a stud or rafter in a house frame) was floated down the Susquehanna River to Middletown in 1789, 43 years after the first raft appeared on the Delaware River (Livingood 29).

In 1790, 150,000 bushels of wheat came by dugout canoe and keel boat or Durham Boat (Livingood 29). Middletown forwarded most of the wheat to Philadelphia, 100 miles, over very poor roads. To reduce the total weight, Middletown built grist mills and ground the wheat into flour before shipping. It cost 5 shillings, 6 pennies per hundredweight to ship goods from Middletown to Philadelphia in 1794 (Livingood 30 footnote). A barrel of flour weighed 196 pounds or two hundredweight. The exchange rate in 1794 was $4.75 U.S. per British pound (Officer). Therefore, it cost $2.61 to ship a barrel of flour from Middletown to Philadelphia. Flour prices in Philadelphia and Baltimore fluctuated with the world market, but transportation costs remained stable.

Across the river from Middletown on the western shore, York Haven grew up using money from Baltimore millers. It wasn't long until York Haven began shipping flour by wagon to Baltimore, 80 miles away.

After the turnpike was completed from Columbia to Philadelphia in 1803, the transportation costs were cut to $1.35 a barrel, but by then it was too late to save most of the Susquehanna Valley flour trade; it was going to Baltimore. The turnpike cost about $6,000.00 a mile to build because it was built with a base of large cobblestones topped with multiple layers of different-sized crushed stones so it would be an all weather road (ExplorePAhistory.com). The transportation costs included the sum paid to the owner of the wagon and team and tolls for the use of the turnpike. Traveling the turnpike and paying its tolls was cheaper that using the unimproved dirt roads of the day (Ringwalt 33). However, the turnpike had about 1,000 Conestoga wagons using it each day, hauling other goods.

Baltimore

By 1789, Baltimore was the fastest growing city in the country because of its strategic location in the middle of the wheat growing area, and wheat was out-selling tobacco. The large supply of capital realized from exporting flour during the Revolutionary War and the development of a banking system made Baltimore mill owners independently wealthy (Kulhmann 39).

After the war, Great Britain restricted trade with their West Indian colonies, but the non–English islands imported the flour and sold it to the British islands (Kulhmann 39). War in Europe was always good for the flour trade in America. The European wars cut off the flour coming to France from the Baltic and they relied on America to supply them. The French Revolution from 1793 to 1801 would keep the price of flour up in Baltimore.

The cradle became popular in the 1790s, replacing the sickle, making the farmer's job easier, and the first threshing machine was shown in Baltimore in 1791 (Sharrer 44). About this time two types of millers became prevalent. The first, known as the customer miller, ground grain for the local farmers, usually taking part of the grain for the grinding process. The second, the merchant miller, purchased the grain, ground it into flour, and exported it. The merchant miller of Baltimore often owned several capital grist mills, each grinding up to 200 barrels of flour a day (Kuhlmann 44).

Oliver Evans, an inventor from Philadelphia who was neither a miller or millwright, published his book *The Young Millwright and Miller's Guide* in 1795. This book explained his ideas for building a nearly automatic grist mill. The design used water power to move the grain through the mill using conveyers and elevators. It also incorporated a hopper-boy to spread the flour for cooling after grinding. Most of this was done by manual labor before Evans' methods were adopted. The top producing mills in Baltimore ground 200 barrels a day, which required 934 bushels of wheat a day, or 56,000 pounds lifted several times before being barreled (Kuhlmann 44).

Evans stated that a mill producing 40 barrels a day, not using his method, would require four men and a boy. If they used his design, the miller could produce the same 40 barrels using only two men. Each mill laborer was paid seven dollars a month and received free board, worth $40.00 a year. The boy received board and clothing worth $50.00 a year. This represented a $298.00 a year saving using his methods. However, it did cost more to build his type mill. Bigger water wheels were needed and the buildings were at least three stories high with the conveyers, elevators and hopper-boy. Dennis Griffith's 1795 map of Maryland located 172 mills in the state, but excluded those in the Baltimore vicinity as too numerous for insertion (Sharrer 65). Evans got his patent in 1791, and first tried his method in the Philadelphia area, but Baltimore adopted his method first.

2

The Susquehanna Is Opened
to the Chesapeake Bay

This chapter explains how, in 1791, one courageous miller opened the Susquehanna River to the Chesapeake Bay. This provided the stimulus to open the Susquehanna Watershed to the early American worldwide flour trade. Eventually this contributed to making Baltimore the "Flour Exporting Capital of the New World." Flour did for the colonial and early American economy what oil does today for many middle eastern countries.

Cryder's Run

Until the Spring of 1791 all Susquehanna River dugout canoes and Durham boats came down the river to Middletown, about ten miles below Harrisburg. Here the wheat and flour were loaded onto Conestoga wagons to be driven over one hundred miles of poor roads to Philadelphia. The canoes and boats were stopped at Middletown since it was just upriver of the Conewago Falls. Until that time it was believed that the falls were impassable. The Susquehanna River "public highway" law had opened the river to traffic to Middletown, but below Middletown to the Chesapeake Bay the river was so dangerous that it was thought that Baltimore would never profit from the Susquehanna Valley trade.

Eighteen to twenty years before, in 1771 or 1773, Michael Cryder, a German miller from Lancaster County, came to Standing Stone, as Huntingdon was then known, to build a gristmill on the Juniata River. His home and mill were near the present site of Second and Penn Streets in Huntingdon. Mr. Cryder, with a warrant from the proprietary government for this land, possessed the knowledge to build a mill and had the money to finance his venture. He eventually had seven sons and two daughters. During the Revolutionary War, from 1776 to 1783, Michael Cryder was an ardent patriot; in the daytime he worked his mill and at night was a guard at the local fort. Several of his sons served in the Continental Army during the war. Additionally, he gave liberally of his funds to aid the patriot cause. After the war was over, he was paid back by the government, but he found himself deeply in debt because of the depreciation of the Continental currency. It was a staggering burden but he was determined to repay all claims against him. Grinding flour for the local pioneers

Cryder's Run.

would not get him out of debt. Running his extra flour to Middletown and selling it to the brokers there, who would then send it to Philadelphia, was profitable, but not profitable enough (Rung 150 to 152).

Baltimore was fast becoming the flour exporting capital of the colonies; the exporters were paying higher prices than could be had in Middletown. Five years earlier, in 1786, the Baltimore market paid 35 shillings for a barrel of flour (Sharrer 34) worth $7.96 (Officer). That was a lot of money when a mill worker was only paid $7.00 a month (Evans). Maryland started statewide inspection of export flour in 1771, 20 years earlier, and this improved their export quality and sales (Sharrer 15). In addition, the inspectors in Baltimore were not as biased as those in Philadelphia. The Philadelphia inspectors were known for rejecting all wheat coming from Virginia and Maryland (Hollingsworth Nov. 1794). If they rejected wheat from outside the Philadelphia area, they could easily reject his flour from the Juniata. Then his whole winter's work would have to be dumped for a loss. Cryder's chances were much better in Baltimore. All he had to do was get there.

But Baltimore was 110 miles as the crow flies from Cryder's Mill. It would take four Conestoga wagons to haul over 20,000 pounds of flour out of the valley and down the Maryland turnpike to Baltimore. The most direct route to Baltimore was down the Juniata River for 16 miles and then 20 miles across five mountains—the Blacklog, Shade, Tuscarora, Kittatinny and Blue—to Shippensburg in the middle of the Cumberland Valley. Even today there is no road that goes directly over these five mountains. These mountains are so close together that there are no open valleys between them. Once a traveler is through the Cumberland Valley, he must cross the South Mountain before getting to Gettysburg on the Piedmont. From Gettysburg it was 50 miles to Baltimore. The pioneers living in the Cumberland Valley, which contained the towns of Shippensburg and Carlisle, were already shipping their excess wheat and flour to Baltimore, where they were getting better prices for their goods than they would at Middletown. Three years later it was noted that it cost a dollar a barrel to ship flour from Carlisle to Baltimore (Livingood 48). There was no way Cryder could ship his flour over the five mountains and on to Baltimore. In 1790, Philadelphia was the only market for flour from the Juniata and upper Susquehanna Rivers.

In the fall of 1790, Cryder struck upon an idea which solved his transportation problem, turned his financial situation around, and made him a legend along the Susquehanna River and its tributaries, to say nothing of his instant notoriety in Baltimore. A public recognition problem at the time was that almost no one spelled his name correctly. In Cecil County, Maryland, east of the Susquehanna River, they called him Richard Breider (Miller 107). Throughout Pennsylvania and lower New York State they gave credit to a Kryder, but several places in Pennsylvania they correctly called him Cryder. None got his first name correct. And the dates in historical accounts varied from 1794 to 1796.

During the winter of 1790–1791, Michael Cryder conceived a unique boat hull design that would suit his purpose. It would be made of three squared pine logs. The middle log would be 75 feet long and serve as an internal keel for the boat. The two side logs would be 55 feet long and four shorter logs would be mitered into the side logs, with the end of the center log forming a mitered point at each end of the hull. Most sawmill trucks of the day could only cut a board sixteen feet long, so his craft would be sixteen feet wide. (A sawmill truck was the car that the log rested on during sawing.) His craft, simple to build, would be capable of carrying a cargo up to 25 tons, whereas the dugout canoes could only carry nine barrels of flour (Ringwalt 9). The Durham boats could carry 15 tons (Ringwalt 12). Also, these boats and canoes took skilled boat builders to make and thus were expensive, and after unloading at Middletown they were poled upstream to be used the next year. Cryder wanted a simple boat that anyone could build, because he wasn't going to bring his boat back. He would sell it for the lumber.

The craft would float with the current, and oars or sweeps about 30 feet long were mounted, one on the point of the bow and the other on the stern point, like the rafts first seen on the Susquehanna River the year before. The two oars were used to move the craft back and forth in the current to miss dangerous obstacles. They could not propel the craft up or downstream.

We are not sure what Michael Cryder's original craft looked like, but within nine years copies were made of his craft in New York State and they were called arks. Based on an 1838 description of ark building (see appendix), the method of building changed very little in the next 60 years; however, the use of arks changed considerably. One thing we do know is that the ark's roof was waterproof. In 1781 in Philadelphia a law was passed requiring wagons hauling flour to have a good and sufficient covering (Kuhlmann 21). If the flour barrels drew moisture, the airtight seal would break and the water would make the flour ferment. Ark roofs were made of boards sealed with pitch pine to prevent the spring rain from getting on the barrels. Arks also had a false bottom to protect the barrels against water seeping through the ark's bottom.

When the spring freshets came after the ice had broken and flowed out of the river, Michael and his two oldest sons, Israel, the eldest, and Daniel, loaded the craft with 104 barrels of flour. Rung and Africa both stated Cryder had on board 104 barrels (151 and 31). However, McCullough said he had 170 barrels (5). Both Africa and McCullough spelled his name with a "K," most likely because the Baltimore newspaper had spelled his name as Kryder when reporting the event.

A barrel of flour weighed 196 pounds, so the craft was carrying little more than ten tons of flour, far below the maximum load of 25 tons. However, this made the craft more maneuverable, something the Cryders would need. With a son on each oar and Michael as the pilot, giving orders for a pull on the oars one way and then a pull the other way, the Cryders left Standing Stone and floated down the Juniata. The 91 mile trip to the Susquehanna River was apparently uneventful. The Juniata River, with a gradient of less that nine inches per mile, is a gentle flow with very few hazards, especially during a spring freshet. This gave Michael and his sons a chance to learn how to maneuver their craft.

When they entered the Susquehanna River, they most likely rowed their craft across the nearly mile wide river to the eastern shore where the channel to Middletown was less hazardous (Yates' *Charts*). During the ten mile run to Harrisburg the river gradient increases to 2.62 feet per mile, which is 3.5 times the gradient of the Juniata. All water craft move faster than the water current and in this situation about four miles per hour.

As the Cryders approached Middletown on the eastern shore, a crowd gathered expected the strange craft to make its way to the beach for offloading. They had never seen a boat like this one, which was 15 feet longer than a Durham boat and twice as wide, with only three men on board. The strangest thing was the cabin covering almost the full length of the vessel. The boat remained in the main stream heading for the gurgling white waters of the Conewago Falls.

The crowd must have been wondering: "What are they thinking? There is nowhere to sell your products downstream — maybe Baltimore?" But first they would have to run the impassable Conewago Falls and the first 26 miles of the

Susquehanna Gorge from Columbia to Peach Bottom. Even if they did make it to the Peach Bottom, the 20 miles to Port Deposit were just as dangerous as either the Conewago Falls or the run to Peach Bottom. The crowd must have felt sure they were watching three men going to their death.

The Conewago Falls are at the lower end of the Three Mile Island and the York Haven Dam. Here the river drops rapidly for about three quarters of a mile. What makes the falls so treacherous is the river bottom is covered with the most expansive pothole field in the United States. Potholes are cut into the black and gray hard biabase rock, some as small as a marble and others deep and wide enough to hide a bear. Rocks covered the falls, some the size of golf balls and others the size of a trailer on an eighteen wheeler (Brubaker 167–68).

Mitchell tells us that the pilot exercised great care to get his craft lined up to pass through the very narrow Sweet Arrow Gap just below Sweet Arrow Creek, so that he would enter the Conewago Falls correctly (36). (Sweet Arrow is the name all West Branch raftsmen used for Swatara.)

Yates' chart of the Conewago Falls gives details of how the pilot would line up his craft to enter the falls. Approaching the falls, about halfway between Swatara Creek and Three Mile Island, there was a rock sticking up out of the water. Raftsmen called such a rock a "pilot," because the pilot guided on this rock. Yates instructed: "Keep the big chestnut tree in the field, and the barn on the hill in range before you come to the pilot in Swatara." The tree and barn probably were on Three Mile Island, and his use of the word *range* meant keeping the two lined up. Many boatmen today use this technique to get their craft in the right position. "The water draws to the left at the pilot in Swatara," Yates said, warning that the current would draw them down between Three Mile Island and the eastern shore. "Look back over the old red tavern and keep the hollow in the mountain in range." This was a second check to make sure the craft was in the right place as it passed to the right of the pilot. Yates shows the path between two sets of submerged rocks and to the west side of Three Mile Island.

Mitchell said, "Leaving the falls on the left side was the Lancaster Bar and on the right side was the York Bar." The bars, rows of rocks on each side, made stoving (wrecking) a very possible outcome. "Some raftsmen claimed their rafts reached a speed of a mile a minute, and in later years the local pilots kept a boat at the foot of the falls to pick up survivors" (36). Stoving was raftsmen's vernacular for staving their ark or raft.

Yates showed the Lancaster Bar below the falls, and to help the pilot guide his craft between the two bars he wrote on his chart: "Keep the trees on the point ahead and the barn in the orchard in range." Yates' information is dated 1855 and Mitchell's the later 1800s. None of this information was available to Michael Cryder in 1791.

The passage down the Conewago Falls is underwater today, covered by the slack water of the York Haven Dam. But today the backside of the Lancaster

Bar can be seen from the state operated boat launch on the eastern shore at the foot of the falls.

Below the falls the river smoothes out and is calm until it reaches Turkey Hill, just below Columbia, Pennsylvania. Here the Cryders entered the Susquehanna Gorge and the run down the river to Peach Bottom at the Pennsylvania Border. Through the gorge the hills rise up 200 feet to 500 feet on both sides of the river (Brubaker 199).

Most of the run was along the eastern shore, except at two places, Weise Island and at Reed and Hartman Islands, where the pilot needed to cross the river to the western shore to get around these islands, with an immediate return to the eastern shore again to prevent running onto rocks.

Miller (110) quoted a pilot who said he usually made the run from Marietta to Peach Bottom in three hours, and Strong said merchants made the 25 mile run from Columbia to Peach Bottom in three hours. We will use the information from Strong's journal (see Strong's *Voyage*, Chapter 5).

The raft route from Columbia to Peach Bottom measured on the U.S. Geological Survey map is 26.2 miles, and Columbia is 5.9 miles upriver from Turkey Hill. The run around Turkey Hill is fast (Kelly, Brubaker and others) because the river narrows and the gradient increases. (The gradient over four hundred miles of the upper river averaged 2.5 feet per miles [Brubaker 175] and rafts usually traveled at four miles per hour [William Penn Museum and Yates' *Charts*]). The run from Columbia to the swift water at Turkey Hill took about one hour and fifteen minutes to cover the first five miles, leaving one hour and forty-five minutes to make the run from Turkey Hill to Peach Bottom, 21.2 miles down the river. From Turkey Hill to Peach Bottom the river drops 147.5 feet or a gradient of 6.96 feet per mile (E. Shank 85). This is 2.8 times greater than the average gradient on the upper river. The trip from Turkey Hill to Peach Bottom was made at an average speed of 12.1 miles per hour, three times faster than on the upper river.

Kelly tells us there are four places in the river between Turnkey Hill and Peach Bottom where the water was so fast the dancing on the raft had to stop until it had passed through the riffles. The four places he named were Turkey Hill, Fry's Rock, Connolly's Break and Cully's Falls. Riffles are usually three quarters of a mile long (Buttermilk Falls on the West Branch and Conewago Falls), therefore, 3.0 miles of the trip were down riffles and 18.2 miles of the trip were on smoother water. If the average speed on the smoother water dropped to 11.0 miles per hour, then the average speed down the riffles would have to increase to 31.4 miles per hour to make Peach Bottom in an hour and three quarters. If the average speed on the slower water was 10.7 miles per hour then the average speed down the riffles had to be 61.1 miles per hour.

It is possible that the ark reached speeds of 30 miles per hour or higher going through the most dangerous parts of the river, a speed not achieved any other way in 1791. Michael Cryder's ark weighed over 35 tons loaded. If he hit a rock traveling 20 miles an hour, his wooden craft would have been ripped apart and he and his sons would have drowned in the raging water. He most certainly had to know how to position his ark to make it through the torrents without destroying his ark and killing himself and his two sons.

A very treacherous spot was Fry's (also Frey's) Rock. In later years, if one raft stoved on the rock, the rafts following often stoved also (Kelly). At McCall's Ferry the river narrowed to 264 feet from shore to shore with a depth of 40 to 60 feet. The deepest trench was between the Bear (Bare) Islands and the eastern shore, where it was 130 feet deep, 30 feet below sea level (Brubaker 170). Nearing the border between Pennsylvania and Maryland at Peach Bottom, the water slowed to a calm pool.

The nine mile stretch from Peach Bottom to below Smith Falls was another test of the pilot's skill. The gradient on this stretch of the river is 4.49 feet per mile (E. Shank 85), 35 percent less than the upper gorge, but still much faster than on the upper river. Before entering Maryland the mile wide river narrowed to 32 navigable feet at Fanny's Gap (Magee 200). Beyond Fanny's Gap was Bald Friar Falls in Maryland, in which lay the infamous Hollow Rock, which claimed many lives in later years. At Amos Falls was the notorious Job's Hole which, if a body were dropped into it, it was never seen again (Brubaker 171). Smith's Falls was more a barrier against going up river than a riffle, for it consisted of numerous rocks protruding from the water. The local people call Smith's Falls the "rock bridge" because at low water it was almost possible to walk across without getting wet (Brubaker 227). Smith's Falls was named for Captain John Smith. He entered the river in 1608, and the falls prevented him from going farther up the river.

All the turns and narrow points in the river required a pilot to position his craft to take the best advantage of the current and the way the water tossed his craft about so that he would miss the hazardous rocks. Often the best position for the craft could not be determined until it was too late. The pilot needed experience to navigate from Turkey Hill, Pennsylvania, to Port Deposit, Maryland. Michael Cryder had learned the river when he was a young man and might have walked these 39 miles of the river before trying it with his two sons.

On the fourth day of their voyage the Cryders reached Havre de Grace, Maryland, where the Susquehanna River drains into the Chesapeake Bay. Here Mr. Cryder loaded his flour on a shallop headed for Baltimore overnight. (A shallop is a shallow draft sailing vessel used in coastal waters.) At noon the next day they reached the Baltimore docks, where they were cheered by a crowd of entrepreneurs eager to have the Susquehanna Valley wheat and other products available by water to Baltimore.

The jubilant flour merchants paid Michael Cryder a generous price for his 104 barrels of flour. That year flour averaged $5.00 a barrel in Baltimore (Sharrer 63). They also awarded him a bonus of $104.00, one dollar for each barrel, for showing the farmers of the Juniata Valley and the Susquehanna's North and

West Branches a new and better market for their goods. In subsequent years an ark this size would carry about 250 barrels. Some authors stated that arks averaged 400 barrels of flour on each run (McCullough 6). But this would require the ark to be 190 feet long. Some coal arks were reported to be this large.

Ringwald stated: "Some of those [arks] used in Pennsylvania were large enough to carry 500 barrels of flour.... Arks used in transporting coal from the Wyoming Valley were rudely constructed craft, ninety feet long, sixteen feet wide, and four feet deep, with a capacity of sixty tons" (12). Cryder's costs were about $75.00 to build the ark; it took two men about two weeks to build an ark — their wages, plus the material. He sold the ark in Havre de Grace. The wood was worth about $35.00, which probably paid for his transportation to Baltimore on the shallop.

Cryder's success spread up the river like a wildfire, and each year saw more arks appearing on the spring freshets which would carry them over the snags and rocks. Arks, which only drew 18 to 20 inches of water, could carry up to 25 tons of wheat, potatoes, whisky, corn and all kinds of produce, as well as coal and iron from the North Branch, Penns Creek and Juniata. Additionally, lumber rafts and spar rafts started to run the white water of the Conewago Falls and Susquehanna Gorge. Lower New York State farmers brought their produce to Baltimore, where they received 50 percent more than in Albany, New York.

Men living along the lower river saw an opportunity to make money as pilots to the upriver watermen when they wanted to run the Conewago Falls and the gorge. In the summer when the river was low they piled driftwood over the bigger rocks and burned it until the rocks were very hot. Then they threw water on the rocks, splitting them so they could be removed. When they started doing this is not clear, because in 1771, when the Pennsylvania Assembly designated the Susquehanna River a public highway, they also stated that no money should be spent on the river below Wrights Ferry. This law only prevented improvement to navigation on the river; it did not prevent navigation on the lower river. Also, the "no money" clause may have been interpreted as state money, not private money. Eight years after Cryder made his voyage, in 1799, the Pennsylvania legislature felt it needed to reaffirm its position on the Susquehanna River, and its tributaries were again designated as public highways. However, legislators made it against the law to make improvements to the river below Columbia-Wrightsville to the Maryland border. The fine for violations was not less than $200.00 or more than $2,000.00. This law was only in effect for two years until 1801, when Philadelphia wanted to build the Chesapeake and Delaware Canal across the isthmus between the Delaware Bay and the Chesapeake Bay. The canal would cross both Delaware and Maryland, and the repeal of the law was part of the agreement for building the canal (Livingood 33).

A canal was dug around the Conewago Falls in 1793, but few watermen used the canal, opting to use a local pilot to guide their craft though the falls.

By 1805 the Susquehanna Canal was opened, connecting the Maryland border with Port Deposit below Smith Falls. This canal did see a lot of crafts that wanted to avoid the very narrow Fanny Gap, Bald Friar Falls with Hollow Rock, and Smith Falls. That year Baltimore was paying $7.50 for a barrel of flour (Sharrer 136).

Five years after first running the Conewago Falls, Michael Cryder had paid off all his debts and moved his youngest five sons and two daughters to Ohio, near Chillicoths. He died in 1816. Israel, his oldest son, remained in Huntingdon area until his death in 1845. He and his wife, Hannah Seivert Cryder, lived on a farm Israel purchased from his father near the mouth of the Little Juniata, where they raised 11 children.

As the news of Cryder's success spread along the Susquehanna River and its tributaries, most communities prospered from his adventure. Large stone warehouses were built along the banks of the Juniata in Lewistown, 44 miles down the river from Huntingdon, to house the wheat and other farm produce, until the spring freshets made it possible to send arks down the river to market (Frysingher). Local farmers brought their goods to these warehouses and turned them over to the owners, getting only an IOU in return. The owner couldn't pay the farmer until he had sold the goods. Water Street in Lewistown became the business district of the community, with warehouses large enough to require 6,000 perches of stone (144,000 cubic feet), coopers to build the barrels, blacksmiths, nail making shops and various stores selling goods. And of course, where there are financial dealings there are lawyers.

Kitchen, bunk and horse arks (front to back), late 1800s. The kitchen ark fed up to 250 log drivers four times a day. The men slept in the second ark, and the third was used to bed horses at night. Oars are supported on logs extended from the main hull. Arks changed little from 1791 to 1900 (from the collection of the Lycoming County Historical Society and Thomas T. Taber Museum).

Arks remained a popular form of moving farm goods to market until the 1850s, when railroads made it possible to move farm goods right after harvesting, not having to wait until the rivers had swollen. Even the canal boats didn't replace arks, since the canals closed in November and didn't open until March because of freezing. The farmer could run his ark on the spring freshet and get a direct sale nearer the consumer.

Today the run from Middletown, Pennsylvania, to Havre de Grace, Maryland, is obstructed by four hydroelectric dams: York Haven, Safe Harbor, Holtwood and Conowingo.

After the log drive was finished, arks were usually towed upstream during the summer to be used again the next spring.

Information about the Cryder adventure varied widely from one author to another. The Huntingdon County Historical Society provided *Rungs's Chronicles*, which I considered the definitive source for dating the use of arks on creeks and rivers.

3

Arks on the Penns Creek

This chapter presents what happened along only one of the Susquehanna River's tributaries where farmers and millers had access to Baltimore's worldwide flour market. Penns Creek was chosen because data was available; however, the same could be said about the North Branch of the Susquehanna River in New York State and its tributaries, the Chenango, Chemung, Cohocton, Tioga and Casisteo. In Pennsylvania it also represents the West Branch of the Susquehanna River to Lock Haven and the Juniata River. All along the river farmers and millers collected their spare wheat and flour to ship to Baltimore to obtain higher prices than could be had locally.

The Creek

The first part of this information is based on J. G. Shively's *Navigation on Penns Creek*, and the second part is taken from Karstetter's article, "Running Arks on the Famous Karoondinha," in French's *Rafting Days in Pennsylvania*. Shively's article was written in 1963 and the Karstetter article was dated before 1922. The two articles give a history of running arks on a tributary of the Susquehanna River. This author has added information to supplement where needed. This Penns Creek is the one that drains into the Susquehanna River below Selinsgrove, as Pennsylvania has more than one Penns Creek.

Named for John Penn, William Penn's son and governor of Pennsylvania, Penns Creek's begins in a cave in the middle of Penns Valley about fifteen miles east and north of State College, Pennsylvania, where Penn State University is located. This location is almost in the geographic center of the state of Pennsylvania. This Penns Creek is also known by its Indian name, the Karoondinha, and flows through the ridge and valley section of the state where the flat valleys provide excellent land for farms. To move from one valley to the next, even today, requires driving over narrow, steep, winding roads. From its source the Penns Creek flows east over 50 miles until it empties into the Susquehanna River.

For the first eight miles Penns Creek flows along the southern side of Penns Valley to the village of Coburn. Elk Creek flows through a gap in Brush Mountain into Penns Valley. Elk Creek joins Pine Creek and flows into Penns Creek

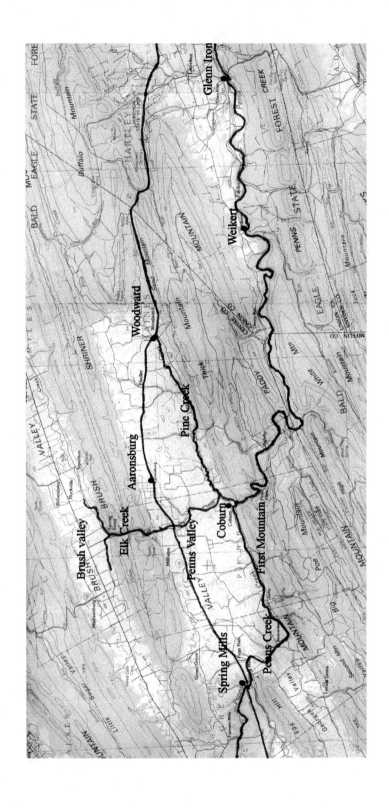

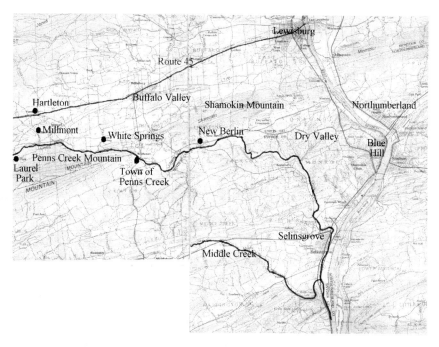

East end of Penns Creek.

at Coburn. At Coburn, Penns Creek starts through a gap in First Mountain. Ten miles downstream it flows into the western end of Buffalo Valley. This is the most difficult passage, with sharp turns that double back.

In the next 20 miles Penns Creek flows along the southern side of Buffalo Valley past the villages of Weikert, Glen Iron, and Millmont. At White Springs it flows between Penns Creek Mountain and Shamokin Mountain into Dry Valley. After passing the village of New Berlin, the creek turns slowly to the south to parallel the Susquehanna River. Just north of Selinsgrove it turns 90 degrees to the left, flows east for about a mile, and then turns right 90 degrees to flow south, only three city blocks away from the Susquehanna River. Five miles south of Selinsgrove it flows into the Susquehanna River.

Before the French and Indian War started in 1755, the area along the Penns Creek was sparsely settled. Then, on October 17, 1755, French-led Shawnee Indians from "The Ohio" struck along the Penns Creek between what is today the village of New Berlin and Selinsgrove. Twenty-six people were either killed, wounded or taken hostage and the remaining settlers fled the valley until after the war.

Between the French and Indian War and the American Revolution, the

Opposite: West end of Penns Creek.

disposal of surplus grain and other products was no problem for the settlers along the creek, since they had no surplus. In fact, most of the settlers were hard pressed to produce enough for their own needs during their first years in this wild country. New settlers coming into the valley were glad to buy anything that their already established neighbors could spare.

Then came the Revolutionary War, and those who remained to defend their homes and communities found little time to cultivate their land, much less to increase their tillable acreage. The autumn of 1781 found the region along Penns Creek almost deserted. Not until after the Revolutionary War, in the summer of 1783, did most of the original settlers return to their homes. Now that the danger from Indians was past, many new settlers arrived, and the carving out of farms from the virgin forest began in earnest.

In 1786, viewers were appointed by the Northumberland County Court to lay out a road from the eastern end of Penns Valley to Sunbury, across the river from Blue Hill. By November of that year it was reported that a road from the eastern end of the Seven Mile Narrows had been opened to the present village of Hartleton. Three years later the road was opened to the second hollow in Blue Hill. This road served the purpose of moving settlers into the territory, but lacked the usefulness of moving farm products to market as roads do today.

The Society for the Improvement of Roads and Inland Navigation reported at the end of the decade: "In the year 1788 large quantities of wheat and flour were carried up the river (Susquehanna) for use of the settlers in Northumberland County (which then included the entire course of Penns Creek). In 1790, after the month of March, 30,000 bushels of wheat returned down the river from the same county."

Now that there was a surplus, especially of wheat and rye, some means had to be found for getting it to market. The nearest overland market was Philadelphia, by way of Middletown. Even east of the Susquehanna it was not considered profitable to transport wheat by wagons for distances over 75 miles, and west of the river there were no roads worthy of the name (Shively 1 & 2).

Thirty thousand bushels of wheat made 200 dugout canoe loads or 60 Durham Boat loads, to be taken 60 miles down the river to Middletown. This was the easy part; getting the canoes or Durham Boats back home was work. Until the Pennsylvania Canal was opened in 1831 the creeks and rivers would have to serve as highways to take farm products, coal, lumber and pig iron to market.

The act passed by the Pennsylvania Legislature March 9, 1771, making the Susquehanna River a public highway also made the Penns Creek a public highway 20 miles along its course from its mouth (Everts 433). This would provide public highway access to the flat farm lands west of its mouth and up the creek to Dry Valley and the western end of Buffalo Valley. We don't know when the first ark went down the Penns Creek, but we do know that it wasn't before the spring of 1791, when Michael Cryder ran the first ark down the Juniata River.

The men coming down the river in their dugout canoes and Durham boats were always looking for a way to make their work easier. The ones who did see Cryder's ark in 1791 probably made copies to be used on the freshets the next year. When one man made an improvement to his ark, the next year there were many copies on the river. With most of the arks arriving down the river at the same time, any new good idea in ark construction was used the next year all along the river.

In 1792 another act was passed by the Pennsylvania Legislature extending Penns Creek's public highway to the mouth of Sinking Creek (Spring Mills). Spring Mills is on Route 45, less than a mile from Penns Cave, the source of the Penns Creek. This was 21 years after the creek was first made a public highway and one year after Cryder ran the first ark down the Juniata River. This act effectively made the whole length of Penns Creek a public highway and gave the farmers access to the Baltimore flour markets.

We can assume that when Penns Creek was included in the acts of 1771 and 1792, the state legislature thought the creek had enough traffic to warrant being mentioned.

Building a Dam Across a Public Highway

Anthony Selin, a professional soldier, migrated from Switzerland to assist George Washington with the Revolutionary War, much like Lafayette, von Steuben and Pulaski. Selin, who served as a major during the war, married Catherine Snyder, a sister of Simon Snyder. The town of Selinsgrove was named for him.

Simon Snyder, a lawyer for whom Snyder County was later named, had served as a delegate to the 1790 convention to draft the state constitution. In 1797 Snyder was elected to the Pennsylvania House of Representatives, and in 1808 he was elected the third governor of Pennsylvania, the only man to serve three three-year terms. He held the post until 1817.

On the 23rd of December 1792, a petition was presented to the Senate on the part of Simon Snyder and Anthony Selin's heirs (Selin died that year) to enable them to maintain a dam across Penns Creek of the height of two and a half feet. Both men lived in Selinsgrove and their mill was at the eastern end of Mill Street on Penns Creek, just upstream from today's railroad bridge. This aroused the settlers along the Penns Creek and produced a remonstrance, read in the Senate on March 4, 1793. It stated "that Simon Snyder and Anthony Selin, before his death, erected a dam across the main current of Penns Creek; that there were not less than ten mills within nine miles of Snyder's, some of which grind the year round unobstructed by ice, and they subjoin a list of the mills with their distances from Snyder's" (Lynn 275–276).

Although most of these mills were not on Penns Creek, all of their own-ers were no doubt interested in using it to transport their flour and other products. This petition, signed by 27 prominent men of the area, mostly mill owners or ark pilots or future ark pilots, is especially interesting because it provides that canoes, Durham boats and maybe arks were running in worthwhile numbers at this early date. Lynn and Shively gave no reason why the settlers were unhappy and wanted to prevent the building of the Snyder/Selin dam, but it may have been too constraining for boats and canoes going upstream.

The act authorizing the construction of the dam was passed on April 10, 1793. It required

> to maintain and keep in good order, on the body of said dam, in a convenient part of the same for rafts to pass through, an opening of at least twenty-five feet wide, the bottom of which shall not be more than twenty inches above the common level of the water below said dam, with a sloping way therefrom, to extend twenty feet down stream before it reaches the bottom of said creek, and also erect, or cause to be erected and kept in good repair, a compleat lock of twenty feet wide, through which boats and canoes may at all times safely and conveniently pass.... If these conditions were not met in keeping the Penn's Creek public highway open, then the court could fine the owners up to fifty pounds [Dallas, Vol. 3, 354 & 355].

The act mentions rafts, boats and canoes, but no word of arks. Arks were only two years old and perhaps the legislature thought of them as rafts or boats. A fine of 50 pounds for not maintaining the lock and chute was a very stiff fine. A laborer in a mill only made about 19 pounds and board a year (Sharrer 77). The legislature considered each dam as a separate entity, and stated special requirements for maintaining the chute according to how the situation dictated. The day before the legislature approved the dam at Selinsgrove, it approved another dam on Swatara Creek, about four miles above Middletown, but required fifteen feet of chute for each foot of dam height (Dallas 348). This would have required the Snyder/Selin dam to be thirty-seven and one half feet long. However, this dam was not required to have a lock for boats going upstream. Snyder/Selin got to build a shorter chute of only twenty feet, but had to maintain a lock. Some dam owners provided a block and tackle to pull boats up through their chutes. The chute was only required to be twenty inches deep. Shively tells us that arks usually drew about 18 inches, giving only a two-inch clearance through the chute (7).

This restriction would limit the ark's displacement and therefore its load. Penns Creek is a very shallow creek and 18 inches of draft is most likely the maximum for any boat during a three foot freshet.

Three Sides to the Chute Controversy

Shively states the mill owners' side:

> When the first arks went down Penns Creek there were already some grist mills and saw mills along its course. These made navigation slow and difficult,

so it was not long until legislation was enacted requiring the owners of all dams to "make and leave open space of twenty feet near the middle of said dam at least two feet lower than any other part thereof." The act also provided that throughout the same width should be made a platform of stone or timber allowing a gradual descent, lowering the water of the dam etc. This had the effect of greatly lowering the water of the dam, and to overcome this, most mill owners placed planks across the open space. On approaching a chute thus closed, the arksmen, as was their right, steered for it, the impact tearing out the planking and sometimes a part of the dam also. They went their way, but the mill owner was obligated to wade into the icy water—for rubber boots were unknown—and again close the chute. This sometimes happened a number of times in one day and caused ill feelings between the arksmen and the mill owners. This was especially true of the saw mill owners. The grist mill owners were obliged to make use of the arks, so they just grinned and bore it [10].

The arksmen's side: They only used the creek, at most, three times a year during the spring, summer and fall freshets. The spring freshet occurred right after the ice went out and the snow in the mountains melted. This only lasted about two weeks before the creek receded, and it was their only way to get their products to market. Also the state, by law, had made the creek a public highway and they were entitled to cross the dam in either direction any time of the year. Usually they only used it in the early spring when the creek was about three feet above normal. If the mill owner built such a small dam that he required a plank across the chute to back up the water far enough to run his mill, then if he had to wade into the icy water, that was his problem. Sometimes when a heavy rain flooded the creek in June and late fall the arksman could catch the flood if he had an ark ready, but this had too many ifs for arksmen to depend on a flood.

The state's side: The state wanted to encourage commerce and the only way farmers, millers, miners and lumbermen could move their products to market was to use the creeks and river. The state tried to be fair and did not charge the arksmen or the mill owners for the use of the creek water, and in the case of Snyder's dam at Selinsgrove, it required the owners to provide a lock for boats going upstream. There was no mention of Shively's grandfather maintaining a lock in his dam. By that time there were few boats and canoes going upstream and probably a lock was not required.

Shively makes note of the first recorded ark on Penns Creek: "In 1794 Thomas Cooper wrote: 'In that year a boat with 1,600 bushels of wheat has gone down the Penns Creek to Baltimore'" (4). This was just three years after Michael Cryder ran the Juniata and Susquehanna Rivers to get to Baltimore. By 1794, the men of the Penns Creek were running wheat to market in arks, for no one boat could carry that amount of wheat. Since 1,600 bushels of wheat weighed 48 tons, it was usually loaded into two arks 75 feet long, each capable of carrying 25 tons.

Ark Navigation

David Scott, writing in 1827 says:

A voyage across the Atlantic does not invoke so much danger to life and property as the navigation of the Susquehanna [and the same might have been said of Penns Creek] from the New York line to the tide-water. Property can only be floated down in time of high floods, which seldom occurs except at the breaking up of the ice and melting of the snow in the spring season. During these floods the river is not navigable with any degree of safety for more than a week or ten days. The consequence is, that the whole trade of the Susquehanna descends at nearly the same time; the markets in the towns and villages along the river are overstocked and the owners are frequently obliged to sell at ruinous sacrifices.... The loss occasioned by accident to river navigation is estimated at five percent per year [Shively 9].

The Baltimore newspapers stated that two-thirds of all arks going through the Shamokin Dam chute the first year were wrecked (Livingood 66).

The best figures on cargo losses came from the Baltimore Commission, appointed in 1823, to estimate the feasibility of building a canal from York Haven, just above the Conewago Falls, to Baltimore. In their report they stated that the cost to insure the cargo for a trip down the river from Oswago, New York, to Conewago Falls, Pennsylvania, was about one-half of one percent of the cargo's value for the 250 mile trip (Livingood 57). If the insurance companies used one half the money they collected to pay administration costs and half to pay off claims, then only about one in every 400 insured cargos was lost. However, from Conewago Falls to the tidewater, a distance of about 65 miles, insurance costs jumped to seven to ten percent of the cargo's value (Livingood 57). Using the same criteria at ten percent, about one in 20 cargos was lost or the five percent cited by David Scott in 1827, four years after the Baltimore Commission's report. No figures are available on what percent insurance companies used to pay claims in 1823, but actuaries confirm that 50 percent is a good estimate.

Studying Thomas Yates' charts of the Susquehanna River dated 1855, it can be determined that the river has changed very little, unless there has been some major construction project since, especially Yates' map of Lazy Man's Gap (see Strong's *Voyage*, Chapter 5). Small islands and rocks on his charts appear the same as they do today, 150 years later. However, we can assume that the streams rose and fell more slowly due to the deep layer of leaves and decayed vegetation that covered the primeval forest floor.

Mr. Shively questioned if the building of the Glen Iron Bridge in 1832 hindered the running of arks on the Penns Creek. The bridge was only 11 feet above the normal water level and arks were only run when the creek was at a flood stage (7).

If the ark had a draft of a foot and one half, that left about ten inches for freeboard. Two-inch thick planks were used to build the ark's bottom. Another layer of two-inch thick planks were placed on top of the two-foot thick square timbers used to build the ark's sides, to provide the decking over the false bottom. This would put the ark's deck ten inches above the water line. The 27 inch tall flour barrels were stacked on this deck. The maximum number of barrels a 75 foot, pointed ark could carry was 250. These barrels could be stacked on the ark using only one level. Therefore, the roof of the cabin on the ark covering the barrels only needed to be about three and one half feet above the water level to protect the barrels. Any additional height of the cabin's roof was for crew comfort. They used the shack for sleeping and cooking. Watching *Video of the Last Raft, 1938*, we see that the raftsmen removed the roof of the shanty to go under a wooden bridge.

Arks and rafts were only run when the freshet was three or four feet higher than normal water level. Higher water was too dangerous; the unpredictable water could put the ark out in the middle of a field where it could not be returned to the creek, or smash it against a rock, ruining the ark and its cargo. Therefore, we can assume the Glen Iron Bridge did not hinder the running of arks.

Shively tells an amusing story about running whiskey to Baltimore:

> An ark pilot had been employed to take an especially large cargo of whiskey from the vicinity of the present village of Laurel Park. It was the usual procedure for most of the pilots, to employ a local river pilot to guide them through the treacherous waters of the Conewago Falls. Here a perfect knowledge of the location of boulders, often almost submerged, was necessary, if the passage were to be made with any degree of safety.
>
> The Penns Creek pilot had imbibed rather freely of his cargo during the voyage and upon approaching the falls, announced to his crew that he could run them as well as any man on the river. Realizing the danger, his crew made every effort to dissuade him. Failing in this they landed against his orders and he continued on alone. Hardly had the ark entered the falls when it crashed against a rock, spilling the pilot and his cargo into the roaring water. For a time he disappeared among the barrels and debris, but finally appeared near the shore and was rescued. Blowing the water from his lungs, he said in Pennsylvania Dutch (German), "Mein Gott! Ich hob gamaind ich het's letsch'd brode in bauch kot." (My God! I thought I had the last bread in my belly.) As a result of this experience, the old pilot went on the "water wagon" for the rest of his days (9).

John Fisher, owner of the largest distillery in western Buffalo Valley (at Laurel Park), would ship as much as 8000 gallons annually to Baltimore. The whiskey was worth from 25 to 50 cents per gallon. Eight thousand gallons of whiskey weighed 66,760 pounds, required 250 32-gallon barrels and was worth $2,000 to $4,000 in Baltimore. The standard barrel used to ship 196 pounds of flour also held 32 gallons of whiskey (Shively 9).

Shively makes this assertion: "It is doubtful however, that arks longer than 30 or 40 feet came down from Centre County, for it would have been impossible for them to clear the sharp curves of which there are many down through the mountains" (5). The West Branch raftsmen brought rafts 130 to 180 feet long and 26 feet wide through Rocky Bend and Chest Falls, which is about the same width as the Penns Creek at Coburn. In 1938 the last raft came through this area and it was 116 feet long and 26 feet wide. The video from the William Penn Museum in Harrisburg, Pennsylvania, shows the old raftsmen successfully navigating the bend and falls, missing the flat rock, and coming out of the falls by only 18 inches. Certainly arks 75 feet long or longer were run down the Penns Creek from its upper reaches.

Butter Rock

Shively tells this story about Butter Rock:

Back of Little Mountain, about two miles west of Weikert, there is a large rock known as "Butter Rock," because of the wreckage of an ark coming down from Centre County, partly laden with butter. When the casks containing the butter were thrown against the rock, some of them burst, covering the rock with butter; and as "Butter Rock" it has been known ever since.

The right side of the creek (Penns Creek Mountain side) had been cleared for navigation, and all of the pilots knew that they must hug the right shore immediately after rounding a sharp curve, just a short distance above the rock. During the previous night there had been a great storm and downpour of rain, which caused a large tree to fall from the Penns Creek Mountain side, entirely obstructing the cleared channel. A number of arks had started from "The Forks" (now Coburn), at daybreak, so spaced that there should have been little danger of collision. The teller could not recall the exact number of arks involved, but

Model ark on Penns Creek. About two miles west of Weikert on the Penns Creek is Butter Rock. Arks coming around the bend in the creek would stay near the right bank to keep from hitting the rock. However, one laden with butter hit the rock and several casks were tossed onto it, breaking them open and covering the rock, giving it its name.

thought there were at least four. The current was bearing the lead ark along at a good rate of speed — for there is considerable fall at this point — when on rounding the curve only a short distance above the rock, the fallen tree loomed in front of them. There was no time to attempt a landing and the pilot had make a quick decision between striking the giant tree or trying to pass through the uncleared channel. He chose the latter course, and in the parlance of arksmen "stoved." Unable to warn those following, the next ark crashed also, and so on until all were piled up. One or more of them struck the giant boulder, "Butter Rock," which projected from the left bank. A barn was built from the timbers and bottom planking of these arks. [The year the wrecks occurred is not known, and today there is no trace of the barn] [8].

In Aaronsburg, three miles north of Coburn, a barn is built of the same planking without the holes. Also, the original home of George Meyer, the miller at Blue Rock, was built with two inch thick white pine siding.

Ark Stoving (Wrecking)

Whenever an ark stoved, people for miles around congregated on the banks of the creek, searching for damaged cargo. As long as the barrels and casks did not burst open, allowing the contents to become damaged, persons finding them were obliged to restore them to their owners; but damaged cargo, whether by statute or custom, became the property of the person who salvaged it (Shively 10).

Ark Cargos

Shively listed some ark cargoes:

WHEAT AND FLOUR— Some of the first arks going down Penns Creek carried mostly wheat as cargo, but it was not long until there were enough mills to convert the wheat into flour, thus reducing its bulk and at the same time increasing its value. Flour was then packed in tight barrels. They were made by local coopers, which for many years was a flourishing trade. One writer says that at one time almost every other man in the village of Weirickstown (Today Penns Creek, P.A.) was a cooper [11].

RYE AND WHISKEY— The first crop usually planted on new or "wild" land was rye. While it yielded more bushels per acre than wheat, when sold as grain it brought only about half as much. For this reason most rye was converted into whiskey, thus reducing its weight by about two thirds, while increasing its value considerably, although not as much as one might suppose. In 1810, the price of whiskey varied from 20 cents to 50 cents per gallon and flour averaged about $2.10 per barrel [11].

Shively does not say where these products were sold. In 1811, Baltimore was paying nine to ten dollars a barrel for flour and this price held until June of 1812 (Sharrer 141).

Shively continues:

CLOVER SEED—After several years of cultivation the soil produced enormous crops of clover, the second crop being allowed to ripen for seed. At first, like wheat and rye, it was threshed with a flail, but after a time stationary clover mills were built and it was hauled there to be hulled [12]. [The quantity of clover seed exported from Union County, 6,000 bushels in 1825, indicated that it must have formed an important part of the cargo carried by arks, especially in earlier years.]

MEAT AND BUTTER—A considerable quantity of cured meat and butter was carried as cargo, much of it, especially butter, coming from Centre Co. [13].

POTASH AND PEARL ASH—Land was cleared much faster than a market could be found for the timber; in fact for many years there was no market for it. Many of the settlers bore a sort of hatred toward the trees because of the amount of toil necessary to dispose of them. The finest of trees were often cut down, rolled on great piles and burned. These "log rollings" were usually carried on at night, the people of the neighborhood gathering together and making merry by the light of the great fires, which could be seen for miles. Enormous piles of ashes were produced and this was often leeched and boiled until dry in large kettles. The black potash which resulted was sold for manufacture into pearl ash, which sold for two to three hundred dollars per ton. It may be presumed that these products, too, formed an important part of the cargo [13].

SPLIT SHINGLES—Suitable logs, usually of clean white pine, were sawed to length and split into shingles, for which there was ready sale in the eastern markets. A special tool was used for splitting these shingles, consisting of a knife-like blade about fifteen inches long with a hole in one end for a wooden handle. The blade, which was somewhat wedge-shaped, was struck with a mallet, thus causing the block to split with the grain. These shingles being of light weight were sometimes piled on top of the load of other items or used to fill vacant space [13].

The Costs to Get Products to Market

Shively quotes the March 26, 1825, *Union Times* newspaper of New Berlin: "Union County [Buffalo Valley] sends annually to market a surplus of about 150,000 bushels of wheat, 2,600 barrels of whiskey, 6,000 bushels of clover seed and 200 tons of pork.... Centre County [Penns Valley] spares for foreign consumption about 180,000 bushels of wheat, 6,000 bushels of clover seed and 1,000 barrels of whiskey" (15). In 1825, it was still six years before the canal opened and 30 to 40 years before railroads were available to haul the farmer's products to market.

The 210 miles of dirt roads from Penns Valley to Philadelphia wound through mountains and across Penns Creek, the Susquehanna River and the many small creeks that crossed the countryside. Shipping flour over that terrain by wagon was not profitable. There was only one way to get the flour to market and that was by ark. To run this quantity of goods down the Penns Creek it would take about 230 arks from Penns Valley and 210 arks from Buffalo Valley, to say nothing of the arks from west of Selinsgrove along the Middle Creek, if all were shipped by ark.

In 1822 Baltimore was paying $6.64 a barrel for flour; however, in 1830 the price of a barrel of flour in Baltimore was only $4.94. Usually the prices in Baltimore were a little higher than in Philadelphia (Sharrer 222). To ship the flour by ark to Baltimore it cost only about 40 cents a barrel. It cost about $75.00 to build an ark (Shively 7 and Rinwalt 12). Three hands running the ark to Havre de Grace, Maryland, and returning to Penns Valley cost $6.00 a hand. It would cost $8.00 for a pilot to run the Susquehanna Gorge (Missimer 42).

The ark would be sold for its wood for about $35.00. Hopefully that money would pay for transporting the 250 barrels of flour from Havre de Grace to Baltimore. If the flour sold for $6.64 a barrel, the ark's load brought $1,660. If it cost $101 to transport the flour to market, then $1,559 would be taken back to Penns Valley. Often this was a cooperative effort between the farmer, miller, ark builder, the warehouse owner and pilot, with no one getting any money until the pilot returned.

Today the villages of Coburn in Penns Valley and New Berlin in Dry Valley have many large, beautiful old homes. Where and how people made their money to build these homes is no longer a mystery.

What Was 180,000 Bushels of Wheat Worth?

If Buffalo Valley sent annually to market a surplus of about 150,000 bushels and Penns Valley sent about 180,000 bushels of wheat, what did that mean to the economics of these two valleys? Baltimore was paying approximately $6.00 a barrel for white flour in 1825 (Sharrer 222 and 223).

A bushel of wheat yields about 42 pounds of white flour, therefore 180,000 bushels of wheat made about 38,571 barrels worth $231,426.00 in Baltimore. In 1825 a laborer worked 12 hours a day, 6 days a week at $1.00 a day, for an annual income of $312.00. The 180,000 bushels of wheat represented about 742 annual incomes in 1825.

Today the minimum wage in Pennsylvania is $7.25 per hour, and to pay for 72 hours a week for 52 weeks, it costs $27,144 annually. To buy 742 annual incomes at that amount would take $20.14 million. The 150,000 bushels of wheat from Buffalo Valley sold for about $192,858.00 in Baltimore or about $11.9 million in today's money.

Warehouses, Landings and Ark Construction

Much of the grain, whiskey and produce carried by arks from the western end of Buffalo Valley was first stored in a large warehouse that stood on the creek bank just west of the mouth of Laurel Run (about one mile south of Laurelton). This warehouse was owned by Henry Roush, who also owned a mill and distillery at the entrance of the Seven Mile Narrows. All traffic to and from

Penns Valley passed by. Farmers for miles around sold their grain and other produce to him. Many from Penns Valley preferred hauling by land through the narrows rather than risk losing their cargo on the water route (Shively 13–14).

When the first mill at Laurel Park was built by Peter Fisher in 1793, a large platform was constructed in connection with it for the purpose of loading arks. Next to the mill was a large stone near the south bank of the creek where arks were built. The stone had a deep depression in its center for the platform on which the ark rested during the first part of its construction (Shively 14). The rock was probably used the same as a log in other locations. This was done so that the bow and stern ends of the timbers would bend earthward, and when the builders turned the ark over the calked seams between the bottom boards closed tightly (French, Colcord 66).

Sampsell's dam was another landing place. The mill powered by this dam was built by Peter Kuhns about 1814. Kuhns sold to George Sampsell in 1823 and Sampsell's dam it has remained (Shively 14). The dam and mill are near the village of Penns Creek.

Penns Valley Arks

The following report was dictated by Daniel Karstetter to Herbert J. Walker and published in *Rafting Days in Pennsylvania* under Karstetter's name and in the Pennsylvania Alpine Club under Walker's name. The article was titled *Running Arks on the Famous Karoondinha* (sometimes spelled Kayarondinhagh) and was published before 1922.

At age 35 in 1827, George Meyer moved to Penns Valley and located on Pine Creek, south of Aaronsburg, Pennsylvania, where he built his mill. Therefore, the period of this report was after 1827 and before the Civil War (Meyer 118). His mill used water from Elk Creek.

The report stated:

> Daniel's father, Leonard Karstetter, and Johnny Strahan, residents of "The Forks," built large arks toward spring in which to transport the flour to Selinsgrove by way of Karoondinha, now called Penn's Creek. These arks were made of first-class timber. Mr. Karstetter was the owner of the first saw mill on Penn's Creek. The floor of the ark was made of hewed timber [he meant sawed] and was packed with tar and pitch so that it was perfectly watertight.
>
> In the spring when the freshet came, each ark was manned by a pilot, a steersman, and a bowsman, when they were put afloat and proceeded to Selinsgrove. When the arks came through the Seven Mountains where an old lady kept a restaurant, the arksmen would stop for the noon meal. She sold the old-fashioned ginger bread and small beer.

According to the report, the trip to Selinsgrove from "The Forks" was made in one day. The arks were sold there, and the flour and the arks were then manned by other crews and proceeded to market.

The arksmen who had taken the arks from Coburn to Selinsgrove then returned by night through the Seven Mountains, ready for another trip, so that these fleets of arks might be dispatched while the freshet lasted. That was their only outlet to the market with their grain.

The Manufacturing of Wheat

The early lumbermen referred to the process of making trees into various types of marketable products as manufacturing; therefore I will use the term manufacturing of wheat to describe the process of harvesting the wheat and preparing it for the gristmill. Daniel Karstetter described the process: The plowing was done with oxen and horses; the better class had horses. The harvesting was done by means of sickles.

Karstetter probably meant a scythe with a cradle attached, commonly called a cradle. Later when he describes cutting the wheat, the description is that of using a cradle. This farm instrument became popular in the 1790s and replaced the sickle, making the farmer's job easier. With a sickle one man could cut about three-quarters of an acre a day; with the cradle he could cut 2.5 acres, or 3.5 times more. The first threshing machine was shown in Baltimore in 1791, but it would take years before Penns Valley would see one (Sharrer 44).

From the report:

> The farmers would go together and help each other. They would commence at one farm. Usually there were from twenty-five to thirty men and women. The women were as proficient with the cradle as the men. Two cradlers cut together, one on each side, the one on the right side laid the grain with the butts toward his partner, and the one on the left laid the grain with the butts toward his partner, thus forming a sheaf that required four handfuls of grain for one sheaf. It was the custom in those days to go to work with the rising of the sun without breakfast. They would work until 7 A.M. when they would retire for breakfast. The company would make their toilet usually at a large watering trough, after which the good women of the house would announce the time for partaking of the meal.
>
> After they resumed their work at harvesting, they worked until 10 o'clock when a young girl would come out into the field with a lunch which consisted of dried venison that had been smoked and cured, and had been provided for during the preceding winter.
>
> Buck skin was used for making trousers for the man of the house to be used during the harvest season. These trousers were worn when the wheat was moved into the barn. Each sheaf of wheat was placed and the mower would get on his right knee and press it into position. That was a trade in itself. In those days the men usually did the mowing for the whole settlement.
>
> Threshing the grain was a very slow process, since there were no threshing machines in those days. The wheat was placed on the threshing floor and a boy rode a horse around in a circle over the wheat, until the grain was tramped out of the wheat. It usually took from one and one-half to two hours, after which

the old-fashioned shaking fork was used to shake the grain out of the straw. This grain was run over a homemade fanning mill to clean the wheat, after which the year's supply of wheat flour was made at the grist mill above Blue Rock, now called Meyer's Mill, on Pine Creek.

The surplus wheat was also ground into flour and barreled in home-made wooden barrels ready for shipment.

4

Waterways from 1791
to the Early 1800s

This chapter presents the history of rafting and the running of arks along the rivers and streams from 1791 until the 1850s. By 1860 most of the wheat and flour was going back to Philadelphia, and Baltimore started drawing wheat from the Midwest (Kulhmann 43). However, rafts (board, timber, spar and round log) would continue to use waterways until about 1900.

Arks and Rafts in New York State

There are two branches to the Susquehanna River in New York State. The North Branch and its tributaries drain lower eastern New York State and the Chemung River, and its tributaries drain the western end.

After the Revolutionary War in 1787, immigrants flocked to the Chemung Valley in large numbers. Then in 1793, Judge Christopher Hurlbut, Frederick Bartles, Captain Charles Williams and eleven other prominent men held a meeting at Painted Post, New York, to devise ways and means to improve the navigation on the Chemung River and its tributaries, the Cohocton, Tioga and Canisteo (Near 236). The group had been reading William McClay's reports on navigation on the Susquehanna River in Pennsylvania. McClay had been making reports on the river for the Pennsylvania Assembly, so they could appropriate money for improvements to facilitate the use of Durham boats, scows and rafts on the river. This meeting was just two years after Cryder opened the lower Susquehanna River to the Baltimore market. Near had Cryder's last name spelled correctly, but he was off by one year when he said Cryder had run the river in 1792 (Near 245).

The Painted Post group felt that they could benefit if navigation on their four rivers was improved. They subscribed and paid $1,500.00 to make navigable the Chemung and the three streams meeting at Painted Post to form the Chemung. The three streams to be cleaned were the Tioga to the Pennsylvania state line, with its tributaries, the Canisteo to Hurlbut (today Arkport), and the Cohocton to Liberty Corners. Fifteen hundred dollars was a considerable amount, when men worked a 12 hour day for a dollar.

Pine was the one product merchants could convert to money at the time.

To get their product downstream they imported men from the Delaware and lower Susquehanna Rivers to teach the art of spar and board raft construction. Sawmills were built along the streams and in the fall after harvesting their crops, the men cut logs and skidded them to the sawmills on the snow. At the mills logs were cut into 16 foot boards and in the spring when the freshets came, board rafts were built and floated down the river to markets. This is the first mention of cutting spars on the Susquehanna Watershed; however, if men were imported from the Delaware and the lower Susquehanna River to teach the skills, then other areas of Pennsylvania had already started before 1793. Spars were skidded on the snow to the river bank to be made into rafts after the ice went out.

Three freshet seasons provided enough water for people to take their products to market. They called freshets a "rafting pitch" (in the vernacular of the watermen), known as the "spring fresh" (just after the ice went out), the "June fresh" and the "fall fresh." The fall fresh occurred in late October and early November, but the June fresh was the most popular because of the weather and water temperatures.

In 1795, Frederick Bartles built a dam at the outlet of Mud Lake, about five miles east of Bath, New York, to power his gristmill and sawmill. In 1798, he sent a board raft with ten platforms down the creek by opening a gate in his Mill Pond Dam, creating his own freshet and driving his raft down the creek to the Cohocton and then down past Painted Post into the Chemung River. This may be the first recorded use of a splash dam.

In 1800, Judge Christopher Hurlbut obtained the passage of an act by the New York State Legislature making the Canisteo River a public highway. New York State would never declare all waterways as public or free highways, but they would have individual streams and rivers declared when requested. The state declared the Chemung River a public highway in 1820, with the Cohocton River being declared the following year.

By 1800, the land had been cleared of trees and was producing corn (75 bushels per acre), oats, wheat, potatoes, livestock and whisky. The winter of 1799–1800 saw many New York watermen building arks. That year Judge Christopher Hurlbut built and "turned" the first ark on the Canisteo River and took it to Baltimore loaded with wheat purchased from the farmers in Danville, Mount Morris and Geneseo areas, west of the Finger Lakes area in Western New York (Near 243). On the Cohocton River, Messrs. Swing and Patterson left White's sawmill, five miles below Bath, with a cargo of wheat. The dimensions of three of these arks were 72 feet by15 feet, 71 by 15 feet and 70 feet by 15. All had pointed ends (Near 159).

The judge was so successful that he built a warehouse along the Canisteo River at Arkport to store the products until the spring freshets. Some years he sent as many as 11 arks to Baltimore. Several warehouses were built at the town of Canisteo to store and ship goods also. The arks' cargos consisted of flour, grain, pork, whiskey and shingles, and most of these were shipped to Baltimore, although some made their way to Philadelphia and New York City.

Arksmen were paid 75 cents to $1.00 a day, and the trip down the river and what they saw more than compensated for the walk back home (Near 242). *A Town in Rafting Season* details what they would see, and Schuyler S. Strong describes the route the arksmen walked to get home. They came up the river to Northumberland, then up the West Branch to Williamsport and over the mountains to Painted Post (see Strong's *Voyage*, Chapter 5).

The Canisteo River was narrow, crooked and so full of riffles that board rafts were kept to five platforms, about 90 feet in length, until they reached "Jack's Eddy" at the junction of the Canisteo and Tioga Rivers. They called these small rafts Canisteo Colts, and at Jack's Eddy they lashed two colt rafts end to end to form a full raft, ten platforms long or about 180 feet long. The watermen lashed two rafts side-by-side below Elmira on the Chemung River to form a fleet. This was done to save manpower for the long trip down the Susquehanna River.

Men of the North Branch of the Susquehanna in New York State had started running board rafts down the river in 1795 from the town of Unadilla, about 40 miles down the river from Cooperstown and Lake Otsego, the source of the North Branch. Captain David McMaster was the pilot who took the raft to Harrisburg (Bath, *Plaindealer*, March 12, 1887).

Daniel P. Fitch, a veteran waterman, furnished this interesting account of the first launching of an ark in 1803, a short distance above the village of Sherburne, which is on the Chenango River about 55 miles above Binghamton, New York. At Binghamton the Chenango River flows into the North Branch.

Fitch reported:

> It was built to convey lumber down the river, with the expectation of finding a market in Baltimore. Nathaniel Austin and his brother were engaged in the enterprise. A tax was levied upon the town to clear the river of obstacles. The day of the launch was celebrated with as much eclat as the launching of an ocean steamer at a later day in one of our seaports. As soon as the craft was afloat, it was loaded down with the crowd, all eager for a ride. It was towed up the stream a short distance and then allowed to float down with the current, thus affording the crowd an opportunity to test its merits. The ark was then loaded with staves and shingles [Bath, *Plaindealer*, March 12, 1887].

When the Capitol at Washington, D.C., was rebuilt in 1816, pine and hardwood lumber was taken down the Susquehanna. Some came from New York State and more from Pennsylvania. Anson Seymour of Chenango Forks, New York, had a large quantity of seasoned lumber which was stored at Baltimore. Government contractors were glad to buy largely from him, at good prices, for the new legislative halls of the nation (French 40).

The Northumberland *Public Press* reported that in 1804, 552 rafts containing 22,000,000 feet of lumber — besides a large number of arks, loaded with wheat, flour, staves, whiskey and shingles, the whole aggregating in value $500,000 — passed out of the North Branch at Northumberland. Northumberland is at the confluence of the North Branch and West Branch of the Susquehanna Rivers. However, in 1804 almost all of the river traffic came down the North Branch.

Before the War of 1812

Magee stated that in 1800, the Baltimore newspapers heralded the arrival of the first ark to pass through the treacherous last 40 miles of the Susquehanna River to bring a load of wheat to their city. We know that Michael Cryder had brought the first ark to Baltimore in 1791, and since the newspapers had spelled his name with a "K" we know that reporting at the turn of the century or the recording of history was not always an exact science.

The city businessmen had spent money clearing the 37 mile stretch of the river between Columbia and Port Deposit, the most dangerous part. This had to have taken place after 1801 when Pennsylvania repealed the law on improving the Susquehanna River below Columbia and Wrightsville. Afterwards the trade between the Susquehanna and its tributaries with the city of Baltimore increased rapidly.

The Napoleonic Wars caused a wheat shortage in Europe, inflating the price of wheat and flour in Baltimore. By 1805, Baltimore's merchant millers were paying $7.50 a barrel and $6.00 to $7.25 in 1807. But when both England and Napoleon tried monopolizing American flour at the expense of American shipping, President Thomas Jefferson placed an embargo on sending flour to both countries. This hurt the United States' economics more than theirs and Baltimore flour dropped to $4.50 a barrel in the summer of 1808. After the embargo was lifted flour prices went up to $9.00 to $10.00 a barrel (Sharrer 141). McGrain reported flour at $11.00 a barrel in 1811 (7).

In 1810 Brazil was open for trade and the wealthy of the country demanded a high-grade flour made from the very best wheat, with relatively low moisture and high gluten content, such as would sustain the sea passage (Kulhmen 40).

In 1811 merchant miller Robert Gilmore chartered the *Orizimbo* to carry about 1,500 barrels of flour to Lisbon to sell to the British and Spanish troops fighting the French. The Lisbon price was $18.00 to $20.00 a barrel with Gilmore realizing a 100 percent profit or $15,000.00. The *Orizimbo* was one of 802 American vessels to reach Lisbon in 1811 (Sharrer 141). Exports of flour reached an all time high in that year with a half million barrels going to Spain.

With the flour trade booming in Europe, the Caribbean and now South America, flour from the Susquehanna Valley was welcome in Baltimore. Roughly a million barrels of flour were exported annually from Baltimore, of which about half were manufactured in the city and the rest brought in from tributary territory such as the Piedmont in Maryland, the Cumberland Valley, lower Pennsylvania and those brought down the Susquehanna River. About half a million barrels were exported overseas each year and the remainder sold to the Southern states (Kuhlmann 43).

In 1799, the state capital in Philadelphia was moved west to Lancaster, and 11 years later in 1810, it was moved to Harrisburg. From the Capitol building in Harrisburg the state legislators could see the arks and rafts passing down the river on the spring freshets and would have a better understanding of the river's commerce.

Vying for the Susquehanna River Trade

Baltimore, with the help of the Maryland Assembly, improved its harbor and built good roads into the surrounding countryside so that wheat and other farm products could be brought to the city for export. This included a road from Safe Harbor across the river from Middletown and just above the Conewago Falls on the Susquehanna River. This road was to bring the Susquehanna trade coming down the river to Baltimore instead of Philadelphia. The introduction of the Conestoga wagon made possible the movement of greater quantities of goods to Baltimore. By 1825 Baltimore was shipping flour to all parts of South America (Livingood 62).

The Pennsylvania Legislature responded by opening the Conewago Canal around the falls in 1797 (Shank, W. 69). This canal was one mile long and would get the river traffic down the river to Columbia where it could use the Lancaster Turnpike to Philadelphia.

In Maryland the Susquehanna Canal was opened in 1801 to provide a bypass around the narrowest point on the lower river, the treacherous Fanny's Gap just below Love Island, which was reported to be only 32 feet wide. It ran from the Maryland–Pennsylvania border to Port Deposit about 12 miles (Livingood 34).

Maryland also authorized the company to clear the river, which ran parallel to the canal, and to pay for this effort they planned to collect half tolls. Pennsylvania objected to Maryland charging tolls for the use of the river, since Pennsylvania had made the Susquehanna River a public highway 50 years earlier and Baltimore had benefitted from the Susquehanna trade since 1791, when Michael Cryder had opened the lower river for arks and rafts. Maryland complied with Pennsylvania's wishes and declared the Susquehanna River in Maryland a public highway.

The financially successful Erie Canal in New York State opened in 1825 and then goods moved across the state from the Great Lakes to New York City. This enticed Pennsylvania and Maryland to build canals, both wanting to capitalize on the western trade. Steamboats began plying the Ohio River and those on the Great Lakes brought great wealth to New York City. Both Pennsylvania and Maryland wanted to get a piece of the western trade as well as the Susquehanna River Trade.

The Steamboat

In 1807, Robert Fulton successfully navigated the Hudson River in a steamboat. Within a few years every river and large lake had its own steamboats. This invention would do almost as much for moving goods by water as the Conestoga wagon had done for the movement of goods overland. Since arks and rafts could be towed from the mouth of the Susquehanna to Baltimore at anytime, the men didn't have to wait for the wind and then hope that it would be blowing in the right direction. Canal boats could be towed to Philadelphia if there were a canal that crossed the Delmar's Isthmus between the Chesapeake Bay and the Delaware Bay.

The Susquehanna River is "a mile wide and a foot deep" during the dry seasons and too swift during the freshets. In Pennsylvania the steamboats worked well in the slack water of dams, but they couldn't move up and down the Susquehanna River and its tributaries. So, the state had to build canals along the river.

Baltimore During the War of 1812

As the war approached, British agents in America were openly issuing licenses to American ship captains so they could enter Iberian Peninsula ports to supply Wellesley's army in Portugal with flour. In 1809 Baltimore exported 105,000 barrels to Portugal and 835,000 barrels in 1811, in 802 American ships, an average of 1,041 barrels per ship. That year a barrel of flour could be purchased in Baltimore for $9 or $10 and sold in Lisbon for $18 to $20 (Sharrer 141). Some Baltimore merchants had to combine stock from other cities to fill their orders.

In June of 1812, the Congress enacted an embargo on flour, but even with the war, embargo exports increased to 938,954 barrels in 1812 and 972,560 barrels in 1813. Baltimore printers were busy manufacturing counterfeit British licenses to trade with Spain, Portugal, St. Bartholomew and other British ports in the Caribbean (Sharrer 141).

In 1813 flour trade with the Iberian Peninsula was suspended, but trade with the West Indies continued (Sharrer 142–3). Then in June the British blockaded the Chesapeake Bay, cutting off all trade, so several of Baltimore's merchants applied for letters of marque and outfitted privateers. Privateering proved very profitable also, with 58 prizes between 1812 and 1814 (Sharrer 144).

In September of 1814 the British fleet sailed up the Chesapeake after burning Washington to punish Baltimore for privateering. After being repelled at Ft. McHenry they withdrew and the war ended in February 1815 (Sharrer 143).

The war of 1812 did not touch the Susquehanna Valley, and in 1812 the Baltimore newspaper stated: "Many large rafts are coming down the Susquehanna to Baltimore. One large float (four rafts on top of one another) said to contain 2,500,000 feet of lumber arrived. The lumber which composed this raft came mostly from the counties around Binghamton, New York, a distance of over 400 miles from Baltimore, where seven-eighths of the lumber that comes to Baltimore is collected. It is sold mainly to foreign buyers, and brings prices ranging from $9, $17, and $23 per thousand" (Magee 196).

Arks on Other Public Highways

The West Branch of the Susquehanna River

Peter Arnold Karthaus was born in Hamburg, Germany, in 1765, and emigrated to Baltimore, Maryland, in 1805, where he invested in the flour trade by purchasing several clipper ships during the War of 1812 (Gilliland 1). In 1811 Karthaus purchased six tracts of land in what today is known as Karthaus Township in Clearfield County. This area and the village of Karthaus lies along the north side of the West Branch of the Susquehanna River, halfway between Clearfield and Lock Haven in the middle of the Appalachian Mountains.

COAL • Coal was the first product exported from the Karthaus area. The Allegheny Coal Company and Karthaus purchased land in 1811, and in 1815, Karthaus and his son arrived in the village. It was about this time that they started mining coal by the strip mining method of removing the soil covering the coal and digging the bituminous coal with picks. At that time bituminous coal was preferred over anthracite, and Harrisburg and Columbia purchased all the coal they could transport down river by ark, at 37.5 cents a bushel in 1859 (Row). A 75 foot ark, built as described in the Appendix, could carry 25 tons of coal or about 769 bushels of coal, which brought about $269 at market. Compare this with an ark of the same size filled with 250 barrels of wheat that sold for about $2,500 in Baltimore.

Gilliland states that it cost about four dollars a ton to transport goods by ark down the river or $100 an ark load (14). This figure is the same used by Shively (7) and Rinwalt (12). Coming home with $169.00 wasn't much compared to what the wheat farmers acquired, but it was one way of raising money and carrying some manufactured products home.

Coal arks ran out of the West Branch of the Susquehanna River until replaced by the railroad in the 1850s. Anthracite, which is found along the North Branch, was also run down the river in arks until 1831 when the canal opened.

Arks were replaced by two canal boats, each carrying 120 tons, or 240 tons in tandem canal boats. Five mules and a crew of three men moved coal the year round, except for the three winter months when the canals froze over. The West Branch Canal only extended to Lock Haven, 60 miles from Karthaus, and thus didn't provide transportation for the West Branch coal.

PIG IRON • Bog-ore, found four miles below Karthaus near the river at Buttermilk Falls in 1816, is a brown iron ore found in boggy or swampy land. Peter Karthaus purchased the land and built a furnace at Karthaus in 1817. The ore was brought upriver by boat and made into pig iron, using charcoal to melt the ore. He also built a foundry to make stoves, large kettles, tea kettles, pots and skillets. The pig iron was shipped to Harrisburg in arks and the manufactured items went to Havre de Grace, Maryland, where they were shipped to Baltimore, New York and Boston.

Karthaus and his partner Geisenheimer operated the furnace until 1822 when they abandoned the iron operation, producing about one thousand tons of iron in the seven years it operated. This was only about six ark loads a year. Karthaus and his partner had several problems. First and foremost, they could only ship iron down the river during the spring freshet, which lasted just two to three weeks out of the year. Second was the cost of producing the charcoal for firing the furnaces. An average furnace would consume from 600 to 800 bushels of charcoal every 24 hours. This required about 30 to 40 cords of wood from trees 25 to 30 years old. Some furnaces consumed the yield of an acre of woodland each day. The furnace had to employ many men to cut the wood and a master collier and one or two helpers to make the wood into charcoal. The process of making charcoal was considered an art and the charcoaling skill was called the "Mystery of Charring." It cost about $15 to $20 to turn out a ton of pig iron during those years when pig iron sold for from $28 to $45 a ton. If the $15 to $20 manufacturing costs and the $4 transportation costs per ton are subtracted from the sale price, it can be seen that manufacturing and selling pig iron was not very profitable (George Washington and Jefferson National Forest website).

In 1836, with the price of pig iron climbing to $55 a ton, Peter Ritner, brother of the Pennsylvania governor, and John Say leased the furnace from Karthaus and installed a cupola to use coke instead of charcoal. The British iron industry had used bituminous coal for fuel, and with steam engines to run the blast furnaces, they could produce pig iron for as little as $11.75 per ton. With the bituminous coal mines at Karthaus it seemed logical that it would be profitable to try this method. A cupola was ordered from Boston and delivered to Havre de Grace, Maryland, by ship. The cupola, a cast iron cylinder eight to ten feet in diameter and up to thirty feet high, weighed several tons. With the use of coke made from coal and a blast of air from a steam engine, the furnace turned out superior grades of iron. The cupola pig iron could be pounded thinner to make iron objects. Gilliland says the cupola came up the Susquehanna River to Karthaus (14).

By 1836 the Pennsylvania Canal ran from Columbia, 25 miles above the southern Pennsylvania border with Maryland, to Lock Haven, 60 miles from Karthaus. They could use the Susquehanna Canal in Maryland to get the cupolas into Pennsylvania. Then the 25 miles upriver through the Susquehanna Gorge would have been the worst part of the trip. Using the canal from Columbia to Lock Haven would have been a necessity.

The 60 mile run upriver from Lock Haven to Karthaus was a relatively easy task compared to the Susquehanna Gorge. The most difficult part was coming up through Buttermilk Falls, four miles below Karthaus. Buttermilk Falls, about three quarters of a mile long, was considered the roughest spot for passage of rafts or arks between Clearfield and Lock Haven. This was going down the river. The cupola had to come up the river, which was more difficult.

To go up the river through the Susquehanna Gorge and Buttermilk Falls, the men would have had to hold the flat boat off the shore with poles while a large crew of men pulled the flat boat upstream from the shore. Often they used a block and tackle to do this, reducing the number of men needed.

During the panic of 1837, the price fell from $55 to $22 per ton, and by December 30, 1839, the fires in the furnaces were extinguished for good when the canal was never extended above Lock Haven. According to legend the last arks were loaded with pig iron and sent down the river, where two sank in the eddy at the foot of Buttermilk Falls. Ritner and Say had spent $80,000 to produce 400 tons of iron. This was a cost of $200 per ton to make the iron.

No reason was ever given for the sinking of the arks, but pig iron weighed 450 lbs. per cubic foot and only 111 cubic feet of pig iron weighed 25 tons—an ark's load. An ark load of coal consisted of 961 cubic feet or almost ten times the space as an ark load of pig iron. It would have been easy to overload the arks with pig iron, and if the arks took on water going through the falls they would sink in the eddy below.

The North Branch of the Susquehanna River

In 1839, Pennsylvania began constructing along the North Branch of the Susquehanna River near Danville iron furnaces that used anthracite coal — this innovation reduced production costs. The Danville area had all three ingredients required for successful iron making: iron ore, anthracite coal to make coke for the furnaces, and transportation to markets. Work on the North Branch Division of the canal began in 1828 and was completed in 1831, connecting the area with markets along the river (Shank 51). By 1840 with the opening of the Susquehanna and Tidewater Canal from Wrightsville, Pennsylvania, to Havre de Grace, Maryland, Danville would be connected by canal to Philadelphia and New York just in time for the railroad boom (Shank 71). Danville imported two

British iron makers who knew how to make the T-rails used by the railroads. The Danville area furnaces furnished the United States with the T-rails for the railroad expansion of the 1850s and 1860s.

The Lehigh River

Ringwalt gives this account of the movement down the Lehigh of six arks of coal in 1803:

The descent of the river, for the first 15 miles from Mauch Chunk, was exceedingly rapid, the fall being some 300 feet. It was a bright and cheerful morning, after the stream had attained the usual high-water mark, that the arks were cut loose, and each equipped with six men, began at once the descent of the rapids. Now the torrent roars, the waves and whirls dash madly around the boats; the men at the oars, faces wild with animation and excitement, and muscles full distended; run to and fro upon their narrow platforms; the pilot, with energetic motion and speech, addresses the steersman — the steersman, with like gesticulation and vehemence of manner, responds to the pilot — and then all hands make desperate plunges at the oars! Now the boat, shaking and cracking, swings its cumbersome form around a villainous rock; now it sheers all; in a counter-current towards the shore, and then bending round, again dashes forward into the rolling waves, when-cr-a-sh! je-boom! it rises securely upon a ledge of rocks half concealed beneath the surface of the water! A moment serves to contemplate the wreck, and then the men, seizing oars and planks, make good their exit to the shore — leaving the broken and dismembered ark to its fate, and the cargo to the curious speculation of the catfish and eels. Of the six which embarked, but two reached Philadelphia, and even these presented a very dilapidated appearance [12].

In a letter describing early efforts to transport Lehigh coal to Philadelphia, written by Mr. Charles Miner in 1833, he says that in August, 1814, the firm with which he was connected started off the first ark they had constructed. It was 65 feet long, 14 feet wide, with 24 tons of coal. The expenses here, I post as follows:

Expenses of the passage and hands down and returning $28.27
Wages, including three pilots. 47.50
Total $75.77
Ark (cost high, from inconvenience of building) $130.00
Twenty-four tons coal. raising from mine 24. 00
Hauling nine miles to landing, at $4 a ton 96.00
Loading into ark. 5.00
Total $330.77

So that, in the first experiment, the coal cost about $14 a ton in the city. He adds: "I have been somewhat minute in giving you these details, because this ark was the pioneer, and led off the coal trade by the Lehigh to Philadelphia, now so extensive and important. This effort of ours might be regarded , I as the acorn from which sprang the mighty oak of the Lehigh , Coal and Navigation Company." In a note he says: "The fact may not be uninteresting that we were obliged to pay $4 and for much of the coal hauled $4.50 a ton over an exceedingly rough road of nine miles, where now, by railway, it is transported for twenty-five cents a ton" [Ringwalt 12].

The Main Branch of the Susquehanna River

Ringwalt describes the magnitude of the ark and raft traffic on the Susquehanna River:

> An illustration of the extent to which arks and rafts were used is furnished by the fact that a report presented to the Pennsylvania legislature in 1829 quoted the following statement: From an accurate account, kept by a respectable citizen of Harrisburg, it appears that between the 28th of February and the 23d of June, 1827, there passed that place: Rafts, 1,631; arks, 1,370.
>
> Two hundred of the arks were laden principally with anthracite coal, averaging 55 tons each, making 11,000 tons.
>
> The remaining 1,170 arks were loaded principally with flour and whisky for the Baltimore market, and carried, on an average, 400 barrels each, making 468,000 barrels.
>
> It is supposed that about 300 keel-bottomed boats, carrying from 800 to 900 bushels of wheat each, descended during the same period; say 800, makes 240,000 bushels of wheat, at 35 bushels to the ton, makes 6,857 tons.
>
> Annals of Luzerne county say that 30 lumber rafts passed down the Susquehanna in 1796. In 1804, sawed lumber went down — 552 rafts, with a total of 22,000,000 feet.
>
> In six days, from May 18th to 23d, 1833, 3,480 rafts were floated down the North Branch of the Susquehanna by the village of Catawissa. In 1840 the lumber floated down the Susquehanna in rafts was estimated at 250,000,000 feet [12].

Baltimore After the War of 1812

After 1815, England, France and Spain enacted corn laws (import tax on grains), greatly diminishing American export to Europe. U.S. exports were directed toward the Caribbean and South America, Cuba before 1823 and Brazil afterwards. (Sharrer 264). In 1818 Baltimore paid $9.50 a barrel and by 1822 flour had dropped to $6.64 a barrel (Sharrer 222). However, by 1823 U.S. consumption was greater than exports, reducing Baltimore's reliance on exports. Then in 1838, England revised its corn law, partially reopening its market to America.

By 1820, the ark traffic had increased so that a Baltimore newspaper reported that "200 arks carrying 11,000 tons of coal, 1170 carrying 41,718 tons of general merchandise, 300 Keel boats carrying 500,000 bushels of wheat and 1638 rafts containing 25 million feet of lumber arrived in Baltimore from the Susquehanna Valleys. Here again there is no mention of spar rafts or timber rafts, for they could have stopped in Port Deposit" (Magee 196).

The following year the Susquehanna River brought 40,000 barrels of flour to Baltimore, 8 percent of the flour inspected that year. Additionally, 200,000 gallons of whiskey were also brought down the river (Sharrer 226).

After 1850, railroads would start changing the point of sales for wheat and flour from the Susquehanna Valley. Able to haul farm products anytime of the year and not relying on the spring freshets, the Pennsylvania Railroads started hauling wheat and flour to Philadelphia right after the harvests.

The Canals

To capitalize on the Susquehanna trade, the state of Pennsylvania built the Union Canal connecting the Susquehanna River at Middletown to Philadelphia. But soon after it opened in 1826 (Shank, W. 12), the state realized that when the spring freshets brought hundreds of arks and lumber rafts down the river, the canal was too slow to move all the products to Philadelphia. Canal boats did have their advantages because they could move up to about 120 tons of coal or other products in one boat and often they ran two boats in tandem, or 240 tons, using several mules and a crew of five about the same size crew as a raft or Durham boat. Canal boats were the preferred way of moving heavy material long distances.

However, canals only ran along the Susquehanna and Juniata Rivers, and many farm products were grown along streams such as the Penns Creek, miles from the canal. Once the farmer had built his ark to take the wheat, flour and other products downstream to the nearest canal port, why not run the arks all the way to Baltimore, where they would get a higher price? Additionally, canals closed down for the winter months when they froze over, shortly after the wheat was harvested. The canals opened after the spring thaw or about the time the spring freshet occurred and arks could go down the river.

In 1829 the Chesapeake and Delaware Canal opened across the Delmar Isthmus. Products such as timber rafts, spar rafts and coal arks could be towed from Port Deposit through the canal to Philadelphia, New York City and on to Boston (Livingood 93). The Columbia to Philadelphia Railroad, built by State Works of Pennsylvania, opened in 1834 and connected the canal along the Susquehanna with Philadelphia (Shank, W. 41).

The State Works of Pennsylvania started building canals about 1828 which were operating by 1834, and had to abide by the law the state had enacted 60 years earlier in 1771. This law made the Susquehanna River and many of its tributaries public highways, thus each canal feeder dam was required to have a chute to allow water craft to pass through the dam in either direction. However, when the State Works contracted to have the canals built, they only gave general requirements for building the canal and feeder dams. The details were left up to the contractors.

The first dam, constructed at Clarks Ferry, was known to the raftsmen as Greens Dam and was just above the confluence of the Susquehanna River and the Juniata River. The builder, Abbott Green from Buffalo Valley along the Penns Creek, had been an ark pilot before taking the contract to build the dam.

His chute was wide enough to accommodate a fleet (over 56 feet wide) and long enough so that there was no problem with wrecking in the chute. However, the approach to the chute required the raftsmen to negotiate the dangerous Lazy Man's Gap.

The second dam to be built was the Shamokin Dam, two miles below the confluence of the North and West Branches of the Susquehanna River. No record exists as to how long or wide the chute was, but in the first spring it was open in 1829, the Baltimore newspaper, *Niles' Weekly Register*, reported that two out of three arks that tried to pass through the Shamokin Dam were wrecked (Livingood 66). The dam was washed out the first year by a flood, and the rebuilt dam and chute significantly reduced the number of wrecks. The rebuilt dam was 9.5 feet high with a chute 650 feet long (Snyder, Canals 111). Snyder also said the chute was 62 feet wide, but Chatham and other sources stated that rafts had to be uncoupled to get through the chute. This would make its width less that 56 feet.

The reason for wrecking in the early chutes can be found in a study conducted in New York State when builders had trouble with a chute for the Chemung Dam near Elmira. A team of engineers, sent to Pennsylvania to study their dams and chutes, determined that wrecks were usually the result of building the chute too short, causing swift water to dig out a deep trough at the end of the chute (Whitford Chapter 14). The deep water rolled back on itself, stopping the arks and rafts, breaking them. Canal feeder dams in Pennsylvania were usually about ten feet high with plenty of water running through the chute, causing this problem within a year or two of construction. Dams in New York State, with only 21 feet of chute for every foot of drop, caused wrecks and had to be rebuilt. The state determined that a chute would need almost 70 feet in length for each foot of drop in the dam water to prevent the trough that would cause wrecking (Whitford Chapter 14).

Chatham reported that the Shamokin Dam chute, a single chute, was not wide enough to have a fleet of rafts to pass through (French, Chatham 29). A fleet was two rafts lashed together side-by-side to run the rafts down the river with fewer raftsmen. Square timber and log rafts were usually built about 26 feet wide to pass through the narrow chutes in the rivers above the canal. A fleet, 52 feet wide, would require a chute about 56 feet wide. Chatham said the Lock Haven Dam and Shamokin Dam had single chutes and the rest of the dams were wide enough to run double to Marietta. Chatham helped to run rafts from Lock Haven to Columbia from 1862 to 1873, making four trips a year.

The Clinton County Historical Society in Lock Haven has a newspaper ad seeking a contractor to rebuild their dam the year after it was originally constructed — no one at the society knew why. Was it because the chute was too short also? Billy Byers said the chute at Lock Haven was nine hundred feet long — the interviewer thought Billy was telling another whopper — but he may have been much closer to the truth than anyone thought (Byers' oral history 6).

This is a splash dam under construction. All dams were constructed the same way, including feeder dams for the canals. Logs were stacked like a log cabin with no chinking, then rocks were dumped into the frame to give the dam weight and hold it in place. Planks were laid up against the logs on the slack water side, and dirt and manure were placed on the planking to keep the water from seeping through the planks. This dam appears to be about ten feet high, the same height as many of the canal feeder dams (courtesy Clearfield County Historical Society, Clearfield, Pennsylvania).

The chute at Shamokin Dam remained a dangerous passage, according to Strong. This was for two reasons: A look at Yates' *Charts* shows the shore coming out on the right below the dam. (Even today, at the site of the old dam, rocks can be seen along the right side where the chute used to be.) Second, the wind caused a problem getting into the chute (see Chapter 8).

The West Branch section contained the Muncy canal feeder dam, 23 miles above Northumberland and about 12 miles below Williamsport. This dam, when first built about 1830, caused rafts and arks to be wrecked. The raftsmen and arksmen took matters into their own hands and destroyed the dam so that the arks and rafts could safely pass (Livingood 69). How this was done was not given, but all dams were made of logs stacked like a log cabin, and axes were carried on all rafts and arks.

5

Rafting on the North Branch

Rafting in New York State started in the 1790s, and there were two men from the North Branch of the Susquehanna River who left us chronicles of their trips down the river. The first was Schuyler S. Strong, who kept a journal of his voyage down the river and his return. He was a 42 year old lawyer who watched each spring as many rafts passed Painted Post, where the Cohocton, Tioga and Canisteo rivers merged to form the Chemung River, wondering what it would be like to make the trip down river. In 1838 he signed on as a "light hand" on a board raft. Information about who Schuyler S. Strong was and how his journal was found is included. Reading his words, one will feel the chilling wind on the face, the pleasure of a warm sunny day on the river, the excitement of running a falls and the various characters he met on his trip.

The second man was Thomas Yates, who drew charts (dated 1850) of the channels the pilots used to safely run their arks and rafts down the river. He made two trips to log points on the river and recorded the times when he passed the points. He also recorded a list of items needed to make the trip. His charts have been used to explain the dangerous run through the Conewago Falls and the course with its options past Girty's Notch and through Lazy Man's Gap. His timetables are given below so today's paddlers can gauge their progress.

Strong's Journal

In 1986 I visited the Northumberland County Historic Society in Sunbury, Pennsylvania, and was shown WPA Folder 80. During the depression in the 1930s, the Works Projects Administration provided work for both blue and white collar workers; this was a white collar project. Some white collar workers were hired to capture information for the archives. Folder 80 was only four and one half double spaced pages, but it contained a half dozen excerpts from a reported diary of a Judge Strong, who in March and April of 1838 signed on to run a raft from Painted Post, New York, to Port Deposit, Maryland. All the excerpts from Strong's diary were eloquent descriptions of his trip down the river.

A search of every library and historical society along the North Branch of the Susquehanna for the original diary proved fruitless. I was told the diary, if it ever existed, was lost to history. Then I made contact with Virginia Wright of the Painted Post Historical Society in New York. I sent her a copy of Folder 80. About a year later she sent me 11 articles published in the Bath *Plaindealer* from March to May of 1887. While doing research on another project she had run across these articles and remembered Folder 80. She copied the articles and sent them to me. With the help of the Steuben County historian, I determined the diary's author was lawyer Schuyler S. Strong.

Who was Schuyler S. Strong? In 1838, when he made his voyage, he had practiced law in New York State for over 14 years, winning recognition for his leading role in the murder trial of Robert Douglas at Bath, New York. He died in Springfield, Illinois, in 1845, seven years after the trip down the river. His wife's obituary, in 1882, stated: "He was a leading member of the Bar and an orator of distinguished ability in the political field." Strong was about twice the age of his fellow "light hands."

The *Plaindealer* published his journal five years after his wife, Frances Minerva Cruger Strong, had died, and 42 years after Mr. Strong had died. The *Plaindealer* did not identify the author of the journal. However, the article from the Northumberland County Historical Society referred to the author as Judge Strong from Steuben County, New York. The Northumberland article contained a half dozen quotes that were identical to those in the *Plaindealer*. The Steuben County historian said there was never a Judge Strong in Steuben County; however, there had been a Schuyler S. Strong who practiced law in their county during the period this voyage took place. The six eloquent quotes and the fact that Strong was "an orator of distinguished ability," and that many legal terms are used in the journal convinced me Schuyler S. Strong was the author.

Strong's Voyage

There are parts in this journal that have been written or rewritten since Strong died. I have excluded the gory parts about the Wyoming massacre and background on other nonessential persons, as they did not lend themselves to furthering a knowledge of rafting on the Susquehanna River. Perhaps in 1887 the changes made the article more readable. Brackets are used for author's comments because Strong's journal included parentheses.

Below is the journal as Virginia Wright found it with the exceptions noted. The first two articles covered background and ark and raft construction. Most of this information is included in other places. The third article started with Strong's journey.

> It seems ordained, whatever it is needful that man should do, however hazardous and laborious, he should be impelled thereto, by a seemingly strange influence and infatuation. When the long roll beats and the squadrons deploy, the brawny youth is instantly seized with an unaccountable impulse to fall into

Strong's voyage.

line, and does. When unexplored wastes, people by wild and savage denizens, are made known, the professed disciple of peace has a consuming desire to go amongst and become the associate of the bloody man-eating outcast, and goes. So, too, in the spring-tide, when the booming of the coming flood is heard and the great rafts, with their jolly crews, shouting and halloing, come dancing down the swollen river, the home-bred rustic is inspired with an irresistible inclination to jump aboard to relieve the weary raftsman, and hie away to the salt-sea, and jumps. It was neither patriotism, devotion or charity, that brought about these several results, but the God-given pleasure, in danger, adventure and excite-ment. If it were not for the strong desire to gratify these impulses, the state would be undefended, — new regions unexplored, the resources of the county, undeveloped. It is meet that the plundering pirates, who would lay waste and destroy our homes, should be received "with bloody hands and laid in hospitable graves." It is proper that the merciless savage, who refuses to cultivate the fair fields that lie at his door, should be wiped out; as he surely will be, when the missionary opens the way for civilization. So also it is for the common weal that the great forests should be cleared away so as to make homes and plenty for the coming of generations.

Many a time, and oft, when a boy, have I taken a convenient station, during the Spring freshet, and watched for hours, the rafts and arks sweeping out of the Conhoction (today spelled Cohoction) and Tioga rivers in quick succession; their rollicking stalwart crews— stripped to the shirt, — necks and bosoms bare, with stout arms, when the pilot shouted, "Right! Left! Jump to the work," rais-ing the huge oars to the utmost. Force them through the resisting flood with a will, then lower them and with a run carry them back, ready for another stroke. So they fly from side to side with brief breathing spells, like the cannoneers in an engagement. When the crafts were safely landed at McBurtey's or Big Eddy, the crews came trooping up the banks of the several rivers in long battalions, with a run, shout and jump, to their respective quarters, to repeat the same operations, like frolicking tobogganers.

How I long to be dancing upon the same tide and be one with them; and I resolved, when the first opportunity offered, I would be. In the latter part of March 1838, I chanced to be at Painted Post. The ice had gone out, and the lum-bermen were getting their rafts ready for a move. I casually met Gabriel Har-rower.

Gabriel T. Harrower was born September 25, 1816, in Chemung County, New York. In 1852 he was the sheriff of Steuben County, and during the Civil War he held the rank of colonel in the Union Army. The Civil War was 16 years after Schuyler S. Strong's death. In 1871, Harrower was a New York state sen-ator. He passed away while living in Lawrenceville, Tioga County, Pennsylva-nia, in the fall of 1895. In March of 1838, Gabriel Harrower would have been 21 years old. This was not young, for some pilots of the West Branch of the Susquehanna River were as young as 15.

From Strong's journal:

I had long known him, and then learned that he was getting his rafts out of the Tioga (river), so as to be ready for a final start on the 27th. I offered him my services as a hand, and was accepted. Being what is termed a light hand, I was to receive only five shillings per day [a shilling is one 20th of a pound sterling or about 25 cents], and found, besides the allowance of four days for the return trip with four dollars for expense money. Weight as well as muscle was material in forcing the heavy oars against the current and added value to service I had learned when a boy, the sleight in handling an oar, and generally "Knew the ropes" in sailor parlance.

The Captain was a trained waterman and expert pilot, having been bred to the business from his infancy. His father, before him, was a notable raftsman in the North, as well as the Chemung branch of the Susquehanna, for more than thirty years. The captain had hurriedly collected four rafts, two of which were in charge and piloted by Sam Patterson, a veteran in the service, with a crew of young blades, who were making their first voyage. The other two he piloted himself. He had already employed three hands as assistants besides myself. They were strange to me, and not of the vicinage. One — a printer, a tramping jour, who, at some time had starred on provincial boards. He belonged somewhere below Harrisburg and had the winter previous, joined the Insurgents of Patriots at Navy Island under the command of the notorious General Sutherland. When the Canadian authorities made it too hot for them, he took leave of absence, without pay, and tramped it to Painted Post, so as to work his passage at small wages, homeward. He favored us occasionally with his rendering of passages from "Robin Rough Head," Bombastes Furioso, and other favorite plays of nomadic theatrical troops. He evidently was a vagabond and wanderer, yet was plucky and not uncivil; but being a Pennamite, became the butt of our crowd. The Yankees and Pennamites have never been cordial since their bloody warfare in Wyoming Valley. He was known by no other name than "Pat," derived from his late military service in the Canada unpleasantness. [The unpleasantness was the capture of Navy Island in 1838.]

The steersman, who carried the left hand stern oar, and which was mainly my post, was a burley coarse-grained fellow. He was called "Joe," but no one seemed to know whether he bore any other name or where his domicile was. He boasted, chiefly of his fighting qualities and claimed to have chawed off many an ear and gouged out eyes without number. No bull dog ever spoiled so much for a fight as he, yet to me he was as good and kind as could be. He took especial pains to relieve me, whenever possible on the laboring oar.

The third man was smaller that the others and a rare character, he had a cock-eye and wry nose, and was the personification of mischief and fun. His comical phiz was provocative of mirth and his glibes and jeers kept all in good humor. He appropriately bore the name "Familiar," as the old Dutch name of Veimilyea is commonly pronounced, and belonged somewhere in the county. At home, I have no doubt he was a worthy and reputable citizen, but when on the water he gave loose to his appetites and all manner of pranks. He would fearlessly go into any crowd and stir up a fight, which he would settle for the drinks. It may be proper here, to state by way of apology for him, that persons living in a higher plane, even wearing from home influence and social restraints, give loose also to riot and debauchery of the grossest kind, while on their perennial trip. Owing to their conduct and general reputation of raftsmen in the river towns, they were as much the terror of women and children, as a band of Indians would have be. If the confessions of my associates were to be believed, they were indeed a hard lot; but from an intimate association of ten days, I came to the conclusion they were arrant hypocrites and not what they pretended to be. I never fell in with a kinder or more generous set of fellows in my life. They persisted in giving me the coziest corner in the cabin, the first dip in the dish, voluntarily assuming much labor that might fall to me. Their kindness and good offices were the more appreciated because we were strangers to each other and could not reasonably expect ever to meet again, and never have. My outfit was simple enough, though somewhat more elaborate than the others had. It consisted of a spare shirt and an extra pair of stockings, a large clasp knife for cutting my meat and stirring my tea. I had also provided myself with an old camelot cloak to take about me at night and serve as a "*robe de nuit.*"

DAY ONE

Tuesday, March 27th, I was on hand early this morning at the raft. I was without money and had an order for some upon an individual two miles below. The captain was anxious to pull out so as to get through the canal chute before the crowd, and suggested that I meet him at Shoemaker's Eddy six miles below, where he intended to land and lash up and build the cabin if there was time. So I trudged down to Knoxville. The order was not honored and so I concluded to trust my good fortune for a supply of the needful and pushed on through mud and mire for Shoemaker's. When I reached there, the captain was ready to pull out. The stage of water is not promising and he is anxious to be moving, though the cabin is not built and he has yet no provisions except some raw pork and black bread, but no cooking tensile. I jumped aboard and we were off.

We had run only a short distance when we passed Patterson with the other two rafts upon a bar. We landed as soon as possible and a part of our crew went back to render assistance. A cold drizzling rain commenced which lasted several hours; notwithstanding those of us who remained, set to work putting up the much needed cabin or shanty. It was constructed in this way: Six pieces of scantling about 8 feet in length, three on each side, and opposite, were placed against the coupling plank on each side of the raft, and in the center platform, and so beveled at the upper ends, as to join together, brace-like, so as to support each other. They were then sided over with boards from bottom to top forming a complete roof. A small aperture was left to the back end, for the smoke within to escape. The sides were boarded up tightly with the exception of a narrow opening in front for the door, which was made of rough boards and hung with leather hinges. Four boards, six inches wide and four feet long were made into a bottomless box against the back side, filled with earth, and constituted the fireplace. A large stone was set against the cabin's side to protect it from the flame. We had just completed the job when our men returned. They were not successful in their efforts to get Patterson's fleet off the bar. When they got aboard the order was to "tie loose" and we were soon afloat and on our winding way. The rain had ceased and we glided gaily along rounded Newtown Island beautifully, and swept by the unpretending village of Elmira without call or even a hail, and just before dark landed on the left bank, six miles below under the shadow of the famous Hogback, the scene of Sullivan's brilliant victory over the Indians and Tories for which Wilson, as he passed it nearly forty years ago thus prophetically wrote.

> "To thee brave Sullivan! who scourged this crew.
> Thy countries gratitude shall be due.
> And future ages on there summits rear.
> Honors to HIM who planted Freedom here."

Without fire or straw in our cabin, cold, wet, and weary we were compelled to seek shelter for the night in a rustic Inn hard by. It was already crowded beyond its capacity, by previous comers and every bed taken. I am tired and sore, every bone in my body aches, with the severe labor and exposure during the day. I have some misgivings about my ability to endure the work and fear I have undertaken more than I can stand. To what pains and penalties does this adventure subject us! I can not back out — must go through, I had no alternative but to find a corner. I then selected a smooth board, elevated one end, wrapping my old cloak about me, and wet as I was, made it my bed and lie down to pleasant dreams, if dreams will come to one so jaded, in such comfortless quarters. We are told they do come by contraries. That the hungry dreams of rich feasts, the weary of downy bed, and the freezing of cozy firesides. My fellow raftsmen seem to be jolly notwithstanding their discomforts and promise to make the night hideous with their roistering and noise.

DAY TWO

Wednesday, 28th. At dawn the pilot shouted, "all aboard," we had no toilet to make and were at our respective posts at once and commenced to pull out, but in our haste one of our oars struck a raft at the shore and snapped a blade. We had to hold up, unship the broken oar and repair the damage, which detained us a full hour. At last we were underway and kiting, but it was hard work for us. We had to be constantly on the alert, to dodge the islands, skip the bars and clear the bends. It was pull first one way and then the other. The pilot kept a running fire of "Right! Left! Heavy up behind! Give her headway." As hard as we had to work, it was difficult for me to keep warm, the sky was covered with dense clouds and the weather was cold and sour. I was so stiff and sore that it was with difficulty I could raise my arms for a strong pull. Cold pork and bread with river water for two days began to tell upon me, accustomed as I had been to generous diet and warm beverages. I felt really weak and faint and craved some stimulant. I hailed a passing raft and enquired of an acquaintance on it, if they had any tea on board, and if he would be kind enough to rap up a drawing and toss it to me. He did so. We had a fire going in our rude fireplace, I filled a tin cup with water, set it thereon and soon as it came to a boil — put in my tea. After it was sufficiently steeped and cooled, I took hearty drafts of the delicious beverage. I was at once upon my feet, cheered, but not inebriated, and all right. Every disagreeable sensation had passed away and I was myself again. Never while I live shall I cease to honor thee! Celestial weed! We reached Tioga Point about noon — discarded supernumeraries and entered the big river, as watermen designate the Susquehanna here.

Rafts would carry extra light hands to make it down the Chemung to the North Branch of the Susquehanna. The extra light hands were sent home when the fleet of two rafts was ready to enter the Susquehanna River. The main branch of the Susquehanna River, being wider and straighter, required only four light hands, one for each sweep, with two on the stern of the fleet and two on the bow of the fleet, plus a pilot who commanded the crew and helped out on the forward sweeps when necessary. One of the crew on the aft sweeps was designated the steersman who was second in command of the fleet, and in charge of the other crew members on the other rear sweep.

From Strong's journal:

This beautiful intervale where the bright waters of the Chemung and North Branch so lovingly meet, has ever been an important and notable place and the scene of many memorable events. Here the Iroquois from the East and the West met, marshalled their clans more than three centuries ago, preparatory to a descent upon the Indians of Virginia and the South. The bloody Queen Ester had her seat here. It was here that the British and Indians met in 1778 and planned the expedition against Wyoming [Valley]. In 1779 Gen. Clinton formed a junction here with Gen. Sullivan on his march to the Genese Country for the purpose of punishing the authors of that terrible massacre. It was also a prominent point during the early emigration of the country. In the broad stream we have more sea room, but heavier pulls. I had no time to note the scenery. We pass to the right of Gore's Island and then to the left of Break Neck. Then we take to the right of Gregory's Broad Head Island. Sweep by Towanda Village, hug the slope wall and point for the opposite shore. We run by Wysox and as night was approaching, we shot into a little eddy on the right hand shore a short distance above Standing Stone, a noted land mark, and made a landing. [This Standing Stone was a different place from the one on the Juniata River.] There are rough and rugged mountains on either hand with sweet vales between, rendered historic by the heroic deeds here enacted. The beautiful plateau just across the river was the scene of one of the most daring feats history ever recorded. Major Moses VanCampen, two men and two small boys were being held captive on April 3, 1780, by ten stalwart Indians. That night during their sleep VanCampen overcame nine of the Indians and saved the four hostages. No nobler deed was performed during the Revolutionary War.

As soon as we made everything fast, two of the men went to a farm house and procured some straw for our bedding. Two boards, six inches wide were set up on each side of the fireplace running clear across the cabin, forming wide berths to hold the straw. A rousing fire was built and while they were gone I roasted a slice of pork by thrusting it into the fire impaled upon the end of a hickory stick, and basting it upon a thick piece of bread, made a satisfactory supper. I am about fagged out, but my comrades having all gone up to the Inn to have a time and I shall seek repose on my pallet of straw.

DAY THREE

Skinner's Eddy — Raftsmen's Stew — Buttermilk Falls —
Crossing the Line — Vale of Wyoming

Thursday, March 29th. So tired was I that I slept most soundly in the straw, moving not till we were all routed out upon the first gleam of day. After a hasty breakfast we pulled out, and in the course of an hour reached Asylum, or Frenchtown, where some exiles from France at an early day sought to make themselves homes. As we rounded the bend turning to the east, the morning sun with its grateful beams burst upon us. It was greeted by one and all with rousing cheers. There is nothing like sunshine to dispel clouds and vapors. All were at once in the best of humor, singing and dancing, and awaking with their shouts the sleeping echos of the mountains. We ran into Skinner's Eddy and landed so as to give the captain an opportunity to make some purchases. He soon came aboard with a large tin pail, filled with a needed supply of tea, sugar, eggs and crackers, and in addition, a small bag of potatoes. All unanimous vote of thanks was tendered him with three rousing cheers and a tiger. We could now snap our fingers in the face of all the pot-bellied publication from Tioga [river] to tide [Chesapeake Bay]. I have greatly missed my favorite beverage at meals and have been sorely tempted to take something stronger in spite of my temperance pledge, but like stuttering Mat. B — "Stuck it out," and am the better for it. We were again under weigh upon a broad and smooth current, so that only two were required at the oar to keep the raft straight; and the rest, in honor of the day and occasion, set to work preparing for dinner the lumberman's favorite dish — a pork stew. Some potatoes were nicely pared and quartered and put in the tin pail, partly filled with water, choice slices of side pork were intermingled and the whole put over the fire to boil; when the potatoes and pork were sufficiently cooked and the water largely evaporated, slices of bread and crackers were added sufficient to absorb the remaining fluid, and the dish was ready. The pail was then placed upon a bunch of shingles, and each one having provided himself with a clean shingle for a plate and forged from similar material a wooden spoon or paddle, seated upon his hunkers around the board and fell to without grace. For raftsmen, Delmonico [steak] could not have furnished a more savory repast.

When dinner was over, it was announced with much concern that we were approaching the most dangerous point on the river, the wonderful Buttermilk Falls. No one was allowed to bear the title of Waterman, until he had passed them. It was the freshwater equatorial line. The knowing ones began to wag their heads and talk ominously of the fearful disasters that had befallen careless and inexperienced raftsmen who allowed their oars to be caught by eddies and swirls, and had been instantly swept into kingdom come. The pilot gave his orders as solemnly as the leader of forlorn hope. He shouted, "Make fast all the loose lumber and shingles! Tighten the wedges! See to the couplings! Prepare a scaffold for our bedding and provisions!" It was done. Our fire must be preserved, at all hazards, as we might not be able to get any at the next landing. So, I was ordered to carry Pat's oar, and he, having never sailed through the terrible Charybdis, was directed to take a brand of fire, mount the cabin and keep it waving until the danger was passed. As soon as the sound of falling water was heard, all jumped to their posts, jerked up their waistbands, spat upon their hands, and Pat mounted the cabin, fire brand in hand and there sat astride waving the same to and fro. He was so intent upon his task that he did not observe the beautiful snow white cascade tumbling down the mountain side on his left, until the loungers gathered on the shore, hail him with jeers and laughter, in this wise: "Ho; Spooney? How does she ride? Is her back sharp? Do you see anything green? Get down you-d—fool, etc." Then the pilot announced, "The danger is passed; you can dismount." He was quickly on his feet, swearing that it was the d—est suck ever come over him, and with audible muttering, wagging his head like the flogged school-boy returning to his seat and threatening that when the opportunity offered, somebody would catch it. There was much merriment over the affair. Some congratulated him on his wonderful feat: others commiserated him on his misadventure. Last year a noted raftsmen of Bath, Jim French, took with him on his trip down some law students from this place, to one of whom was accorded a similar honor.

While floating down the broad smooth river Sam Patterson with his fleet overtook us, and we lashed together, having plenty of sea-room. The wind arose which plagued us exceedingly; so two hours before sunset we were forced to run into Lackawanna Eddy and tie up ten miles above the town at the head of the magnificent Wyoming Valley. On this very spot Gen. Sullivan, Aug. 1st, 1779, made his camp on his memorable march to the Genesee country. Much has been said and sung of the beauty of this charming valley, yet comparatively little is actually known to the public of its history. That a terrible massacre was once perpetrated here and that the fearful tragedy has been commemorated in the undying numbers of Campbell in his Gertrude, everybody knows. But few of our people realize that this valley, as well as those which form the Susquehanna for a hundred miles above and below, have been the theater of more historical events and are invested with more historical interest than any other district of equal extent in the United States. How few of the thousands who float down this magnificent stream every spring know, that almost every island, headland and eddy they pass is made memorable by some heroic deed or bloody scene.

Soon after landing I climbed far up the steep hillside surmounted by the wonderful Dial Rock — or Campbell's Rock, as it is sometimes called, because the poet described Gertrude and her lover standing upon it, watching (in the vale below) the merciless slaughter of the patriots by the "monster Brant with all his howling desolating hand." I, too, from an open ledge caught a view of the landscape, more grand and glorious than art ever painted. At my feet lay a valley, sweeping away for miles to the West and South, embosomed by dark and rugged mountains and intersected by the wide and winding river, here and there dotted with green islands and fretted with dancing ripples. Everywhere could be seen broad and fertile fields and charming homesteads, the plowman slowly turning the long furrow, the sheep and cows homeward plodding, after the days ramble in the pasture. The monument erected on the field of blood and spires of Kingston in the distance were lighted up with the golden rays of the setting sun. A single glance at this fair scene was a rich reward for all the toil and discomforts I had suffered, yea a thousand fold. For while life lasts the picture will never fade from my memory. As the shadows fell and gloaming stole on, visions of the past came welling up, and all that I had read and heard came reaming through my brain. I found myself unconsciously repeating these beautiful lines of Campbell:

"Delightful Wyoming! beneath thy skies,
The happy shepherd swains had nought to do
But feed their flocks on green declivities,
Or skin perchance thy lake with light canoe."

I was warmed by the wild birds seeking their nests that I, too, should to my cabin repair. I followed down a dancing rivulet, called Falling Spring, which poured its water into the river near where our raft lay, and was soon on board and ready for a night's repose.

Gertrude of Wyoming, by Thomas Campbell, is a poem with 837 verses. It is about the Wyoming Massacre of 1778.

From Strong's journal:

DAY FOUR

Aground — The chute at Nanticoke Dam — Humlock Eddy

Friday, March 30th. We were up as soon as it was light, and when we began to pull out, found that our raft was fast aground, the river having fallen considerably during the night. All hands pulled, tugged and pried, but could not move them. The rafts were uncoupled and one dropped down a length. Then all got into the water fore and aft of the grounded one, and with pries, managed to get her afloat. We coupled up and were soon swimmingly on our way. In a little time we reached the head of Monocasy Island, and ran to the left of it. This island was the scene of many a tragic event, during the Revolutionary War. The battle of July 3, 1778, was fought in the plain, on the right bank of the river, where now stands the monument, near which were buried the bones of those slaughtered on that bloody field.

We ran down within two miles of Nanticoke Dam, much dreaded by raftsmen, and where very many are wrecked, and landed in an eddy on the left bank. We uncoupled and double-manned each raft and ran through the chute, without accident. It required two trips, but we got all through by three o'clock, lashed up and dropped down to Humlock Eddy, and landed for the night. At Nanticoke, it is evident, the mountains once formed a complete barrier and what is now Wyoming Valley, was a vast fresh water lake. Its outlet was through an indentation on the mountain, forming a magnificent fall, but in the process of time wearing down the soft shales to the bottom, drained the lake completely. The strata of the mountains on each side of the river is horizontal and corresponding, presenting the appearance of a hill cut through as in railroad construction. It has been a charming Spring day, redolent of bursting buds and resonant of singing birds. We lay in a most quiet and romantic harbor. Dark blue mountains swell up almost from the river's bank on the either hand completely shutting in the view, except for a short distance up and down the river, which flows placidly and quietly as if loth to leave the sweet vale of Wyoming. My companions have all gone to the tavern, which is located somewhere at the base of the mountain, leaving me to keep watch over our fleet. They could not have conferred upon me a greater favor.

The rafts, delayed at the dam, are gliding by in great numbers. No one seemed disposed to drop into our quiet eddy and I am glad of it. Patterson has gone on with his fleet, intending to run part of the night by the light of the moon, it is so still and clear I have had a delicious hour looking out upon the sweet scene around me. The moon rides high, scarcely shadowed by the light fleecy clouds scurrying by, and throws its soft beams fully upon the gently flowing river, when not intercepting by dark mountains. It is so still that the humming of the smallest insect is audible. The roar of the falling waters, from Nanticoke Dam are faintly heard in the distance, but no living sound except the far-off yell of a wild raftsmen, the creaking of the oar of a passing craft or the constant thud and splashing coming from the bailing of a leaky ark, landing some distance below, all which are echoes from cliff to cliff. I have improvised a light from a pitch-pine splinter, stuck in a crevice of the cabin, and now writing up the events of this charming day on my notebook, together with the historical association connected with the localities passed.

DAY FIVE

Berwick — Danville — Northumberland

Saturday, March 31. Last night was quite cold and frosty, so that we were not altogether comfortable in our cabin. Our fire went out and we were destitute of blankets. When the first gleam of light broke over the eastern mountain, giving token of a fair day, we pulled out. We were chilled and cheerless, but when the golden sun, with its cheering beams rose above the hills, all were revived and forgetful of the discomforts of the night. The wooded shore was alive with the early birds and resounded with their merry songs. Our jolly crew sought to imitate them with their coarser notes, equally enthusiastic over the promise of a good day. We soon passed Shickshinny, shot by safely the fourth pier of the Berwick bridge, ten miles below. The current below Berwick is quite strong, and was the scene of a fearful disaster some years ago to a small steamer that was testing the feasibility of steam-navigation on the Susquehanna. In attempting to stem the rapid current, her boiler exploded, wrecking the vessel, injuring many. No further attempts were made in that direction.

The day was warm and our labor light. We virtually slept upon our oars. In raftsmen's mythology the stretch from Nanticoke to Shamokin is their idea of paradise, where there is nothing to do but sing songs and bask in the golden sunshine. [The river drops only about 64 feet in 56 miles for the Nanticoke Dam to the slack water of the Shamokin Dam, a gradient of 14 inches per mile.] The mountains gradually recede and the interval broadens. The whole country is changing.

We pass successively Catawissa and Danville, with its smoking furnaces and irons works. Just before dark we crossed the mouth of the West Branch and landed against the slope wall opposite the grand old town of Northumberland, having made a run of fifty miles, and the easiest we have had. [The slope wall was Blue Hill which rises about 500 feet above the river.]

The town occupies a beautiful and commanding position at the confluence of the north and west branches of the Susquehanna River, two miles from Sunbury. The scenery combines the charms of river and mountain views in great variety, and in high degree. It was laid out in 1772. Its location at the junction of the noble stream, draining an immense area of rich valuable territory, made it a village of some importance at a very early period. It was the radiating point for Durham boats and Conestoga six-horse wagons, conveying freight and passengers to the north and west. When the state Capital was removed from Lancaster [in 1810], it came within one vote of being selected, instead of Harrisburg, and that vote was cast by a representative from the little village of Sunbury, just across the river, growing out of an absurd jealousy of rival. But for that Northumberland might now have been the foremost interior city in the Keystone state. Many notable persons have their homes here, whose names the world would not willingly let die. Here lived and died Joseph Priestly, the famous chemist and scientist, whose fame was, and is coextensive with the civilized word. [Priestly, 1733 to 1804, the first man to identify oxygen, probably lived in the town when Strong lived there as a youth.]

His broad views and liberal opinions, while living in England, convulsed that little Kingdom to [its] centra. King, noble and prelates breathing free, when he departed for America. To me, this old place awakens more than ordinary interest, for here commences my earliest recollections, the first mile-stone in my life's journey. Here I attended my first school. I remember well the tall and angular teacher. "Mistress Boodry," whether maiden or matron, I can not say. She was kind and considerate, and not at all to be feared, notwithstanding the long wand she wielded to prod refractory urchins to duty. I remember too, Ben Reeser, a clever lad, my devoted henchman, and how on the "Glorious forth," he got drunk and fell into the river, was taken out, laid on the grass in the old graveyard near by. How when I come to him, he threw his arms around my ankles affectionately, how his fallen and forlorn condition touched me as keenly that I could not hold the evidence of my sorrow. Poor Ben! What came of him I never knew. Nearly a score of years have gone by since I last looked upon the old quaint town before me. I scarcely can see any change outwardly, the unpretentious habitations, look a little browner, the white chinking in the square log houses, has partly dropped out, the streets are narrow and quiet, the ponderous covered bridge across the North Branch still stands, but somewhat dilapidated, old John Mason's leaning tower or house on the very verge of the high precipitous cliff or mountain on the south shore of the West Branch, still threatens to topple down at any moment. I well remember with what wonder and amaze-ment I viewed it, astonished at the marvelous skill and daring required to con-struct it in that frightful position. When I have watched intently while a storm was raging and the clouds flew by, to my youthful eyes, it seemed to move and tremble, and I surely expected to see it come crashing into the town. There, too, is the magnificent island, which Calypso and her nymphs might have longed for. Montour Ridge and the Blue Mountain; here meet, after a wide separation, the two branches of the Susquehanna in loving embrace, like brothers long parted. Time brings few changes here.

DAY SIX

Girty's Notch — Through Lazy Man's Gap

Sunday, April 1st. We pulled out in good time and passed the Shamokin dam and reef of rocks, without accident. [Coming out of the chute at Shamokin Dam the water could throw a raft into a string of rocks along the right side. This was one of the reasons they waited in the slack water until morning.] The morning was lowering, but we had not run many miles before it began to rain and then snow, which continued till near noon, after which it cleared up and was warm and pleasant. We passed Sunbury [the town is on the eastern side of the slack water] the county town, the site of Fort Augusta, built in 1756, as a protection against the French and Indians, and Selins Grove on our right. We kept dogging the rocks, which are scattered everywhere, shot over McKees [Half] fall, run by Mohontongo Creek. About noon we reached that noted land-mark, too well known and sorely remembered, by all raftsmen, Girty's Notch.

We hugged the wall on the right, caught the breakers and pointed for the islands, near the lefthand shore. The river here was nearly a mile wide, and we were compelled by man strength with slight aid from the current, to crowd our rafts nearly that distance in running a few miles. It was pull — pull — pull with-out cessation or breathing spell. No galley slave ever had to work harder. We could plainly see other unfortunates in the same condition, sweating and tug-ging. Sam Patterson was close by us, and his tyro's began to wilt. He shouted and swore. And with a great hickory goad threatened to scourge them to their task, if they let up. By the skin of our teeth, tainting and breathless, we made the point. Many of ours were not so lucky. Some dashed on the islands and some escaped through the gut between them only to be caught up by the rocks below. [Here he is talking about making it through Lazy Man's Gap.]

This place was so named from a notorious Tory and outlaw, one Simon Girty, who either had resided, or committed some outrage here. [Girty's Notch is 4.5 miles upstream from Lazy Man's Gap.] It is said he was the offspring of crime, and during the Revolutionary War was adopted by the Senecas and became the fiercest savage of the tribe, and exercised his innate wickedness to its fullest extent. For long years the name Simon Girty, to the women and children of Pennsylvania and Ohio, (where he was last heard from), brought terror and detestation. We soon pass the mouth of the "Blue Juniata," made classic by song and story, and then shoot the great dam erected for canal purposes.

As the shades of evening fell we ran into the eddy at Coxestown and landed for the night, having made fifty-five miles according to the captain's navigation.

Strong has the points on the river reversed. First they passed Girty's Notch, then they went through Lazy Man's Gap, then under the Clark's Ferry Bridge, then he passed the confluence of the Juniata and Susquehanna Rivers.

From Strong's journal:

DAY SEVEN

A Layover at Coxes Town

Monday, April 2. Last night we all came near cremation. The straw in our cabin became quite dry and combustible. It being very cool, the fire was kept up in our wide fireplace to make ourselves reasonably comfortable. Either a spark or a brand fell into the straw and there was a blaze at once. My place being near the fire, I was first aroused and alarmed the rest. We were all out in a trice and water being handy, we subdued the flames at once, but our beds were gone. My old robe protected me and was that materially suffered from the flames. When morning came the wind was blowing so strongly that our pilot considered it unsafe to pull out until it abated, as the run below was the most difficult on the river, and so we lay to. This miserable hamlet was formerly of more consequence. It was a convenient stopping place for raftsmen who were uncertain as to where they would make their market, whether at Harrisburg, Yellow Britches [Creek at New Cumberland], Codarus [Creek in York County, 5.5 miles upriver from Columbia] or Columbia. It being only five miles above the first mentioned place, all the vagabonds of both sexes, free from municipal supervision, in the spring of the year gathered here to prey upon the raw and unsophisticated raftsmen. As soon as breakfast was over my comrades sought their favorite resort, the well supplied inn. [Coxes Town was just south of where the Rockville Railroad Stone Bridge is today. With a description like Strong's, one can see why no historical society was eager to preserve the village.] I tried to make myself comfortable in the cabin, but the chopping wind drove the smoke within, instead of without, which became unbearable, and I, at last, was forced to seek shelter elsewhere. The only accessible place near by was a dingy antiquated brick tavern. I walked in and took a seat near the stove. There was a rough and noisy crowd around the bar in the back part of the room. Finding a file of newspapers hanging against the wall, I took it down and was soon deeply absorbed in perusing the journals, old and new, contained in it. I had observed a burly, bleary-eyed vagabond, sitting on the opposite of the stove, but gave him no attention. While thus engaged, amid the din, I heard some one coarsely utter, "A d—d cold-water man." That might mean me, for I had not in ten years drank any thing stronger than small beer. "A d—d cent society man," that was doubtful. "A Whig of 36."

I knew that could not mean me, so I went on with my reading. Then I heard a commotion and on looking over the top of the paper I had in my hands, then I saw the curses were aimed at me, and discovered little Familiar, my shipmate, with drawn fist rush promptly in front of the bully and hiss out "you dirty dog, I have a notion to knock your teeth down your throat." I interjected, "Hold on, don't get into a fight on my account; he has done me no harm, I have no regards for what he says." Familiar replied, "None but a sneaking coward will abuse a stranger." His plucky onslaught perfectly paralyzed the fellow and he sneaked off without showing the least fight, and was seen no more. I never saw a man so completely cowed by one not half his size. The wind continuing in the afternoon, the captain determined not to pull out till morning. Pat, the Navy Island hero, took his discharge, his wrongs unavenged, and started for Harrisburg, five miles below, near where he belonged. I am inclined myself to throw up the sponge, but my comrades urged so hard for me to continue the trip, that I have concluded to do so.

DAY EIGHT

Harrisburg — Going Aground Again

Tuesday, April 3. The cabin not being tenantable, I was glad to obtain quarters in the old hostelry. In times gone by it had a bad reputation, having been the fruit (so said), of sin and crime, and stories are hinted of dark doings in the past, — of luckless raftsmen who received here their quietus, and were buried in the dark and seething waters of the river, which rushed madly through Conewago Falls to the unfathomable sea. There is much, especially on a stormy night, about its antiquated structure — creaking floors — rattling windows — the thud of the heavy wooden-blinds, suggestive of ghosts and goblins grim. Thus, the impression spread that it was a uncanny place,

> "O'er there hung a cloud of fear.
> "A sense of mystery the spirit daunted,
> "And told as plain as whispered to the ear
> "The place is haunted."

So everyone was ready to believe the ghostly stories told. But labor and hard fare had made me oblivious to it all, and I slept soundly until routed out for a start at early dawn. On reaching the rafts, I found all hands prying them off, the water having fallen slightly during the night. The wind still blew, but not so fiercely as yesterday. The captain concluded, notwithstanding, to double the crew and pull out. The Conewago Falls are only twenty miles below, and we all expect sharp work there. They are the Seylla and Charybdis, much dreaded by fresh-watermen.

In Homer's poem *The Odyssey*, Ulysses must pilot his ship through unknown seas, populated by the most famous creatures of myth and legend. Among their challenges they must weather the storms sent by Poseidon, resist the charms of Circe and Calypso, outwit the Cyclops, navigate the straits between Seylla and Charybdis and endure the enchanting songs of the Sirens.

From Strong's journal:

The tall spires of the State Capitol soon loom up, and in a trice we were skimming by the goodly city of Harrisburg. In 1733, one John Harris established a trading post here, then the remote frontier of Pennsylvania. It was a long time known by the name Paxton. Harris prospered in business, obtaining a grant of three hundred acres of land from the Penn proprietors, and afterwards purchased five hundred acres of Shippen. His son, John Harris, Jr., laid out the town and established the ferry, so it came to be called Harris ferry — then, Harrisburg. In 1796 there was an effort made to change it to Louisburgh, after a French king; the county was called Dauphin. The effort failed, and the old name by universal and proper consent was restored. The Harrises were prominent men and historical characters. They figured extensively in the Colonial records of their state.

We had scarcely run two miles below Middletown, when in mid-river we were brought to bay, being caught upon a sunken rock. The ripples caused by the wind having prevented the pilot from seeing the breakers. The right hand raft alone hung on the boulder, so we uncoupled in part and threw out the hind end of the left hand raft to catch the current and so draw the whole craft over. The movement practically accomplished the object, but the three rear platforms parted and were left sticking to the rock. We lashed up as best we could and prepared to seek a landing the first opportunity. We could not go through the falls in our crippled condition. We desired to run to right of the big island above the falls, but were too far to the left and ran plump upon the point of it. There was much clamoring among the crew, cursing to throw the blame on the mishap to the conduct of this one and that. The captain, like a true commander, shouted, "No one is to blame; let us set to and get out of the fix." So we complied and swung round the whole raft, which was not fast, and ran it down to the left of the island and landed it. I remained with the raft and the rest hurried back and were so fortunate as in a short time to get the broken raft off, and run down to the landing place, — so far, so good. We then took our dinner and the men became more cheerful. The captain and a squad were ferried over to the main, and went up opposite the rock, where the rear platforms lay, hired a boat and were rowed to the rock. By three o'clock we were rejoiced to see them kiting down to us, all safe. We landed them along side and set to work in repairing damages. By dark we had accomplished the work and were all right for a start in the morning. All hands are rejoicing upon our safe deliverance and that our mishap was no worse.

DAY NINE

Shooting the Conewago Falls

Wednesday, April 4. Bright and early we pulled out, having made due preparations for the rough water we must soon encounter. We hugged the island closely and struck the first breakers [riffles] below, nicely. Our heavy craft was tossed upon the seething waters, as lightly as a cork. It would bend in conformity to the waves like a great serpent, sometimes dash through a swell, dashing the foam and spray over us and again mounting over another, coming down with a slam. There was quick and heavy work, and the oars had to be handled carefully to prevent their being caught by eddies and swirls, so dangerous to those manning them. Thanks to our skillful pilot and his prompt assistants, we went though safely. The current must run fifteen or twenty miles an hour. Few green horns, if they could see from the shore, the boiling and surging waves, would dare ride through. It was reported that when Jim French's legal hands saw what was before them, they jumped off and made the trip on foot. Law being the perfection of reason, that seemed the sensible course. We had a hard pull to make Marietta, but succeeded and landed to get our dinner. Immediately after we pulled out, intending to run through to tide, but finding it too late when we reached Columbia, we landed just below the town for the night.

"A thousand toils, a thousand dangers past,
"Columbia's harbor shelters us at last.

It is a pleasant village, situated on a high sloping bank of the river and has a population of 2500, and is the principal depot of the lumber rafted down the Susquehanna River for the Philadelphia market.

DAY TEN

Columbia to Port Deposit — down the Gorge

We were at our oars by daylight [April 5, 1938]. The tide pilot [Tidewater pilot] came aboard and we pulled out with a single raft, doubly manned, having four at each oar, upon our exciting trip. The Susquehanna from Northumberland is broad, flowing over a rocky bottom with large boulders here and there. Below this point the river is compressed into a narrow channel, consequently deeper and more turbulent, as it flows over the sunken rocks, like the rapids below Niagara Falls. No man can stem such waters. The strongest swimmer will be drawn by the swirls to the bottom. The raft dodges around and among the breakers, now hugging a huge boulder, cutting closely a point, sweeping around a bend, then making directly for the bald head of another rock, which the divided waters prevented us from striking, and we slide smoothly by. So we go bounding along as if on a race with father Neptune, in his marine chariot. Precisely at 9 o'clock we shot into the tight little eddy, know as Fitz's, safe and sound. We had made twenty-five miles in three hours, for which each hand was paid two dollars and furnished a breakfast.

Soon after our arrival, I met D. H. Bonham, a lumberman and old acquaintance from Big Flats, who desired me to take charge of two rafts, which he wished to forward to Port Deposit, twenty miles below. A pilot was engaged to run them to the head of the canal around rapids, too dangerous to be navigated. [Below here in the river is Hollow Rock with Fanny Gap, where the navigable Susquehanna narrowed to only 32 feet wide and below that was Job's Hole, the famous hole that reportedly grabbed cars and raftsmen and spit them out into the Chesapeake Bay near Baltimore.] This stretch [of canal] is not difficult and fewer hands and a lower and cheaper grade of pilots are employed for the service, who are universally called mud pilots. When I arrived at the head of the canal I found a crowd of rafts and had some little wrangling with those crowding in. The rafts floated along by a gentle current and are kept from stranding on the bank by a setting of and pushing off of a pole, the oars having been removed and that is all the labor required. The banks of the canal are well lined with trees. The day is bright and sunny, the early trees are partly in leaf, the cherries blossoming and the birds are full of song. Some amusing scenes occurred at the several log-ponds I passed, growing out of efforts to get rafts out of them into the canal. Fierce quarrels and sometimes fights occur among the raftsmen in their efforts to get first in. Being an observer of one of these contests it came near bringing me into difficulty. The current having slacked, owing to the closing of the lock to let rafts through, I went on shore and upon a bridge over the canal, and I stood there waiting for the moving of the waters. Four stalwart men came on the bridge and as they saw me, charged me with being one of the party that had interfered with them at the log-ponds. I attempted to explain that I was a mere passer by during the disturbance and knew none of the parties. This seemed to exasperate them still more, and I said nothing further, not apprehending an attack, being alone and in no way a match for either one singly. The foremost one came threateningly toward me and swore he would throw me over the bridge. I had a large clasp knife in my pocket and felt sure if he grappled with me, I would be able to use it to my advantage. The instant I thrust my hand nervously into my pocket, he jumped back, at the same time saying: "I am not afraid of your knives or pistols," but I knew he was and backed up to the parapet of the bridge keeping my hand in place. As others approached, the cowards took themselves off, leaving me master of the field. By this time there was a moving of the waters and on I went. [The log-ponds held the rafts for sale. The raftsmen wanted in first so their rafts were at the right spot to be sold first. It could take weeks for the owners to sell their rafts [see William Lowman Chapter 6]).

While in the last lock, as the water was being drawn off, I saw wriggling upward on the side of the lock millions of little eels from one inch to two inches in length. The water being low was perfectly alive with them, all headed up stream. It proved to me conclusively that eels go to the sea to spawn. For that reason they are found in the fall going down the rivers on their way to their spawning grounds.

Back in the nineteen thirties, before the hydroelectric dams were built in the Susquehanna Gorge, the Susquehanna River had many eel dams. They were built by laying river stone up like stone fences until they protruded above the water's level. The two sides of the dam were "V" shaped with the open part of the "V" upriver and the pointed part down the river, containing a wire basket four to six feet wide. The eels, coming down the river in the fall, would get trapped in the wire basket.

From Strong's journal:

> I arrived with my charge in due time at Port Deposit, a long straggling town under the lee of a mountain, but a place at this time of much importance. It is in the state of Maryland and situated at the head of tide water, within five miles of the Chesapeake Bay. It is one of the principal lumbering depots and has facilities for shipping to the Southern markets. It is estimated that the shipments amount annually to fifty millions of feet. I walked back to Fitz's [Missimer spelled it Fites] in time to meet my old comrades on their second trip. We returned to Columbia by a foot path over the mountains, rough and rocky, the like I had never before essayed. It was a constant scramble, jump and climb. When we had gained the summit of the highest peak, an extensive prospect was spread out before us, a rich rolling country on the one hand in which there were plainly to be seen the spire of churches in the ancient city of Lancaster, on the other, rocks and mountains, within whose dark recesses a thousand feet below, foamed and fretted the wild waters of the winding Susquehanna. The scene was grand description, but I had no time to enjoy it. I had to improve every moment to keep pace with my more vigorous companions. When we reached our inn at Charleston, I was weary and sore and nearly used up.

The raftsmen's path back from Peach Bottom to Columbia ran along the eastern side of the river. The path was the most direct route, because many of the raftsmen made their living running this stretch of the river, and they had to be in Columbia the next morning to ride their scheduled raft. However, a hotel or tavern every mile or two catered to the men's taste when they got thirsty, so that they could stop for a glass of refreshment or stay the night if they so desired (Missimer).

Strong met up with his crew in Fites, which is five miles above Peach Bottom. They had made two runs that day so it had to be after 6 P.M. that evening when he met up with his old crew. However, they made Columbia that night because the next day he started from Columbia. The inn at Charleston must have been in Columbia.

From Strong's journal:

DAY ELEVEN

To Middletown

Friday, April 6. At an early hour, I started from Columbia on foot in the company of a fellow raftsman for Marietta. [From Columbia the raftsmen could walk the tow path along the canals north to Williamsport and Lock Haven on the West Branch, Nanticoke on the North Branch and Huntingdon on the Juniata.]

Notwithstanding my sore and blistered feet, I was able to hobble on and keep up with my companions. The morning was charming, the birds full of song, the blossoming growth of Springtime made nature gay, all which tended to cheer my spirits and sooth the pains of travail. Our route lay in sight of the river. We could see plainly the rafts with their jolly crews, constantly gliding down the river to our left. So there was no alternative for us but to jog on or wait for some chance freight boat. I did not feel like traveling further, and concluded to wait and my companions pushed on. I watched and waited, and in the afternoon I saw a [canal] boat loaded with iron ore, approaching, and I started for the lock, some three miles ahead. It was a hard pull, but I managed to get there and board her. It was as much as I could do in my crippled condition. I was, however, at rest and still moving, though slowly. Scores of raftsmen were constantly passing us at more than a mule's gait. I was content, as time was not of so much conse-quence to me as comfort. The crew were Pennsylvania Dutchmen. So called because their ancestors were from Germany, and they had preserved as much as possible, the language and customs of the Fatherland. Their jargon was a con-glomerate of German and English. Their German was more than a hundred years old and all names for places and things here since that time, had been coined chiefly in English and had to be engrafted upon their tongue. A modern German could not have understood them any better than I, though they pre-tended to speak that language, it is a curious fact that the swear words in all lan-guages are chiefly derived from English. [They were Palatine Germans who spoke a dialect of German that was different than the high German.] Swearing is thought to be evidence of smartness, and we are smart people. Our progress was so slow that I feared I should not reach Middletown in time for the evening train to Harrisburg, so when within a mile of the place I jumped off the boat and hobbled on as fast as I could, but when I reached the station I found the cars had gone. There is nothing attractive about the place, it seems to be rough and dirty, but gives some evidence of considerable business. There is no alternative, here I must stay all night, unless I can strike a chance [canal] boat bound for the Capi-tal, for walk I can not, any further. After waiting and watching an hour or so, I found a freight-boat laid up, that was soon to start, so I boarded her. It was manned by a Quaker family. The good man was captain, the wife, cook and the boys were drivers and crew.

DAY TWELVE

To Harrisburg

Saturday, April 7. It was nearly 9 o'clock last night when the driver cracked his whip for a start from Middletown. We had not gone far before the rain, which had been threatening, came down. The cabin was so small and so filled with the family, it seemed there was no place for me. The hold being uncovered, I sought shelter in the naked fore castle or roofed deck, at the bow, obtained enter thereto through the man-hole. I found a seat on a cross-timber and rested my back against the enclosing partition. There was water under me, over me, to the right of me and to the left of me, but I was dry in my dark and gloomy cavern. There was music in the pattering rain on the roof, in the dash and splash of the parted waters, in the deep and audible silence of my solitary quarters. As dark and dis-mal as my surroundings were, yet the chambers of thought were all ablaze with radiant pictures, real or ideal, that came and went, like the coruscations of a pleasant dream. I felt neither loneliness or discomfort. It was near midnight when the boat reached her birth in Harrisburg, in the midst of pouring rain. I was fortunate in soon finding a welcome inn and a comfortable bed.

I awoke in the morning thoroughly rested and refreshed, and then learned that no packet would leave for the north till night. It was well, for it gave me what I desired, an opportunity to look over the town. I strolled about till 10 o'clock and then in my rough raftman's regimentals, I strode up to the State House, as independent as a Lord, to see the official dignitaries and hear the "lions" of the Capitol roar. I was fortunate as to meet in the vestibule the Governor, "old Joe Ritner," as everybody designated him. He was elected in 1835 on the Whig and Anti-mason ticket, owing to a Democratic split. I remember during the campaign traveling in company with some Pennsymites [Pennamite] on the Erie Canal, who were bitterly hostile to him and every old rack-a-boned horse they saw on the tow-path, they designated "Joe Ritner's roadster." But Joe won the race nevertheless by a good lap. He is a portly, good-looking man, feeling quite comfortable, and I have no doubt is a clever, easy-going fellow in spite of his hostility to secret societies and Specie Payments, Free Masonry and Free Trade. I did not stop to interview him, but hurried into the Representative's chamber. The house being organized after some desultory motions, it was adjourned ostensibly on account of the death of some member, but I more think for a day of recreation and game of ten pins, just now with them a higher game than the Mumbelty Peg of their rural homes. For at once a large number started for an alley and I with them. They were no popin-jay fellows, but beauty rollicking rustica mostly. They addressed each other as "Bob, Bill, Jack, Jim." etc., after the fashion of the country, derived from the Quaker custom. They went at the game with a will and made many ten strikes. There was considerable strife for the championship. A tall, lithe and well built fellow, whom they called "Dave Porter," seemed to take the lead. I really took no interest how the Solons of State disported themselves, and so visited the State Library, where I spent several joyous hours in rummaging through rare books and pamphlets. No one objected to my freedom and gave me full liberty to look for myself. The custodians, I suppose, thought if I was evilly disposed, I would be hanging around some old clothing store rather than coming to works of "Rare" Ben Johnson, of which a very early and fine edition I came across.

Ben Johnson, 1572–1637, English dramatist and poet who wrote:

> "Drink to me only with thine eyes,
> And I will pledge with mine;
> Or leave a kiss but in the cup,
> And I'll not look for wine."

After all the boasting of New Yorkers of their superior culture and intelligence, the State Library at Albany bears no comparison with this one to my mind. When the library closed I had a little more spare time, so I wandered down to the river bank and watched for a while the process of unrafting or taking to pieces the rafts, washing and piling the boards marketed here. Then I followed down the bank, where it is said old John Harris went through the fiery ordeal of expecting death from the Indians, and where his remains now peacefully rest. It is a lovely spot and will ever be a charmed place to those interested in the Colonial history of the State. I have boarded the packet and by six o'clock I shall be on my winding way.

By the time the Packet was ready to start last night [the journal was written the following day April 8th, but was part of day 7], it was loaded down with returning raftsmen who had started from Columbia in the morning and boarded the boat to save their lodgings, and to get a good lift on their homeward way. My prospects for rest and comfort looked gloomy enough. The berths were all taken and there was scarce any room on the floor. A hay loft is by far the more comfortable than a crowded cabin on a packet, reeking with stale whisky and tobacco, besides other disagreeable odors. So I began to prospect. There was a small portion of the cabin in front, set apart for ladies. I soon learned that there were none aboard. They would scarcely trust themselves in such a rough crowd. I cautiously obtained ingress to the vacant and slipped into a comfortable berth. I signaled to a few friends and they came also, and we had exclusive possession and passed a most comfortable night and arose in the morning perfectly refreshed. The traveler to get along well must need keep an eye open and his wits about him.

DAY THIRTEEN

To Northumberland and onto Milton

Sunday April 8th. At 11 o'clock in the forenoon we reached Northumberland, in the midst of a driving rain, and learned that no boat would leave for the north until to-morrow. A mail coach leaves at 5 P.M. for Milton, and it is the first conveyance north. I met at the landing Mr. John Taggart, a native of the place and former acquaintance. I made myself known and he kindly invited me to go home with him and spend the day, which I was quite willing to do. After dinner the rain having in a measure abated, he went with me to visit the tomb of Joseph Priestly, the famous philosopher and chemist, who died and was buried here many years ago. We then walked about the old town. I could recognize many of the old landmarks, familiar to me when a child, — so few changes had taken place. At 5 o'clock I was at the stage office and found every seat had been taken, but I persuaded the driver to permit me to occupy a seat with him on the box. The roads were heavy and our progress slow. It was nearly 8 o'clock when we reached our destination. Here we must remain till midnight. An excellent supper was awaiting us at the Stage House. One to be remembered, flannel cake and honey, choice ham, and delicious Java coffee with the richest cream. One can always fare well at country Inns kept by native Pennsylvanians. They care less for style, but pay more regard for the comforts of the inner man. To be comfortably housed and fed satisfies the ordinary traveler, and I feel that we have struck the right place and need have no care for the morrow.

DAY FOURTEEN

Milton to Williamsport

Monday, April 9. We were routed out at the appointed hour for leaving, before we had hardly finished our first nap. The weather was cold and cheerless and the dark clouds betokened rain. An Irishman had a pavior right to the place on the driver's seat, so I was forced to take a place on the top of the coach over the boot, which furnished some support to my feet. Another unfortunate like myself, took a seat on the bottom of the boot with his legs hanging or dangling down behind, with the loose boot straps. These Troy coaches on swinging through braces are claimed to be a great improvement over wooden springs, but I do not sense it. To be jolted up and down is bad enough, but to be constantly rolling from side to side, as if upon a chopping sea, is infinitely worse. I tossed and nodded like a Knight's plume on my perch, hanging on lest I should roll off. I could not even doze and very bone of my neck ached with constant swaying to and fro, then to add to my comfort, a gentle April shower came down from time to time as a reminder that it would bring, by and by, May flowers. I was not dissatisfied with my position, but as I could not sleep I longed for some one to converse with during the dark and gloomy hours, and the man in the boot below me, was fairly out of hearing. So at the next stopping place, by means of a little blarney, I persuaded my Emerald friend to change places with me. I don't mean to intimate he was green, for it was generous in him, and I took the coveted seat with the driver. For the change I had more reason than one to be thankful, for notwithstanding his night drive, he was a genial fellow quite garrulous, brim full of local legends and scandals and regaled me all the balance of the night with their rehearsal. We passed an old church with its extensive paved yard near Chillisquaqua, where Parson Bryson had preached for nearly half a century, which was the scene of some of his weird stories.

DAY FIFTEEN

Williamsport to Covington

[Tuesday, April 10] We reached Williamsport about nine o'clock in the morning, just in time to take the train on the Ram Shackle Rail Road running northward, upon which I paid my fare to Clendennys at the foot of the mountain, where the wagon road crossed the same to the Tioga Valley. I started alone and on foot. The road was fine and kept up a narrow glen, through which flowed Trout Run, a beautiful mountain stream and well named. It was the old Williamson road cut through by Patterson in 1792 from Williamsport to Painted Post, the whole way through a stark wilderness. I soon was overtaken by other footmen and we made good time overhauling the stage wagon at the summit of every rise. As we reached Laurel Hill, the summit of the range, an elevation of 1600 feet, we were little ahead and gained on it. Winding up that bare and barren crest, largely denuded of timber, whether by tempest or forest fire I could not determine, there were many grand and magnificent views which greeted the wayfarer and rewarded his toils. After passing the last ridge we could see for miles and miles the Tioga winding its tortuous way among the hills toward the Chemung. We reached the Block House, so named from a rude structure erected by Patterson and his pioneers, while opening his road to the Genesee country. For years it was the half way house through the Wilderness, as this region was appropriately named, and was kept by a vagabond German, named Anthony, some times called Anthony Sun. It was regarded as a disreputable place, but was the only shelter for travelers for twenty miles each way. He was noted for his treatment of his guests, furnishing them with dog's milk, cat soup and roast horse, taken from the hock of broken-down roadsters. I was there just in time to take a seat in the old rickety lumber wagon, used by the Stage Company for the conveyance of passengers and mails. The day was waning, as we jolted slowly over the rough road, the driver solacing us, with the information that any greater speed would surely result in a break-down of the crazy vehicle. We, however, reached Blossburgh safely just at dark and after a short breathing spell pushed on. Then it commenced raining and thick darkness came on. As weary as I was from my last night's ride, I could not bob an eye, because every moment it was expected that our conveyance would come crashing down. About nine o'clock the off hind wheel collapsed, down it went and dumped us all in the mud. There was no help for us, but to trudge four miles through the mud and mire to Covington, the only place of shelter. It was a weary tramp, being compelled to keep the open road and wade the sloughs and pools. We reached the welcome hotel of Frank Young about 11 o'clock, where we found warm fires and a bountiful supper prepared for us. We washed our blethered mud covered feet, dried our soaked garments and laid ourselves away in comfortable beds. [Today this is Route 15, from Williamsport to Painted Post.]

DAY SIXTEEN

Return to Painted Post

In the morning [Wednesday, April 11] I was all right and started on foot for Painted Post, where I arrived around three o'clock in the afternoon. I found on figuring up my gains I had just three dollars and some worthless Shinplasters. But for these worthless rags I might have saved more of my small wages. They were the only change in Pennsylvania, and were issued by every borough and corner grocery, which as a matter of necessity, you were compelled to take for change. As they were worthless ten rods from the place of issue, you were forced to unload at the second block, to do so you were compelled to make some purchase, a sugar, a ginger cake or a glass of pop. A rich harvest was thus reaped from the poor raftsmen and thousands lost, for none were redeemed. If my trip has not been profitable pecuniarily, it has at least been rich in experience — of much more value than money.

At this point we should thank Schuyler S. Strong, esquire, for leaving us his journal to enjoy. Strong may have lived in Lawrenceville, Pennsylvania, during 1838, when he made the trip down the Susquehanna. Lawrenceville is on the Tioga River just below the state border, about ten miles south of Painted Post. He had lived in Lawrenceville for about a year before moving to Wheeling, West Virginia, where he remained for 18 months. He then moved to Springfield, Illinois, where he lived and practiced law for over four years before dying in 1845. His wife, Francis Minerva Cruger Strong, returned to Bath, New York, where she lived until her death on August 13, 1882. She and Schuyler had seven children, six girls and the fourth born was a son.

Thomas Yates' Charts

Thomas Yates drew a chart of the North Branch of the Susquehanna River in October 1850, to help him know how to run rafts down the river from Shepard's Landing in New York to Wright's Ferry in Pennsylvania.

Mr. Yates drew his chart in a three by five inch notebook with 46 pages. It consists of 17 separate charts starting at Shepard's Landing, where Shepard's Creek entered the Susquehanna River. The first chart is drawn on the next to the last page of his notebook. The notebook must be turned so that the top is to your left side. This puts the south at the top of the chart, because he was headed down the river to the south. The last page contains his name and a second name Capt. Bishop (Hugo?) Shingles, who I assume was the pilot. To read the charts page from the back of the notebook to the front of the notebook, with each chart covering two pages. In the front of the book are three timetables for travel down the river: one dated October 1850, one dated November 1852, and another dated March 1853.

The first step in finding Thomas Yates was to find Shepard's Landing. A landing was usually a place along a river or a stream where rafts and arks were built and launched. Yates' first chart started his journey from Shepard's Creek, which, according to the chart, entered the river on the right bank, near the border of New York and Pennsylvania, along the North Branch of the Susquehanna River. A perusal of maps of this area did not reveal a stream with that name. The Bradford County Historical Society in Towanda, Pennsylvania, provided information that the 1869 Beers Atlas identifies Shepards' Creek as the creek known today as Cayuta Creek, and it drains the area east of South Waverly just below the New York border in Pennsylvania.

Bradford County Historical Society said there was no Thomas Yates born in Bradford County between 1790 and 1836. However, in Part Second [this is correct], *Historical Gazetteer of Tioga County, New York 1785–1888*, Thomas P. Yates of Factoryville was listed as a lumberman and farmer, and his widow, Emily, was living in Factoryville. He was the only Thomas Yates so listed. Factoryville was part of what today is known as Waverly, New York, and is just north of Shepard's Creek.

The Tioga County historian in Owego, New York, gave me the genealogical information on Yates. He was born on May 17, 1811, and died September 1876, in Waverly, New York, at age 65. On September 22, 1843, he married Margaret Emily Knapp. In October of 1850, when Thomas Yates drew his charts of the Susquehanna, he would have been 39 years old, with probably 25 years' experience on the river.

Below is the timetable from Yates' trip down the river in 1850 on a board raft. We know his raft was a board raft because he had a witch on his list of things to take along. Only board rafts used witches (see Appendix). The raft's speed was an average of about four miles per hour. This is about the same speed the last raft came down the West Branch of the Susquehanna in 1938.

By the 1850s brokers were coming up river from Port Deposit to Wrightsville, Columbia and Marietta to purchase rafts; they got better prices because the watermen didn't have to engage pilots to run the gauntlet from below the Columbia Dam to Port Deposit. The brokers employed their own pilots and thus saved money. This time table is from Thomas Yates' Charts:

October 29th Tuesday 1850		Started Wed. 30th 5.45	
Place	*Time*	*Place*	*Time*
Shepard's Landing	12.30	Tunkhannock	9.00
Towanda	3.30	Falling Springs	12.15
Stony garden	4.00	Pittston Bridge	12.45
Wyalusing Creek	6.30	Wilkesbarre	2.15
Landed at Fafsets (Eddy)	9.00	Water 12 ft 8 in as high as safe to run the chute.	

Place	Time
Landed above the Nole Ferryat Nanticoke	4.00 P.M.
Water fell 18 in.	

Started Thursday 31st 9.00 A.M.

Place	Time
Shickshinny	11.40
Stone Mill	1.00 P.M.
Berwick	2.00
Miffinburgh (ville)	2.55
Aspy or Bloom?	4.50
Catawissa	5.16
Foot of 2nd Island	6.00
Ransoms Rock	6.13
Danville	7.13
Cinders Edy	8.05
Landed above North Bridge (Northumberland)	10.41

Friday Nov. 1st

Place	Time
Started from Bridge	5.00 A.M.
Shamokin Dam	6.30
Penns Creek	8.15
McKees (Half) Falls	10.15

Place	Time
Liverpool	12.05
Berry Falls	1.00 P.M.
Gurty's Notch	1.45
Reeds Riffles	3.00
Landed at Greens Dam	3.45

Started Saturday Nov. 2nd 11.00 A.M.

Place	Time
Furnace	12.10
Coxes Town	1.30
Turnpike Gate	2.18
Water Works	2.55
Between Bridges	3.06
Halfway House	4.10
Landed at White House	5.10

Started Sunday Morning Nov. 3rd

Place	Time
Fogy	10.55
Pilot in the Swatara	12.03
Hog Hole left of Island	1.07
Big Buak	1.15
Trap	2.02
Landed at Wrights	5.30

The water was too high when they reached the Nanticoke Dam and they tied up above the dam to prevent being washed over the dam and breaking up their raft, and perhaps drowning someone. The water was low enough to continue the next day. This 1850 trip required five and one half days from noon Tuesday until late Sunday afternoon.

On his 1852 trip, Yates noted more points on the river, but he did not record the times of passing these points. Most of the points were written in ink with several added in pencil, indicating that he may have made out a list of river points before starting. Also, he did not list a captain or pilot on this trip. From Thomas Yates' charts:

**Susquehanna River
Sunday Nov. 28, 1852**

Place	Time
Chemung Run Mill	3 P.M.
Shepard's Landing	
Athens School	4.40
Athens Bridge	4.42
Mouth of Chemung	
Upper Ulster	
Cash Bar	6.36

Place	Time
Hemlock Run	7.16
Sugar Creek	7.36
Towanda Bridge	8.52
Towanda Eddy	9.22
Pier at Stony garden	9.40
Birneys Bar	10.15
Standing Stone	10.45
Homets Mill	
Dodge Bar	

Monday Nov. 29   A.M.

Place	Time
Wyalusing	12.47
Rocky Forest	2.20
Skinners Eddy	2.53
Fafsets Eddy	3.50
Meshopine	
Horse Race	6.00
Sterlings Bar	
Hunters Bar	
Taigs Eddy	
Tunkhannock	8.00
Stopped half way to	
Ousterouts Island	8.55
Started from	.
Ousterouts Island	1.20 P.M.
Berrels Bar	
First Brothers	
Lower Brothers Point	2.00
Buttermilk Falls	2.40
Mills	
Falling Springs	4.30
Schofield Island	
Pittston Bridge	5.10
Forty Fort	
Landed at Wilkesbarre	6.45

Started Monday 29   8.30

Place	Time
Cripmans Rock	
Sees Eddy	
Nanticoke	11.45
Hemlocks	
Davis Island	

Tuesday 30th   A.M.

Place	Time
Shickshinny	2.00
Stone Mill Wappwallapee	3.20
Wappwallapee House	3.37
Old house and barn	4.16
Berwick Bridge	4.37
Miffinburgh (ville)	
Catawissa	1.08 P.M.
Pine Tree Point	
Lower Island	
Ranson Rock	2.07
Point above Danville	

Place	Time
Danville Bridge	3.30
Started P.M. 30th	11.15
Cinders Eddy	

Crooks Wednesday Dec 1   1.40

Place	Time
Northumberland Bridge	3.35
Shamokin Dam	5.30
Island above Selinsgrove	
Penns Creek	
McKees Half Falls	11.20
Mahantango Creek	12.00
Dry Sawmill	
Landed at Liverpool	1.15
Started from Liverpool	2.10
Berry Falls	
Gurty's Notch	
Muskrat Hole	5.00
Started from Muskrat Hole	6.00
Reeds Riffles	
Greens Dam	7.50
Yellow Rock	8.18
Furnace	
Hunters	
Brushy Rock	10.00
Turnpike Gate	11.11
Water Works Harrisburg	11.50
Between Bridges	12.00
Halfway House	1.12
White House	2.35
Pilot in Swatara	3.45
Landed above the	
upper fish house	4.35
Started from fish house	6.10
Head of Conewago Falls	6.33
Hog Hole	
Landed Trax	7.50
Started from Trax	9.05
Chestnuts	
Vinyars	10.50
Marietta	
Columbia Bridge	
Columbia Dam	
Charlestore	
Turkey Hill	
Frys Rock	
Canistoga	

In 1852, he made the trip in less than four days by running at night. He must have had moonlight. Below is a list of things he took along and stones were on the list. It is unclear what they used stones for, but along the Mississippi River when running at night, if the watermen lost their moonlight, they used potatoes to throw towards shore to determine how far off shore they were. If they heard a splash they were far enough, if they didn't they rowed their raft farther away from the shore. Stones were probably used for the same reason.

Yates gives us no indication how big his crew was on this trip. Monday he stopped for four hours and twenty-five minutes above Ousterouts Island. No reason was give for the stop. He stopped for an hour and forty-five minutes at Wilkes-Barre possibly to pick up supplies. At Danville he stopped at 3:30 in the afternoon, but started again at 11:15 that evening. This was almost an eight hour rest, but his timing for the start put him at the Shamokin Dam at 5:30 in the morning. On the run from the Shamokin Dam to Greens Dam the raft passed through Lazy Man's Gap below Girty's Notch, which was too dangerous to try at night. He stopped at Liverpool for fifty-five minutes with no explanation. He also stopped an hour at Muskrat Hole. This was because he went aground — no one stopped in Muskrat Hole if they didn't have to. Muskrat Hole is one of two safe places to cross the river, the other being Lazy Man's Gap. Both are in the middle of the river between very small islands with no inhabitants.

On this trip Yates picked up a pilot at Swatara Creek. With a Tidewater pilot he may have run his raft all the way to Peach Bottom, since he listed points on the river below Columbia Dam which were in the Susquehanna Gorge. Yates didn't log the times in the gorge, since he most likely had enough trouble maintaining his balance. Also, Yates may have had only one raft, because he said nothing about uncoupling before going below Columbia Dam.

Yates included in his notebook a list of things to take along on his trip down the river. The cinders were wood charcoal cinders to be used in case he needed to restart his fire. I was unable to determine the meaning for the next to last word, quapia. The articles were:

Charts	Auger	Tea	Tar pine (patch the
Watch	Witch (to tighten	Stove	roof)
Lantern	grubs)	cooking tools	Wood
Stones	File	Bread	Spectacles
Cinders	Matches	Salt/Pepper	Pain Killer
Grouzer	Soap	Butter	Quapia ?
Nails	Towel	eggs	Oar washers
Candles	Meat	Shaving tools	
Saw	Potatoes	Trunk (rafting box)	
Axe	Sugar	Straw (for the beds)	

Yates listed pine tar. Pine tar was used to waterproof the roofs on arks to prevent water from getting on the flour barrels and breaking the airtight seals. Yates must have used a similar roof on his shanty. He listed tea, but no coffee. Coffee was not used until much later.

6

Rafting on the Main Branch

The main branch of the Susquehanna River is from the confluence of the West Branch and the North Branch at Northumberland and runs south to the Chesapeake Bay. This part of the river would see rafts as early as 1790 and arks by 1791 (Rung 1949–1951, 150). Arks would run until the 1850s, but rafts would continue to run down the river until about 1905 (Mitchell 27).

There are many points along this part of the river that the raftsmen used in their navigation, sometimes called rafting points. First was the Shamokin Dam only three miles below the confluence, where most pilots stopped over night. They needed to get an early start the next day in order to go by Girty's Notch and through Lazy Man's Gap in daylight, since running through the gap was the most dangerous passage in that part of the river. At the white house below Middletown, they employed pilots to guide them through the Conewago Falls and down the Susquehanna Gorge to Port Deposit, Maryland. William Lowman lets us know what it was like to try to sell your raft. Some people even partied on the river, according to Kelly in "Rafters, or Dancing over the Columbia Dam." Arks would use the river only until railroads were available in the 1850s.

The Shamokin Dam

The Shamokin Dam was nine and a half feet high with a chute wide enough to pass a fleet of board rafts, but not wide enough to pass a fleet of square timber rafts. Rafts and arks were required to take intervals going through the chute so that one raft or ark would not over run another. If they did, they often broke the oars on both crafts, lost control and had to land until the oars were repaired. A board raft required a minimum of 300 feet, which included raft and clearance. If the river water flowed at four miles per hour, then the maximum number of board rafts that could go through the chute in one hour was about 70. Arks, being much shorter, would require less than 150 feet, so twice as many arks could get through the chute per hour.

Timber rafts were up to 300 feet long and required about 50 feet extra on each end or 400 feet, which reduced the throughput rate to only 50 per hour. Timber fleets were too wide to go through the chute, so they had to be cut apart for two trips, reducing the throughput rate to 25 per hour for timber rafts.

The pilot would notice the swift water leading to the chute and keep his craft out of the swift water until he had the correct interval on the craft ahead of him, and then he had his craft rowed into the swift water, which would accelerate his craft through the chute.

In 1833, the *Danville Intelligencer*, an early town newspaper, reported that 2,688 arks and 3,480 rafts passed Danville from May 18 to May 23. That was over 6,100 in a six day period or over 1,000 per day. Danville is 12 miles upriver from the Shamokin Dam and that was only the number of arks and rafts coming down the North Branch. It did not include the arks and rafts coming down the West Branch. This would put over 1,000 rafts and arks in the dam's slack water each night during the height of the rafting season. The Sunbury newspaper reported that the people of their town would sit on their porches in the evening to listen to the watermen singing. As during the Civil War, singing in the evening was very popular when a group of men would get together. The water crafts were tied up along the western side of the river across from Sunbury. With Blue Hill rising up 400 feet behind them, the water carried their songs into town. The people of Sunbury were treated to some wonderful concerts.

The first watercraft to land in the dam's slack water tied up to a tree or a post on the shore, but the ones that followed tied up to a raft or ark already tied to the shore. Up on the West Branch there were reports of half the river being blocked by tied up rafts. This made it easy to visit for songfests. The next morning the last to tie up were the first to lie loose and go down the river.

With no lights on the river and with treacherous rocks and islands like at Lazy Man's Gap, described below, raftsmen seldom ran at night. In the end of May with perhaps 13 or 14 hours of daylight, one can imagine how busy the chute at Shamokin Dam was during the rafting season.

Simon Girty

Girty's Notch was named for Simon Girty, who was born near Harrisburg in 1741, and at age ten saw his drunken father killed by a drunken Indian friend. In 1756, at age 15, he was taken hostage in the French and Indian War and lived with the Indians three years, learning their language and ways. After the war he worked around Fort Pitt (Pittsburgh) as a translator. In 1778, he signed on as a recruit in the Continental Army, hoping to be made a captain. When this did not happen, he switched sides, going over to the British at Detroit, where he organized Indian raids against the colonists. His brutality to his prisoners made him the most hated man on the frontier. When the British withdrew from Detroit in 1796, Girty moved to Canada, where he died in 1816. Historians have never been able to place him along the Susquehanna, however early novelists often wrote about exploits like his along the Susquehanna and Juniata as well as the Ohio.

The reason why this point along the Susquehanna River was named Girty's Notch is lost to history. However, the early settlers would often embellish their stories about Indian atrocities. Many best selling stories of the time were about people being taken hostage by the Indians, and to give credence to the story it was usually titled "From his or her own lips."

It could have been given the name by the raftsmen because they needed something to tell their friends and family at home about after "Going to See the Elephant," their term for getting out of the mountains to see the wonders of the cities. It was better to tell stories about going by Girty's Notch, than telling what really happened in the lumbering towns along the river.

Today, if this place is marked on the map, it is usually called the Susquehanna Water Gap. When Route 11 and 15 was widened by the Notch, the mountain behind Girty's face was dug away. Excavations for the road revealed a cave behind the Notch, setting off rumors among the locals about human bones being found in the cave. The cave was walled up and today the cinderblocks are painted to match the natural rocks.

Lazy Man's Gap

To get through Lazy Man's Gap the raft needed to be in the right channel as it went by Girty's Notch. Thomas Yates' charts indicated that the distance from Shamokin Dam to Girty's Notch is 29 miles, and his log recorded that it took seven hours and fifteen minutes. This was a raft speed of exactly four miles per hour. The men would be traveling downstream at four miles per hour, while trying to row the raft between the islands to the opposite shore.

From Shamokin Dam to Girty's Notch, Yates' chart shows that the rafts hugged the western shore, so that they came down in a line along the west shore of the river like rush hour traffic on a single lane road. The middle of the river has many long islands that can be forded to from the eastern shore in the summertime, making it too shallow for rafts along the eastern shore. A board raft fleet was about 215 feet long, 34 feet wide and weighed 221 tons.

Yates' charts are not drawn to scale, and distances and island sizes cannot be measured on his charts. Everything is relative and often he never drew the opposite shore of the river or islands when he was showing the way down one side of the river. Also, he has the north end or upriver end at the bottom of the chart, so he would see the chart as the pilot would see the river. However, the map from the Notch to Greens Dam is a U.S. Department of the Interior Geological Survey map. The map is to scale and is printed upside down so it can easily be compared with Yates' charts of the same era.

Approaching Girty's Notch, Yates' charts tell the pilot to be within 5 or 6

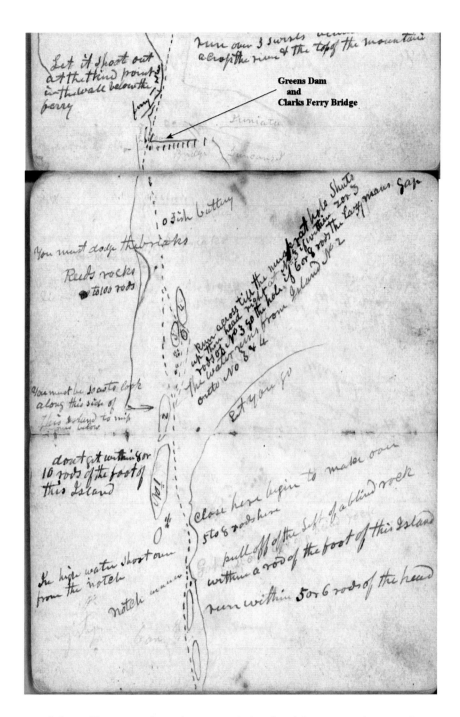

Yates' chart of how to get through Lazy Man's Gap, hand drawn, 1850 (courtesy Pennsylvania State Archives, Harrisburg).

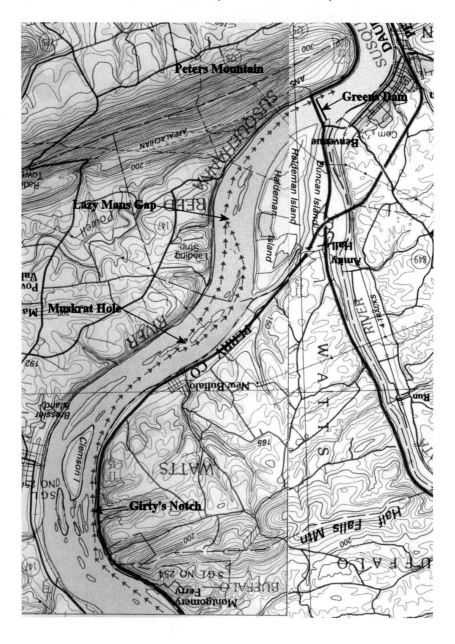

Geological survey map, to scale, of Lazy Man's Gap.

rods off the head. He means to the head of the island. A rod is 16.5 feet so a pilot needed to be 80 to 100 feet from the island's upstream end. At Girty's Notch there is a shelf of black rocks running across and upriver from the Notch about two feet high, which looks like a natural dam. If there isn't enough water, over three feet higher than normal, the only place to get through is one rod (16.5 feet) off the western shore below the island. This is at Girty's Notch. Close to the shore is a natural chute, but the raft had to be pulled to the left to avoid a hidden rock under the water. R. Dudley Tonkin called this rock the sunfish, and noted that it was very easy to hit (265).

The problem: Girty's Notch was 7 miles above Green's Dam, and the rafts were only 17 feet from the western shore. In the next 7 miles, or about one hour and forty-five minutes, the raftsmen needed to row their 221 ton raft about 3,600 feet across the river (about 12 city blocks) to the eastern shore to get through the chute in Green's Dam. Running down the middle of the river are four groups of islands blocking the way across. Yates shows that if there isn't high water, the rafts needed to stay close to the western shore for the first mile, before trying to cross over to the No. 1 Island. Clemson Island and the island behind it appear on Yates' charts as one island labeled No. 1 Island. The two islands across from the village of New Buffalo appear on Yates' charts as Island No. 2. Yates also notes that if the water is high, the pilot could pull to his left and get ready to move between the islands to the eastern shore as soon as he passed Girty's Notch.

With a normal rafting flood, Yates recommended that until the pilot was abreast of the upper end of Clemson Island (his No. 1 island) that the pilot remain 5 to 8 rods off the western shore of the island (83 to 132 feet). At that point the crew had an hour and a half to row 12 city blocks across the river, being careful not to get within 8 to 10 rods (133 to 165 feet) of the foot of this island, the island behind Clemson Island.

Then, if pilots going to go between islands No. 2 and No. 3, which was Muskrat Hole, Yates warns them to run across till Muskrat Hole shuts up. On the left side of the chart he warns: The pilot must be so as to look back upriver along this side of No. 2 Island to miss No. 3 and 4 Islands below. If not, head right at No 3. If within 2 or 4 rods (33 to 50 feet) of No. 3, go the Hole (between Island 2 and 3, the Muskrat Hole is 4 miles above Greens Dam).

Yates' alternative was: If the pilot were 6 or 8 rods (100 to 132 feet) from Muskrat Hole, wait until the raft got to the Lazy Man's Gap between Islands 3 and 4 before trying to cross over to the eastern side of the river. Lazy Man's Gap is about 2.7 miles above Greens Dam, or about 45 minutes to row the heavy raft 1800 feet or six city blocks. Yates does not say this, but if the pilot has to wait until below Island No. 4 to cross to the eastern side of the river, he only had about 20 minutes to row the last 1,800 feet or six city blocks. I could not find how high Green's Dam was, but most of the canal feeder dams were close to ten feet high. If a raft went over a dam that high, it would break up the vessel and dump the crew into the icy water. No raftsmen ever wore a life preserver; most had on heavy woolen clothing and didn't know how to swim.

Finally, he warned the pilots to watch out for Reeds Rocks, 100 to 200 rods (165 to 330 feet) off the eastern shore, before going between the eastern shore and the first pier of the Clarks Ferry Bridge and through the chute at Greens Dam. Harrower, with Strong's help, got his fleet of rafts through this mess during what seem like rush hour traffic. From Strong's journal we do not know which passage they used, but we do know they made it. Both times, in 1850 and 1852, Yates stopped in the slack water of Greens Dam. His trips were during the fall freshets in November. In 1852, he stopped at or near Muskrat Hole either to wait out the traffic or because he went aground. The next day he went through the chute at Greens Dam. In 1850, he landed in the dam at 3:45 P.M. and remained overnight until 11:00 A.M. the following day. He gave no reason for the long stay; however, tying up at 3:45 P.M. put him in the slack water early, with rafts that came in later tying up outboard of him. The next morning the fact that the first out are the last ones in the night before could have kept his raft in the dam until 11:00 A.M.

The following is another story about Lazy Man's Gap. This occurred in the late 1800s near the end of the rafting on the Susquehanna. However, it can be seen that rafting had changed little in over 60 years from 1838 to the 1900s.

Dr. Edwin Lewis Theiss gave this paper before the Northumberland County Historical Society on August 9, 1950. Theiss said he made four voyages down the Susquehanna on rafts, and he related this story about going through Lazy Man's Gap on one of his trips. Theiss didn't say if the vessel was a round log raft or a square timber raft, but it was not likely that it was a board raft. Theiss' fleet of two rafts would have been about 300 feet long, 56 feet wide, and weighed 562 tons. This made the fleet the length of a football field and about one third the width. These rafts usually had a crew of six for the two oars on the front end and two on the rear end. This is one man for each oar, with the pilot to help on one of the front oars and the steersmen to help on one of the rear oars. However, all of Yates' guidelines still applied for getting through Muskrat Hole or Lazy Man's Gap. The following is from Dr. Theiss' paper:

> At either end of a raft was mounted a heavy block of wood. A strong, vertical wooden pin was driven into this. This pin thrust up through the shaft of the oar. The oar's shaft was a small [pine] tree trunk, thinned at the inner end so that men could grasp it. The blade of the oar was a ten-inch thick plank, many feet long. The oar was tremendously strong. It had to be. And it was just as heavy.
>
> Rowing a raft was similar to rowing a footboat. But there was this difference. The raftsman had to be on his feet, and the oar, when held level, was less than two feet above the tide. To dip the blade, the oarsman had to raise the handle high above his head. To lift the blade above water, he had to depress the handle to a level below his knees. To row with the oar, he walked across the raft, his hands high above his head, the terrific strain of the push falling on the small of his back. Then he had to turn, depress the handle, walk back across the deck,

and again elevate the handle and once more push. It was an exhausting effort that could not be sustained very long.

In early days, when lumber was so plentiful, rude shanties were built on log rafts to shelter the raftsmen. Later, tents were used. A most memorable thing about a log raft was the mess kettle. On sand on a platform, amidships, burned a fire — preferably made of that excellent fuel, dry, stolen chestnut fence rails. Over this fire a round-bellied iron pot was hung from a tripod. And in the pot was a "raftsman's stew." This began with the voyage and ended with its conclusion. Bread and whiskey supplemented it.

It was a life saver. Into it raftsmen put whole hams and potatoes, carrots, onions, etc., by the peck. It simmered endlessly. In all the world there is no colder place, seemingly, than the exposed deck of a log raft in a March tempest, when rain is falling and fog dampens everything, and no clothing yet devised will hold the body heat. When his teeth chattered so that he feared they would crack, the raftsman ran for the stew pot, scooped out a dish of it, and packed it away where it would do the most good. The raftsman's stew was indeed a life saver.

Mention has been made of the fact that lumbering was always dangerous. Rafting was no exception. In a single trip down the Susquehanna the writer had occasion to witness two trying situations. These personal experiences are used here because the writer knows the details exactly. Without a doubt there were hundreds of similar or even more stirring experiences on Susquehanna log rafts. And sometimes the outcome was sheer tragedy.

When our raft was nearing Green's Dam, at Clark's Ferry, just above the confluence with the Juniata, the pilot elected to take what the raftsmen call "The Lazy Man's Gap." Coming down the river from Northumberland, raftsmen stick close to the west bank, where the channel is. But to get beyond Green's Dam, they must cross the stream, here probably three-quarters of a mile wide, in order to get into the chute on the east side. A raft can be rowed directly and laboriously across the stream just below New Buffalo, or it can be given an occasional shove with the oars, so that it sidles along, crablike, toward the eastern bank, reaching it just above the chute. This easy course takes the raft between islands. Hence the name, "The Lazy Man's Gap." Our pilot took the Lazys Man's Gap. We had not moved far out into the stream before the pilot suddenly dashed wildly back from his forward oar, tore the tent down like a crazy man, and shouted hoarsely, "Every man on an oar." Every soul leaped to his post. Over the brow of Peter's Mountain, the precipitous cliff that rises from the eastern bank of the river, came a frightfully ominous cloud, rushing before a sudden tempestuous wind. We were head on to it. The wind held us back almost as though we were anchored. Back and forth across the deck we raced with those heavy oars. It seemed as though the raft would never make it. Failing to do so, it would be swept over Green's Dam, broken in pieces, and the crew pounded to jelly between swirling logs. At Inglenook, the villagers were on the river bank watching the seemingly hopeless fight for life. A man in a footboat rowed out from shore to take the crew to land. The pilot grasped the nose of the footboat. "Come aboard," he said to the oarsman. "I want to talk to you." The boatman stepped on the raft. The pilot drew the boat up on the logs. What he said to the oarsman was: "Get on an oar." Aided by this added "slave labor," the clumsy raft was inched toward the shore.

All the while it was being swept down stream with frightful velocity, for it was in the rapids above the dam. As it neared the bank, a big raftsman grasped the end of the snubbing rope, raced across the deck and leaped for shore. He fell short many yards. But he swam desperately to land, and instantly had the hawser tied around a tree that was fully a foot in diameter. The pilot snubbed the raft too hard. Up came the tree and went bouncing along the shore beside the raft. Somehow, that raftsman got the rope untied and fastened it about a huge sycamore. This time the pilot was more cautious. The raft was snubbed gradually, then made fast, just above the chute. And almost before the tent was raised, rain descended in blinding torrents. It was a close race with death.

Two methods of snubbing were used. Along the West Branch above Lock Haven, a sturdy young man on the rear oar would go ashore with a one hundred foot hemp line that was two inches thick, and make two to three wraps around a stout tree.

Lower River Pilots

There were three types of lower river pilots for hire: the Conewago Pilot who guided rafts and arks through the Conewago Falls, the Tidewater Pilot who guided the rafts and arks from Columbia to Peach Bottom, and the Mud Pilot who guided rafts and arks down the Susquehanna Canal from Peach Bottom to Port Deposit, Maryland. The Conewago pilots were employed at the "White House" (a big white house in the town of Highspire, about six miles south of Harrisburg, just above today's Harrisburg Airport at Olmsted Field). The Conewago Falls is located at the lower end of Three Mile Island. It is only three quarters of a mile long, but drops 23 feet in that distance or over 30 feet per mile, the steepest drop experienced by the watermen. The York County Conewago Creek enters the river on the right bank below the falls.

If the raft's pilot didn't have a Tidewater pilot when they got to Columbia, they hired one to run the gorge. None of the pilots ran the river between Columbia and Peach Bottom like Michael Cryder did. At Columbia the fleets were chopped apart and only one raft at a time would be run down the Susquehanna Gorge to Peach Bottom. Rafts were double manned at Columbia; the crew who brought the fleet (two rafts) down the river would man one raft, and leave the second raft behind. The Tidewater pilot guided the raft to Peach Bottom and the crews walked back that evening to take the second raft down the following day. Missimer described the path the crew took home and many of the watering holes they used to keep them going. Additionally, Missimer's maps show the route taken by the rafts and arks to Peach Bottom.

Conewago Falls

Dr. Edwin Lewis Theiss reported a second incident that happened on the same trip, when he had trouble getting through Lazy Man's Gap. This occurred shooting the Conewago Falls.

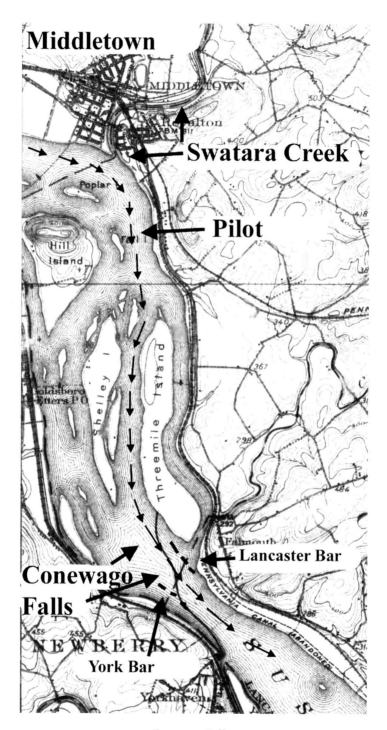

Conewago Falls.

This picture of Conewago Falls was taken in 1963 during a severe drought, years after the local pilots had removed the large rocks by heating them with fire and dousing them with water until they split (courtesy *New Era*, Lancaster, Pennsylvania).

Below Harrisburg a few miles lie the so-called Conewago Falls. Here the Susquehanna rushes down a river bed that is worn to fantastic shape. Elsie Singmater's book, Pennsylvania's Susquehanna, pictures that river bottom on page 185. The photograph, taken during a protracted period of drought, shows the river bed absolutely dry. And such a fantastic, grotesque, amazing array of potholes, perpendicular crags, eroded boulders, upright rocks, one could not even imagine. Well, the spring flood, rushing down over this uneven floor, is torn and whipped and churned into indescribable fury. The water comes tearing down this frightful slope with terrifying speed. Here it leaps upward in a great comber. There it swirls savagely about a sunken rock. Yonder it is churned into blinding spray. The roar of the water is overpowering, benumbing.

Yet, there is a channel through this maelstrom. Probably no one now living knows that channel. Very early in the century, when our raft went through these rapids, only one pilot remained alive of all those who had guided rafts through these troubled waters. He was tall, but old, stooped, and fragile. When finally we entered the rapids, he took his place at the right forward oar. Both oars had been fastened to the deck with strong ropes. The blades were thus well above the raging waters. The ends of their handles rested on the logs. Should an oar be torn loose and its blade drop into the flood, it could swing the raft crosswise of the current in the twinkling of an eyelid, and cause it to be torn to pieces on the rocks that studded the falls. (Rafts surf down water falls faster than the water.) Hardly was the raft caught by the current before something happened to the pilot. He straightened up like a pine tree. He braced his feet for what he knew was coming. His long cloak gave him a peculiarly commanding appearance. He had shaken off senility and become a gladiator. All hands were gathered at the rear oars. From time to time the pilot motioned with his right hand, now gently, for an easy pull, now violently, for a hard push. As the raft hit the first comber, its nose dived under water. The comber swept back over the raft. Yet the pilot, with nothing to hold to, stood as firm as a post. This was what he was braced for.

So the raft drove into the maelstrom. At the very worst part of the passage, with the raft plunging up and down, the waves sweeping over it, the rapids shaking it savagely, the oar at the pilot's side tore loose. But the blade never touched the water. Like a football player diving for a fumbled ball, the pilot was on it, full length, fighting with might and main to keep the blade above the waves. Two of the raftsmen raced forward. One knelt on the handle, to reenforce the pilot. The other speedily prepared the rope for retying. Then the rope was readjusted and knotted so that it could never come loose again. Meantime, the man at the sweeps had kept the raft on its course. The pilot, seemingly unconcerned, resumed his post. The oarsmen hastened back to their comrades. On went the raft through the surging combers. It ran out of the maelstrom into the calm waters in the deep pool at the foot of the rapids. Those aboard had seen another of those close and sudden battles with death that marked every step of lumbering in the early days of the industry.

The raft Dr. Edwin Lewis Theiss was crewing on was sold in Columbia or Wrightsville. Tidewater pilots would have taken the rafts down the river to Port Deposit and the raftsmen would have headed home. But in 1838, the Strong-Harrower raft went as far as Fites Eddy before the Mud pilots took over and moved the rafts to Port Deposit through the Susquehanna Canal along the eastern shore of the river.

Susquehanna Gorge

The run from Colombia to Fites was one of the most exciting parts of Strong's trip, for even he was at a loss for words to describe it adequately. During the building of the Holtwood Dam in the early part of the twentieth century, when builders constructed a cofferdam to divert the water away from the eastern shore, they realized what made the passage dangerous. The exposed river bottom revealed a trench over a mile long, 200 to 300 feet wide and 40 to 60 feet deep. Then, while building the Safe Harbor Dam above the Holtwood Dam and the Conowingo Dam in Maryland, they found five more such trenches along the eastern shore. These trenches ranged from a mile to two miles long and up to 500 feet wide. The deepest trench was between the Bear Islands and the eastern shore. The bottom of the hole there was 130 feet deep — 30 feet below sea level (Brubaker 170).

Folklore about the deep holes told of logs and swimming raftsmen being sucked down into these holes never to be seen again. Old raftsmen would tell these stories at the hotels along the river at Columbia, Wrightville, Marietta and as far north as Coxestown to scare young greenhorn raftsmen. The most famous was Job's Hole just above the Conowingo Dam in Maryland, where

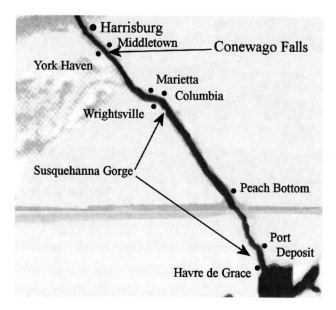

Model ark on Penns Creek. About two miles west of Weikert on the Penns Creek is Butter Rock. Arks coming around the bend in the creek would stay near the right bank to keep from hitting the rock. However, one laden with butter hit the rock and several casks were tossed onto it, breaking them open and covering the rock, giving it its name.

nothing had ever been found after it disappeared into the hole. Some people claimed it had no bottom because it was the upriver end of a subterranean cave that ran into the Chesapeake Bay. A twentieth century story was the most pretentious with a fellow pushing his old automobile into the hole, and a half year later seeing the car running on the streets of Baltimore with his license plates on it. The new owner had said he found it in the shallow waters of the bay, had pulled it out and started it again (Brubaker 171). As you can see not all the big story tellers belonged in the nineteenth century.

Also, the words Conewago and Conowingo are variations of the same Indian words meaning "at the rapids." Many West Branch raftsmen used the two words interchangeably.

Port Deposit, Maryland

Port Deposit is about three miles north of the Route 95 bridge over the Susquehanna River in Maryland. The town is along the eastern shore between the river and the granite cliffs behind the town and just below the fall line in the river. In 1729, Smith's Ferry was operated by Thomas Cresap at the present site of Port Deposit. The ferry had been named for Captain John Smith. Smith had explored the river up to the fall line, today called Smith's Falls, over 120 years earlier, in 1608. When Colonel John Creswell acquired the ferry, the community at the ferry was called Creswell Ferry.

After the first ark ran through the Susquehanna Gorge in 1791, Pennsylvanians began running rafts and arks to the tidewater of the Chesapeake Bay. Creswell Ferry became a natural stopping point where the rafts and arks were held until transportation could be arranged to Baltimore. In the early days sail was used to tow the rafts across the bay, but this was replaced by steamboats in the 1820s.

To eliminate the danger of running the falls near the present day Mason-Dixon line and through Fanny Gap, Bald Friars Falls with its Hollow Rock about two miles below Fanny Gap, Job's Hole and Smith Falls, a canal was proposed to be built from Creswell Ferry on the eastern side of the river north to the state line. In 1793 digging began. Conflicting reports have the canal opening as early as 1795 to as late as 1803. This canal was known by several names, such as the Susquehanna Canal, the Port Deposit Canal, and the Conowingo Canal, and one report called it the Old Maryland Canal. Today the historic markers refer to it as the Susquehanna Canal. It ran from Love Island, below Peach Bottom in Pennsylvania near the present day Mason-Dixon line, to Rock Run in the town of Port Deposit. The canal was nine miles long with nine locks. It never was a financial success since the canal only had traffic in the spring when rafts and arks used it. Boats could not use it to go upstream since when they got to Peach Bottom it would take 30 to 40 men to pull the boat upstream through the Susquehanna Gorge the 25 miles to Columbia. It was this canal that Gabriel T. Harrower and Schuyler S. Strong used when they brought their board raft to Port Deposit in 1838.

In 1812, while searching for a new name for Creswell's Ferry, someone said, "It is a port of deposit for lumber. Why not call it Port Deposit?" In December of 1812, Governor Levin Winder of Maryland signed a bill changing the name of Creswell's Ferry.

In 1826, 1,500 arks arrived in Port Deposit. Between February and June of 1827, 1,631 rafts and 1,370 arks passed Harrisburg, many headed for Port Deposit (Miller 107). Ringwalt (12) estimated that the average rafts contained 25,000 board feet and this number was picked up and used by many subsequent authors without questioning his assertions. However, because early board rafts were made by placing 16 foot boards one inch thick into 16 foot square platforms that had 24 layers (24 inches deep), then each platform contained 6,144 board feet (see Appendix).

A raft constructed in this manner would have over 24,000 board feet in just over four platforms. Most rafts were made up of from 10 to 12 platforms, totaling for each raft 67,584 board feet (11 platforms), or 2½ to 3 times the 25,000 feet.

Jacob Tome's Port Deposit

Eighteen thirty-three was a significant year for Port Deposit for two reasons. About 120 different lumber schooner captains frequented the Port Deposit storehouse of Thomas Bond and William Morgan to purchase food, drink and utensils for their crews. These sailing ships carried lumber to every port on the Chesapeake Bay and through the Chesapeake and Delaware Canal, which had been opened five years before in 1827, to ports on the Delaware Bay. These schooners each carried from 24,000 to 60,000 board feet (Kelso 3).

The second reason was not so apparent at the time, but would become more important. A 23-year-old man by the name of Jacob Tome moved down to Port Deposit from Manheim Township in Lancaster County, Pennsylvania. Tome had first visited Port Deposit as a light hand on a raft running the gorge and recognized the opportunities afforded in the small community. At 16, Tome was left fatherless and had to support the family, but in Port Deposit he drew the attention of Davis Rinehart, a wealthy Pennsylvania banker who recognized Tome's grasp of financial affairs. Rinehart made him a partner in a lumber company where Tome amassed a fortune and 17 years later was Cecil County's first millionaire. Two of his gifts to the people of Port Deposit were the Jacob Tome Memorial Methodist Church and Washington Hall, a school for 200 students, which he endowed with 2.5 million dollars. This school became the Naval Academy Preparatory School, and the Methodist Church still graces the main street of Port Deposit.

William Lowman: A Waterman's Life in Port Deposit

Life in Port Deposit and the problems of trying to sell your raft are illustrated in the following story.

In 1977, Elizabeth Lowman Hall published her grandfather's and grandmother's letters in the June issue of the *Chemung County Historical Journal*. Chemung County is in southern New York State, the area around Elmira. The Lowman family had recently found the letters between their two newly wed grandparents, sent during the first year of their marriage in 1848. The letters tell us about the board rafting trade on the Susquehanna and in Port Deposit, Maryland.

At Port Deposit they had a water storage pond of about 30 acres to store rafts and arks that had come down the river. The arks and rafts were kept in the pound until they were sold and moved by steamboats or sailboats to ports all along the eastern seaboard.

On October 13, 1847, 27-year-old William Lowman married 20 year old

Mary Ann Beers. Lowman made his living building board rafts during the winter and running them to Port Deposit on the spring freshets, where he released his crew to travel back home while he waited to sell his rafts. The wait often meant as much as three months or more because brokers would wait until all the rafts that were coming down river that spring were in the pond or tied up along the river before starting their purchases. They wanted to see what the market was like before they made their offers.

About February 20, 1848, William Lowman kissed his new wife goodbye and made the eight day trip down the river from Painted Post, New York to Port Deposit, Maryland. After being away from Mary Ann almost a month he wrote her a letter and sent it back to her when he found a rafting crew from Chemung County getting ready to return home. His letter from Port Deposit was dated March 18, 1848, saying he had arrived in port on the 28th (February). He told her about how it snowed the second day after leaving Elmira on the raft, but then it cleared up and he had had a pleasant trip, being one of the first rafts to arrive at Port Deposit. He realized that it would take a while before he could sell his rafts and return to her. He hoped he would be one of the first to leave. He wanted her to write him because he was anxious to hear from her.

He wrote to her again on April 12 telling her that he had received her letter on the 10th. William said he was missing his wife very much after being away from home almost eight weeks. And to compound his anxieties Mary Ann had told him that her health had been poor since he had left. However, he resolved to remain in Port Deposit until he could sell his rafts. He had no choice; he owed his workers for their winter's work and the watermen for running his rafts to Port Deposit, and until he sold his rafts he couldn't pay them. His letter also showed how much he loved her. (Early rafters were called watermen in New York and along the North Branch in Pennsylvania. Along the West Branch they were called raftsmen.)

On April 28, 1848, almost ten weeks after saying goodbye to Mary Ann, William wrote her another letter after receiving a letter from her on the 21st, telling him her health was much better. He was much relieved to receive the good news and informed her how lonely he was. In his letter he stated, "I am surrounded with company, but the company I prefer is absent. There is a perfect swarm of men in port. It is really amusing to see the rush when the bell rings, every man is on his tops. It reminds me of a lot of pigs going to a buttermilk trough, everyone for himself. I have given you a limited description of the company that I am surrounded with."

On May 12, 12 weeks after leaving Mary Ann, he sent her another letter telling her it had been raining a lot. The bad part of the rain was it had confined him to his small room, but the good part was that it would bring the May–June freshet and the last rafts into Port Deposit, so that the brokers would complete their buying. He informed her that he had already sold two rafts and was looking forward to selling the rest. He showed excitement in being able to return to her.

On May 20, she sent him a letter telling him she got his letter six days after he had written it, and she, too, was very eager to see him, although she knew it would be a month before he could make it back to Chemung County.

He had to have received this letter in Port Deposit about eight days later around May 28, for his grandchildren found it in his old desk with the other letters. He got home sometime about the first week in June, making his stay about 15 weeks. That fall on October 1, 1848, Mary Ann give birth to their first born — could this have been the cause of her poor health back in March and April? Mary Ann and William Lowman lived together until his death in 1898, and in 1901 she joined William.

We do not know where William stayed in Port Deposit, but histories of the little town indicated that almost every home made extra money by renting out rooms. Several taverns also prospered with the owner trade.

The men in Port Deposit, like Jacob Tome, knew how to make money by waiting until all the rafts were down the river in June before making their purchases. This way they could obtain lumber at the lowest prices. Several of the Cecil County newspapers of the day indicated that the lumber brokers in Port Deposit made their best profits when lumber was plentiful, because they could obtain wood at the lowest prices. When rafts were scarce the brokers had to pay higher prices because they found they were competing with each other to fill their orders.

Dancing Over the Columbia Dam

By 1872 the raftsmen on the lower Susquehanna River in Pennsylvania, had tamed the river and learned its ways. Richard Kelly wrote in his article "Rafting, or Dancing Over the Columbia Dam":

> The big rafts did not exceed thirty-two feet in width to accommodate the narrowest point of the river, Fanny's Gap, below Peach Bottom. The rafts were piloted down the swiftly-flowing Susquehanna, with the sole means of steering usually only two large, long oars some forty feet each in length. One oar was positioned forward, the other aft.
>
> A crew consisted of a pilot, a steersman, and from four to eight additional men according to the size of the raft. Like lumbering itself, manning these rafts was hard and dangerous work. The treacheries of Hollow Rock left more than one widow along the river.
>
> Subject as it was to the vagaries of weather, lumbering was equally treacherous from the financial point of view. Heavy winter snows and ample spring rains were the life's blood of the business. A prolonged dry spell could mean disaster.
>
> The year 1872 looked unpromising. The previous spring, after April, there had been no floods to enable the lumbermen to get their stock downriver to market; and through January of 1872 there had been no snow to enable the men to sled logs through the forest to the streams.
>
> Many firms were discharging their men; but February of 1872 brought wel-

come heavy snowfalls to the northern regions. Then an early spring drought was followed by heavy rains, sufficient to bring out at least some of the lumber which had been stranded upriver. In the second week of June, 1872, when the river traffic once again began to move, about one dozen rafts reached Columbia and were sold there, each purchaser branding each individual log with his mark and arranging for the goods to be taken further downriver to tidewater at Port Deposit. There, still in the water, the rafts were piled atop one another into floats and hauled by barge to their destinations.

George Churchman, of Wilmington, Delaware, was pleased with the turn in the weather. He was a "highly esteemed" gentleman of the lumber trade and well known in Lancaster circles. To celebrate nature's benevolence in the early summer of 1872, he invited a number of his friends from Lancaster to rejoice with him. Hence, at 6 A.M. on Thursday morning, June 20, 1872, a party of about forty ladies and gentlemen appeared at the Pennsylvania Railroad depot in Lancaster. There, in the spirit of anticipated adventure, they settled down to await the arrival of a specially hired railroad car. Arranged and paid for by Churchman, it was to take them to nearby Columbia, where novelty awaited, moored to the riverbank.

Aware that among the waiting group were some whom it was unwise to disappoint too deeply, Boyle advised them to hurry over to the Reading Railroad depot in Lancaster to catch a regularly scheduled train for Columbia. So the party gathered up their belongings and hastened off, arriving breathless at the Reading Railroad depot at 8:00 A.M., where they awaited the Columbia train. In a carefree mood, some of the ladies spent the time daringly walking on the tracks, while others, more sedate, seated themselves prettily on trunks or other pieces of freight in the shade of the platform.

When the Columbia train chugged into the station around 8:25, they boarded it, filling up an entire car. After a pleasant ride toward every point of the compass on that remarkably crooked road, they arrived at their destination, disembarked, and jauntily walked the several squares of streets to the riverbank, while the citizens of the town looked on, astonished at such holiday gaiety on a business day.

At the point on the riverbank where Churchman had told them he would be waiting, they saw the craft which was to take them on their adventure. Floating low in the water, it was about 150 feet long and 25 feet wide. To the forty landlubbers, it looked frightfully unseaworthy. Leading down to it from the steep riverbank was a plank, not overly broad. At the foot of the plank, on the raft's deck, stood their host, waving to them with merry confidence.

In single file the party gingerly began descending the plank. Some shuddered visibly at the ordeal, but Churchman bolstered their confidence with a warm welcome for each as his guests stepped in file from the plank to the deck.

First to board was Churchman's friend, attorney Andrew Jackson Steinman. A solid Yale man, A. J. held strong opinions about Radical Republicans, which he did not hesitate to express in a local newspaper he partly owned. With A. J. were his older brother George and sister Mary. George had taken over the family hardware business when their father, John Jr., had retired from it twenty-three years earlier. Mary shunned the glare of publicity, as did most well-bred Lancaster ladies, unlike their counterparts in New York and Washington.

Next aboard were Mr. and Mrs. O. J. Dickey and Mr. and Mrs. S. H. Reynolds. Messrs. Dickey and Reynolds, both attorneys, had recently been among the five lawyers defending the Northern Central Railway in a suit brought against it for allegedly charging excessive rates.

Mr. and Mrs. Reynolds had the added distinction of having given the most elegant party of that year's social season in Lancaster. Their home had been handsomely decorated with evergreens and brilliantly illuminated by candles and gas lights. The supper table had been prepared by Augustine of Philadelphia, and had been loaded with all the delicacies of the season and adorned with masses of fragrant flowers, which were afterwards distributed among the ladies as bouquets. Everyone had danced and laughed until 4 A.M. to Miller's music. The memorable evening had closed with "the gallop," the new round dance which to the regret of traditionalists, seemed to be replacing the waltz.

Stepping carefully next onto the raft was E. H. Yundt, a busy man whose time had been lately taken up by his determination to convince the people of New Holland to participate in raising cash to extend the East Brandywine and Waynesburg Railroad from New Holland to Lancaster. On a recent visit to Reading, Yundt had been taunted regarding Lancaster's lack of energy in building railroads and embarking on other enterprises. If only $6000 a mile were subscribed, the Pennsylvania Railroad would guarantee construction of the road, and Yundt was among a Committee of Nine to further the cause.

George Steinman was also on the Committee, as was his friend, George M. Franklin, who came aboard the raft next with Mrs. Franklin. All of them were keen to do something about Lancaster's lack of business bustle.

Behind the Franklins were Mr. and Mrs. H.E. Slaymaker. Mr. Slaymaker, an agent for the venerable Reigart's Old Wine Store at 26 East King Street, had problems of a different nature from the other gentlemen. No sane man could doubt that the tide of the future was with railroads, but the future of alcoholic beverages seemed in jeopardy. Last February, the National Prohibition Party had had the temerity to declare, at its convention in Cincinnati, that "traffic in intoxicating beverages is a dishonor to Christian civilization," and its plank demanded suppression by both state and national governments.

Slaymaker, who dealt only the finest brandy, sherry, old madeira, champagne, scotch, brown stout, and domestic wines, felt that only a dunce could declare such superior beverages dishonorable. But the convention had nominated a Lancastrian, James Black, as their candidate for President. As Slaymaker shook hands with Churchman, he was grateful that his host had not invited the fanatic Black on this little outing. Gathered here were the finest citizens in town, and not one of them a professed teetotaler.

Slaymaker stepped aside to make room for Doctor Henry Carpenter and Mr. Peter McConomy. Neither of these chaps was a teetotaler although both were upright, respectable members of the school board. Dr. Carpenter was also Chairman of the Democratic County Committee. Slaymaker was also an active Democrat. A nation trapped between the plundering scoundrels of the Grant administration, on one hand, and the howling Prohibitionists on the other, required steady guidance and good brandy, he felt.

When all were safely aboard, Churchman showed them about a little. The raft was composed of five sections, each about thirty feet in length. Various small cabins had been erected on the raft for the guests' necessities.

Churchman gave the nod to Fred Waller, his pilot, to get underway. Fred's brother, George, was second officer for the trip. Both were seasoned veterans of the river and quite dependable. Rafters were generally hard drinkers, with a penchant for Lancaster County whiskey, but Fred and George and the other men in this hand-picked crew knew the difference between work and recreation.

When the moorings were loosed, the raft began to float slowly down the placid part of the river above the Columbia dam, expertly navigated by the crew handling the three mammoth oars which extended fore, aft, and starboard. Underneath a specially built roof in the middle section of the raft, a boarded dance floor had been laid, around which rows of logs had been placed as seats and bulwarks. To provide music for the trip, Mr. Churchman had hired Keffer's orchestra. As the raft slipped gently downriver, the orchestra began to play, its violins enticing couples to spirited quadrilles.

Presently the raft reached the chute of the Columbia dam, entered its portals, shuddered momentarily, and was swept with rapidly increasing velocity to its exit. The formerly peaceful waters now surged over the front and sides of the raft. An unexpected wave swept over the bulwarks of the dance floor, trounced the astonished Miss Sue Frazer, and sent the rest of the dancers scurrying with laughter for drier places.

Once beyond the dam, the raft's pace slowed again, and the music resumed. Past the town of Washington Boro they danced, flirted, and enjoyed the view. Just below Washington Boro the raft hit the rough and rapid waters around Turkey Hill, one of the more perilous spots on the river. Under the crisp command of the Wallers, the crew ignored the excitement of the guests, and deftly manned the navigational oars while the Susquehanna churned and boiled beneath them.

Once past Turkey Hill, there was a brief respite, but soon a worse place, called Fry's Rock, was neared. Churchman had been endeavoring to have this rock removed from the river and had spent $25,000 on the project with no success. If a careless pilot wrecked his raft here, fifty others behind him might go to pieces on it, heaped up in the narrow channel.

To the uninitiated, the raft seemed doomed to disaster as it sped toward the rock in a roar of rushing water that put an end to the violin-playing and dancing. But with little exertion, the crew steered their craft past the obstacle and through the tortuous channel to calm water once again.

The passage over Safe Harbor dam was next. The fall was said to be five feet; but the dovetailed construction of the raft allowed it to take the fall with a hinged gradation, shipping very little water.

At the next obstacle, a rough piece of river called Connolly's Break, they were not so fortunate. As the craft raced over, the Break water flooded the dance floor. Losing his balance, a deckhand fell overboard, but was deftly rescued with little harm done beyond damaged pride.

By two o'clock, having been on the river for over three hours, the guests dined from the lunch baskets provided by the ladies. As they passed through the calm waters of McCall's Ferry narrows, in flowing bumpers of wine the guests drank to Churchman's health and future happiness. All declared to their beaming host that they had never passed so pleasant a day.

After the food, wine and the toasts came the last difficult section of their trip, Cully's Falls, through which the Wallers and the crew took them safely. In the calm waters which followed they danced until journey's end at Peach Bottom, which they reached about 7 P.M. They had come thirty-two miles by water, wisely disembarking before Fanny's Gap, the narrow squeeze about one mile downriver which took the measure of every raft. Beyond Fanny's Gap was Bald Friar Falls, in which lay the infamous Hollow Rock.

Attending them on shore were omnibuses and a long line of carriages to carry them back to their homes. Through a delicious moonlit night they rode, tired but happy, the sound of roaring waters replaced by the lulling rhythms of endless hoofbeats, while, in the distance and the darkness, Hollow Rock still waited.

Kelly said they took over eight hours (from before 11:00 A.M. to 7:00 P.M.) to travel what he claimed were 32 miles between Columbia and Peach Bottom. All maps have Columbia 25 to 26 miles above Peach Bottom, a difference of four miles or one hour's travel by raft on the open river. Two sources stated it only took three hours to run down the gorge. The crew with Strong made two trips in one day and Miller (110) quotes a pilot who usually made the 28 mile run from Marietta to Peach Bottom in three hours. Kelly did not state where he got the information for his article.

George Churchman was the man who purchased the 100 spars from George William Huntley of the Sinnemahoning Creek on the West Branch of the Susquehanna River in 1875. The "Panic of 1873" or as we call it today, the depression, eventually forced George Churchman into bankruptcy (Huntley 357).

7

Rafts on the West Branch

Pioneers first settled the upper reaches of the West Branch of the Susquehanna River in 1785, and the first board rafts appeared on the river in 1827. John Patchin was given credit for bringing the knowledge of preparing, hauling and rafting-in square timber and spar rafts to the "Little Ditch," as the head waters of the West Branch was known. He sent his first rafts down the river in 1836 (Caldwell's 24). This relative late start and the fact the river and it tributaries, the Sinnemahoning and Pine Creeks, drained a vast area of primeval forest meant that rafting would continue until about 1905 (Mitchell 27).

In 1855 William Langdon wrote a diary describing a raftsman's life in the woods and running rafts on the West Branch of the Susquehanna River.

William Langdon: 1855

Below are William Langdon's diary entries for the year 1855 to his "Daily Journal of the Weather, at the Cherry-Tree, Pa." Langdon's diary is held in record group MG-6, Pennsylvania Archives, Harrisburg, Pennsylvania. The author has added explanations so that the reader can understand what Langdon meant when he used such phrases as "commenced making spars."

Like Strong's journal, Langdon's diary only indicated what was happening to Langdon as he understood it. In the 150 years since he wrote in his diary, we have lost much of what was going on daily in his life that he took for granted. Without this background, Langdon's comments have little meaning to us today. It is my hope that by adding information gathered from numerous sources, it will fill in what Mr. Langdon had in mind when he wrote his diary. Hopefully the reader will understand the vivid meanings that punctuated his life during the end of 1854 and the year 1855. This time initiated a turning point in Langdon's life.

William Langdon, the oldest of six children of Charity and David Langdon, born in England in 1828 or 1829, came to Pennsylvania with his family sometime before he was eight years old. He was relatively well educated, writing essays for the *Philadelphia Dollar*, and teaching school. He supported and may have been a graduate of the Cherry Tree Academy. Academies were the

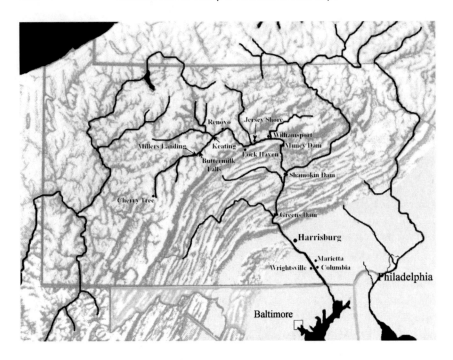

West Branch of the Susquehanna River.

equivalent of today's high schools and were required education for teaching the first eight grades of school. In July, August and September he became very active in the lyceum by reading an essay and delivering an oration at the Presbyterian Church exhibition. Evidently he was very popular because the church was full with a great many people standing outside. This exhibition was for the Cherry Tree Academy's end of the summer term. By 1870 he had left the family farm and in 1880 he was working as a carpenter in Oil City, Pennsylvania, which boomed after people first successfully drilled for oil in nearby Titusville in 1858.

During 1855, when William Langdon kept his diary, he helped to manufacture 20 spars in the fall of 1854, and in the spring of 1855 he delivered the spars to the market in Marietta. Then he returned home to build a board raft, couple it with a timber raft and run it to market at Coxestown, above Harrisburg. The 1850 census lists William Langdon as a 22 year old "lumberman." R. Dudley Tonkin (259) listed William T. Langdon as a head water pilot, one who was qualified to run a raft out of the headwaters of the West Branch of the Susquehanna River.

In 1855 he would have been 27 years old when he piloted two rafts down the Susquehanna River to market. The Langdons had a small water-powered sawmill on their property, called a "Thundergust" by the local inhabitants, because it could only saw after a thunder storm or when the snow was melting. Marietta and Columbia on the lower Susquehanna River in Pennsylvania and Port Deposit in Maryland were his markets.

The process of manufacturing and selling spars and timbers required eight separate stages. These stages were: selecting a pine grove for trees felling, building a hauling road from the grove to the landing, manufacturing the sticks (making a tree into a spar), skidding the sticks to a landing, rafting-in (constructing) the raft, running the raft, selling the raft, and returning home. Each stage was separate and sometimes there were months between the stages.

The process of manufacturing boards and selling them required ten similar stages. They were: selecting a grove of trees, building a hauling road from the grove to the sawmill, manufacturing the saw logs (usually 16 feet long), skidding the saw logs to the sawmill, sawing the logs into boards, placing the boards at the landing, rafting-in the raft, running the raft, selling the raft, and returning home.

William Langdon's diary had entries for every day, but some are omitted because they only gave the temperature and weather, while others were eliminated because they did not further our understanding of rafting. When the rafting season was over on June 28, 1855, Langdon did not return to rafting for a good reason. His activities are summarized for the rest of the year.

EVENTS FROM 1845 · The Langdons owned a large farm just north (or downstream) of The Cherry Tree on the headwaters of the West Branch of the Susquehanna River, which was in the heart of a white pine primeval forest noted for its spar trees. (The town got its name when it was mentioned in the Fort Stanwix Purchase of November 5, 1768. One of the boundaries stated that it ran up the river to Canoe Place at the Cherry Tree. Canoe Place was as far as a canoe could travel.) They probably took trees from their own land. Commercial rafting had only started about 20 years earlier, hence there was a wide selection of trees. Sometime before the ground froze, and before Langdon and his crew started making spars, they would have built a hauling road from the spar grove where the trees grew to the landing where the spars would be stored along the river's edge until the ice went out. If they used an old road it would have been checked and repaired. Also, a live-in shanty was needed while manufacturing the spars.

Entries in Langdon's diary are indented. Other text provides background information to his life and rafting.From Langdon's diary:

Sun. Oct. 15. Commenced making spars.

Langdon lived in the heart of the white pine primeval forest, and most likely rose early each morning, had breakfast, and walked to the site before daylight. In the evening after dark he would walk home for supper and sleep in his bed that night. When the work was too far to walk each day, the men built a shanty to live in at the site. The shanty was usually 12 by 16 feet with a comb roof (pitched), and had two to four feet high sides (Mitchell 33). The sides were single wall construction made from boards or bark. A sheet iron stove was used to heat the shanty and cook the four meals a day demanded by the men, who worked ten to fourteen hour days. Straw-filled bunks lined the walls.

These shanties served two purposes; first to house the men at the pine grove while making spars or sticks, and second, after building their raft the men moved the shanty aboard the raft for shelter while running down the river. A master spar maker was contracted, or someone in the crew acted as the master spar maker, to make the spars.

Wed. Oct. 25. Went to a Whig torch-light procession.

This was the only time that Langdon, in 1854 and 1855, showed any interest in political activities. However, that Wednesday evening was a week and a half into spar making and it must have been important to him to spend this time after dark, when he needed to be up before daylight the next morning to help with the spar making. He was 27 years old, no serious interest in a young lady yet, and perhaps not as difficult to do as we suspect.

Fri. Nov. 10. Finished 20 spars.

It took 27 days to make the 20 spars. We assume that they worked through the weekends because they started on a Sunday. Also, we don't know if the crew made any extra spars to replace those broken during skidding. Now the wait would start for the haulers to move the spars from the spar grove to the landing, where they would be stored until rafting-in.

Sat. Nov. 18. Emma Tuffing and her sister Jessie arrived from Ohio.

This was possibly the most important event in William's young life, perhaps only rivaling the birth of his children. At the time of this diary entry he most likely didn't realize how important this day was since he had met his soul mate, Emma. However, he was reasonably impressed with her so that he noted it in his diary.

January 1855

Mon. 1. Clear; warm. Very little snow on the ground. A good deal of timber hauled to the river.

Thu. 11. Snowing and raining all day; snow two inches deep. Temperate. Very little water for sawing; mill going part of the day.

This was the curse of the "Thundergust" mill owners. Small dams were usually blocked off and the water would back up in the dam during the night, so the next day the men could run the "muley saw," as the water-powered saw was called.

Sat. 13. Raining hard in the morning, then turned to snow — and got cold and windy. A strew of snow in the ground; Water raised.

Sat. 20. Cloudy; sprinkling a little rain the forenoon; rather warm. Snowed a little last night: all gone by evening. Wm. Kneedler's blacksmith shop burned down last night, with two bellowes and all the tools.

Tue. 22. Clear; cold. A little snow on the ground. Went to a party this evening at Amos Johnson's.

Sun. 28. Snowing a little; cold. Took a sled-ride to Robt. Mckaig's [McKeage's].

Tue. 30. Snowing; windy; very cold. Went to Benjamin Pittman's school on a visit. John Barr and family moved away from Joseph Eson's [Eason's] place.

Wed. 31. Cloudy; windy; cold. Snow 6 inches deep. Jacob Breth [Breath] moved on to the Joseph Eson. Dr. Piatt and Jacob Breth having bought it in partnership. Good sleding; people hauling timber busy.

February 1855

Fri. 2. Variable; very windy and cold; snowing a little. Snow nine inches deep.

Tue. 6. Clear nearly all day, very cold. This morning was the coldest morning by 20 deg[rees] of any this winter, the mercury being at 25 deg. below zero.

Fri. 9. Cloudy; cold. Plenty of snow but not good sleding: snow too dry. Very few people hauling.

Wed. 14. Raining all day; warm. 9 or 10 inches of snow on the ground. Indian show at the Cherry tree this evening.

Sun. 18. Cloudy; cold. Emma and Jessie Tufting and George, David, and Mary Ann went to Joseph Tonkin's in the sled.

George was Langdon's younger brother, age 19. Langdon did not include himself on this sled ride. However, since he and Emma would get married in September, it is highly likely he was part of the group. Sled rides were one of the favorite ways young people got together during the winter months; often they went to a house for a party that would last all night. Due to the slow mode of travel these trips were very enjoyable. Many times the young people didn't get home until the sun was coming up.

Mon. 19. Cloudy; cold. Snow 8 or 9 inches deep with a hard crust.

Fri. 23. Cloudy; cold. Amos Johnson commenced hauling our spars, with eight horses. Hauled seven.

Sat. 24. Variable; very cold; this morning the mercury at 15% below zero. Johnson hauled six spars to-day. Got five barrels of flour from Edward King, twelve dollars per barrel. Got one barrel last week. [A good spar was 93 feet long and weighed five and one half tons.]

Tue. 27. Cloudy; cold. Johnson finished hauling the spars, hauled seven. Ten horses. Last night went with sleighing party down to Patchin's; three sleds.

Why they didn't haul on Sunday and Monday was not given. The skidding or hauling took three days using four to five teams. If the snow was too soft to haul during the day, hauling was done at night when the snow froze. John Patchin lived down the river from the Langdons'. Patchin was known locally as the Spar King, because he had brought spar manufacturing technology to the head waters of the West Branch from Sabbath Day Point, New York State (R.D. Tonkin 3).

March 1855

Thu. 1. Perfectly clear all day. Thawing in the sun; freezing in the shade. Very cold this morning, mercury 11% below zero. There is more timber and spars hauled in this winter than ever before & people still hauling. Bought some oats at 75 cts. per bushel, and corn at $1.37½ per bushel; very scarce. [Langdon was right, when he got to Marietta, the market was glutted that year.]

Sat. 3. Cloudy; snowing a little; temperate. Went to a party last night at Mrs. Moore's: dancing.

Elizabeth Ann Moore's husband, William, was washed off a raft while running the chute at the Muncy Dam in 1852. (This was more than 20 years after the dam had been destroyed by raftsmen because it originally proved too dangerous to navigate.) He was buried on the river bank. Running chutes was always dangerous. Mrs. Moore supported herself and her children by running a boarding house for raftsmen and woodhicks. This usually included throwing several parties during the season which provided an additional source of income. This was not unusual during the raft and ark running times, since many people made extra money providing this service. She owned river bank property which she rented out as raft landings. This brought in about ten dollars a raft per season (R.D. Tonkin 101–114).

Rafts were run during the spring thaw when it rained one day and froze the next. Nights were cold and a good warm room was a welcome place to sleep, preferable to the shanty aboard the raft. However, this was not quite as inviting as it may seem. Often a small room was rented for the night to a rafting crew of six. The older men got the bed and the younger men slept on the floor. A Mr. Reed from Clearfield took a trip down the river to Buttermilk Falls to experience rafting. He wrote in his diary that the crew had gone through a chute and got wet. That night they stayed in a river house. It didn't bother the seasoned raftsmen, but he couldn't stand the smell — he went out on the porch to sleep. Usually the meals (evening and breakfast) received at a river house were befitting a man who worked ten to 12 hours a day on the bone chilling river.

Sun. 4. Clear; warm; snow melting fast. Went to preaching at Brillhart's.

Mon. 5. Cloudy; very smoky; raining a little the afternoon, warm. A hard storm of thunder, lightning, wind, rain and hail this evening. Fields getting bare, snow melting fast.

Sometime after skidding the spars to the landing and before his crew started rafting-in the pilot, Langdon would have the crew make four head blocks, four or more sweeps for the two half rafts, and a shanty if needed. They would now wait until the ice went out before starting rafting-in.

Wed. 7. Variable; temperate; warm in the sun. River raised a little; ice breaking up on the riffles. Some people beginning to raft in. Mill started.

Thu. 8. Clear most of the day; warm. Ice breaking up, water raised a little.

Sun. 11. Cloudy; cool. Some people rafting in.

Mon. 12. Cloudy; temperate. Raining some last night. Commenced rafting in the spars. People busy rafting in. Snow all gone out of the fields.

Langdon gave no reason for waiting five days before he started to build his spar raft. Usually the raftsmen rushed down to the river and started rafting-in as soon as they could get into the river, because the spring freshet only lasted ten days to two weeks. He would pay later for being late.

> Tues. 13. Cloudy; raining in the morning but freezing as fast as it fell; turned to snow and hail; cold. People rafting in. Lightning in the evening, and a hard shower of snow; the ground covered in a few minutes an inch deep.
> Thu. 15. Cloudy; raining a few hard showers the forenoon; very windy the afternoon; temperate. About, a half flood in the river. All the dams & dead waters full of ice yet.

A dead water was an area in the water where there was a lack of current. This could be the slack water of a dam or an eddy which had little current. A half flood was a rise in the river of about a foot and a half to two feet, not enough to run from Cherry Tree to Clearfield.

> Fri. 16. Cloudy; temperate; snowing fast after dark. Splash flood in river: people dropping their rafts. [Raftsmen were starting to run their rafts and Mr. Langdon was still building his.]
> Sat. 17. Cloudy most of the day; showers the forenoon; temperate. Ground covered with snow this morning; all gone before night. Raining all last night; tremendous high flood today; higher than has been for some years; great jamb-ing [jamming] of rafts. Got two spar rafts ready to run.
> Sun. 18. Cloudy; rather cold; sprinkling a little snow. River rather too high to run this morning. Ran one raft to Patchin's mill & one to the foot of Colry [Colliery?] ripple. [Colliery ripples is not listed in R. D. Tonkin's rafting points, however there are coal banks in the area.]
> Mon. 19. Variable; rather cold, snowing very fast after dark. Ran one raft from the coal bank to Atchison's bridge; and one from Patchin's dam to Carnel's; water getting low, stuck two or three times. Could not get along well for the rafts crinking [twisting] and stopping up the course. A great deal of timber to raft in yet. [Langdon was five and one half miles from his home and starting place after two days work trying to get the rafts down the river.]
> Tue. 20. Cloudy; very windy & cold, an inch and half of snow this morning. Lay in our cabin last night, just below Atchison's bridge. Water too low to run. Came home this morning. Rec. a letter from Geo. Langdon.

This would start a 16 day delay; it would be April 6 before he would have enough water to move further down stream. It was during delays like this that raftsmen feared their rafts would be stuck in the river until the following spring. During the next 16 days Langdon kept a very close watch on the water level in the river so he could get his rafts moving again. The George Langdon that sent the letter may have been an uncle that his brother George had been named for.

> Wed. 21.Variable; cold; some snow still in the fields; plenty in the woods. A letter came from Ohio, stating that Ebenezer Forsyth died of the lung fever & jaundice.
> Wed. 28. Snowing; windy and cold. Good sleighing.
> Thu. 29. Clear; very windy. Thawing in the sun, freezing in the shade. Some people still making and hauling timber.

Sat. 31. Variable; warm: morning at 60 degrees: warmest day since last summer. Walked down to Patchin. People rafting in all along the river. Snow gone from the fields.

April 1855

Thu. 5. Raining most of the day; very foggy; temperate. Every appearance of a flood. Good deal of snow in some parts of the woods.

Fri. 6. Variable; temperate; raining in the evening. Flood in the river. Ran one raft from Atchison's bridge to the mouth of Chest-creek.

Chest Creek enters the West Branch at the village of Mahaffey. It was the only creek above Clearfield that rafts could be run on. The creek held the title of the "Fightenest creek in the state." R.D. Tonkin (218) quoted one raftsmen's son as writing, "Every old raftsmen of fifty or more years ago (about 1900) knew the Chest Creekers—you could always spot them, as they usually had an eye gouged out, an ear torn off, or most of their front teeth gone."

Sat. 7. Clear; temperate. Ran one raft to Walter's, and one to Goose Island. Stuck on a rock in Ellis' dam; forced to cut a lash-pole and spread the raft, and get another raft to snub it off. Detained three hours. A strew of snow this morning. Aunt Mary Ann Tufting came from Ohio this evening. Brought word that aunt Hannah Forsyth in Ohio was dead. Died of lung fever one week after her son Ebenezer.

Rafting points changed names over the years and on later lists Walter's is not identified, but Goose Island remains Goose Island today. Most likely Ellis' Dam was later identified as Hoyt's Dam.

Sun. 8. Clear most of the day; temperate. Ran both rafts to Lumberville [Lumber City] and commenced to couple. Water getting low. Great crowd of rafts, two jambs at Lumberville within half an hour.

Mon. 9. Cloudy forenoon; raining in the morning; clear afternoon, temperate. Water low. Finished coupling and ran the raft about a mile and quarter below Lumberville and stuck, the water being too low for big spars. Tied the raft to shore and left it in care of Mr. Snyder to run to Scofield's dead water when the water rises.

Scofield's Dead Water was also known as Kelly's Dead Water. The two rafts were coupled in tandem, making one raft 186 feet long. The head blocks were left on both ends of the platforms. Two sweeps or oars were used, one on each end, and two extra sweeps were loaded onto the raft to be used in case a sweep was broken. The raft is about 23 miles down the river from the Langdon Landing, the starting point. It was about a four hour walk back home. This would start another six day delay until April 16.

Tue. 10. Rain, hail and now cool. Left the raft and came home. Met a splash flood and rafts running.

Splash floods were artificial floods caused by releasing water from splash dams. Farmers owning land along a creek would build a dam with a splash gate so that the water of the dam could be released quickly. The water or splash would flush the saw logs out of the creek into the river. In the streams that fed the river above Clearfield, there were about a dozen splash dams. Usually the saw log drivers combined their drives and paid the splash dam owners about $10.00 to open their dam at a specific time, so that when their splash would reach the river it would meet with other splashes that were making their way down the river. In this manner the log drivers would create a splash flood to drive their saw logs down the river. Raftsmen often used the splash flood to get their rafts out of the Little Ditch, also.

During the walk home he saw the splash. If Langdon knew the splash was coming he may have been able to ride it out of the narrow part of the river, but when he saw the artificial flood it was too late to go back to his raft.

> Fri. 13. Cloudy; raining; temperate. Commenced making runners for a board raft. [This would be the second raft he would run that spring.
> Sat. 14. Cloudy; raining; temperate. Plenty water for sawing. Some snow still in the woods. Some people still rafting in timber.
> Sun. 15. Cloudy; raining forenoon; temperate. A flood. Ran a raft for Wm. Irwin, to Smith's dam. Nearly all stoved below the shute [chute]. We started from home at 12 oclock. Walked from Smith's dam to Enos McMaster's. Staid all night.
> Mon. 16. Clear; very foggy in the morning. Walked from McMaster's to McGee's dam; took a raft for Johnson & Camp to Ellis' dam; left it (being too weak handed) and walked to our spar raft in Scofield's dead water by 12 o'clock. The raft was taken' off the point where it was stuck. Ran the raft into Antis' dam. Engaged a pilot to run us to Middletown for 45 dollars.

Even as a passenger on a spar raft a person's life could be in danger. James Batchelder was a cook in Huntley spar camp on the First Fork of the Sinnemahoning Creek and wanted a ride down the creek to the main branch, or the Driftwood Branch, of the Sinnemahoning Creek. Coming down the creek he wanted to be helpful so he used a pike to push saw logs out of the way for the front oar. (A pike is a long pole with a metal point on the end, used to push sticks along during rafting-in and to prevent jams by log drivers.) Batchelder reached too far, fell in and the raft ran over him. Fortunately all rafts run faster than the water's current. Bill Krebs was able to see Batchelder passing under the raft and he followed him to the rear of the raft. When Batchelder popped to the surface, Krebs plucked him out of the water like a drowning puppy (Huntley 328).

> Tue. 17. Raining the forenoon; rather cold. Started from Antis' dam at 6 o'clock with 5 hands. Wm. Hoover pilot. Ran to Plum Island by 11 o'clock, landed for rain. Started again at 12; ran to Sandy Run by 4½ o'clock and landed for night. Good flood. Rafts piled up at the Big Stepping-stones nearly across the river. Did not see many rafts running today.

Big Stepping Stone was upriver from Sandy Run, and that landing was very full. That morning Langdon had passed one of the rafting points on the river with a most colorful history, Rowles' Ducks. The river makes a sharp 90 degree turn to the right just after passing under the Shawville Bridge. In the left-hand corner of the turn is a small island and when the water is low it looks like a sand bar. This is Rowles' Ducks, named for Uncle George Rowles. The title "Uncle" was given to a likeable character who often found himself in embarrassing positions. One day Uncle George Rowles was piloting his raft down around the turn when he shouted to his steersman, "Steer for that flock of ducks." The ducks turned out to be willows above the water from the submerged island. Consequently Uncle George ran onto the island and stuck (Mitchell 14).

One reason Langdon and his crew may have stopped at Sandy Run was to visit the "Pig's Ear" there. A Pig's Ear was an unlicensed tavern and this place would cater to the raftsmen during the season (Dunlap, oral history).

Raftsmen bragged there were only four types of whiskey: Squirrel, Fighting, Sleeping, and Logger's Delight. If you took several drinks of sleeping whiskey you fell asleep, and several drinks of the fighting whiskey you were ready to fight. A few drinks of the squirrel whiskey and you wanted to climb a tree. Probably all whiskey sold in Pig's Ears was made from the same recipe or a slight variation of the recipe for "Logger's Delight." Logger's Delight was made by putting five gallons of grain alcohol into a 32 gallon barrel. Twenty pounds of finely chopped tobacco was added to the barrel and it was filled with rain water. The mixture was agitated three times a day for ten days and left to stand for one month. Then it was strained through a cloth and diluted with water. Pig's Ear bartenders didn't like to serve fighting or sleeping whiskey because the customer couldn't drink these all night. However, if he started the customer on squirrel whiskey and he was just about ready to climb a tree, the bartender switched him to Logger's Delight. This would maintain the customer's readiness to climb the tree and keep him buying whiskey all night (Huntley 486–7).

> Wed. 18. Clear; very warm. Very foggy in the morning. Started at Sandy ¼ past 7. Ran to Stout's; landed at ¼ past 4. Water very high. 5 hands going all the way. A squall blew down the roof & gable ends of the cabin at Sinnamahoning. [Stout's was an island just below the Hyner Bridge and above Lock Haven. Tonkin called it White Island and today the map calls it McCloskey Island.]
>
> Thu. 19. Cloudy; raining a little at noon. Water very high; 3 feet too high. Very warm. Lay at Stout's all day for high water and crowd at the Island. Great many rafts running as far as the Island. A great crowd of rafts in this eddy last night and this evening. Water rose last night 8 inches. A man drowned at the mouth of Sinnamahoning, in jumping from one raft to another.

The three branches of the Sinnemahoning Creek (the Bennett Branch, the Driftwood Branch and First Fork) supplied as many spars as the West Branch of the Susquehanna River area in Clearfield County. It seemed every creek and river had a dangerous point to get through and on the Sinnemahoning it was Tunnel Hill. Tunnel Hill is on the Driftwood Branch of the Sinnemahoning

Creek about two-thirds of the way from Emporium to Driftwood. The creek runs south through the mountains where Tunnel Hill extends out into the area where the creek should flow. Coming down the creek approaching Tunnel Hill a black stone mountain can be seen blocking the path. At the stone face the creek makes a 90 degree sharp turn to the right and runs west for 3,000 feet. Then it makes a 180 degree hair pin turn back to the east. These are the two worst turns on the creek, both within what seems like one city block. Clarence Miller described how the rafts ran through the turns. Tunnel Hill was also known as Hickory Bottom. Miller said they used four men on each oar. The rafts were 26 feet wide and about 200 feet long, with an oar on each end. Coming into the first turn they ran two sticks up on the gravel beach to slow the raft so it could make the turn. (A stick was a spar, square timber, or log.) Across the creek there is a big rock that if hit would tear the raft apart. Then the men would have to get two sticks up on the left gravel beach to get around the hairpin turn, and again there is a big gray bed rock on the right side of the creek waiting to stove the rafts. They were lucky that the inside of the turns did not have large rocks on the beaches. Once they reached the West Branch at Keating the raftsmen fleeted up to go down the river (Miller, oral history 4).

> Fri. 20. Very heavy thunder showers all day; temperate. Raining last night. Water fell last night 7 inches, but commenced raising in the morning and continued raising all day. Lay at Stout's all day on account of high water. Water this evening 16 inches higher than when we landed, and still rising.
> Sat. 21. Clear; temperate. Lay at Stout's all day for high water. River uncommon high last night. Rose 3 feet within 20 hours. Rose last night an inch every 15 minutes for some hours. Staid up all night watching the raft. Whole and pieces of rafts drifting down the river. Water falling a little today. A good many rafts running.
> Sun. 22. Variable; warm: Sprinkling a little rain in the morning. Lay at Stout's all day for high water, which makes 4 days lying at Stout's. Water falling. Several rafts lying in the eddy.

The "lead of the water" is what the raftsmen called the area in a body of water that had the strongest current. Raftsmen depended on knowing the lead because rafts floated downstream in the lead. A rafting flood raised the water level about three feet above normal, providing enough clearance to get over rocks and low places in the streams, but it didn't change the lead.

When the flood got much above three feet, the lead began to change as the stream flowed across fields rather than around bends. If caught in such a lead the raft could be run out into a field, where if stuck would remain there forever. Another dangerous area was at a dam. Raftsmen depended on the lead to pull them into the chute, but a rafting flood that was too high sent the water pouring over a dam and the lead could pull them over the breastwork of the dam. Therefore many raftsmen waited until the water receded to a "good rafting flood" level. Langdon would wait four days for the river to recede.

Mon. 23. Clear; warm. [Left] Stout's ½ past 5 o'clock; got in the head of Fernsville [Farrandsville] dam by ¼ to 10. Great crowd in Big [Great] Island dam. Landed because a lot of rafts broke loose. Saw one go over the breast of the dam. One man on but took him off in a skiff. Started again at ½ past 2. Landed at Carson's eddy 5 miles above Jersey Shore, by ½ past 5.

It was four and a half hours from Stout's to Farrandsville Dam or about seventeen miles, confirming that Stout's was Whites, later called McCloskey Island. Great Island is down river (east) of Lock Haven.

Tue. 24. Very smoky; temperate. Started from Carson's ¼ past 5. The pilot took the billious cholic; and we were forced to land 1½ miles below Jersey Shore. Went up to town for medicine, which cured him. Started again ½ past 1, ran to Long Reach by 4. Landed for night. Great many rafts running.

Wed. 25. Thunder showers; smoky; warm. Started from Long Reach at 5, passed Williamsport at 8. Passed Muncy Shute ¼ to 2. Landed at Lewisburg ½ past 5.

By this time the Muncy dam and chute had been rebuilt after the rafts-men had destroyed it in 1830, because it had wrecked or stoved too many rafts and arks (Livingood 69). Evidently it posed no threat to Langdon's raft.

Thu. 26. Cloudy; windy; temperate. Started from 6; landed at Northumber-land at ½ past 11 for wind. Lay there all afternoon. Wind, thunder and rain. [Langdon waited until the wind died down to run the Shamokin chute.]

Fri. 27. Clear; temperate; windy. Started from North ½ past 4; landed at McKee's Half Falls at 11 for wind. Lay there all afternoon. Blew a perfect storm all last night. [Langdon waited here because he was just above Lazy Man's Gap.]

Sat. 28. Variable, temperate; smoky. Started from McKee's ½ past 4. Ran to Green's dam, got a pilot to run to Coxestown for 4 dollars. Stuck on a rock at Foster's; stopped about 10 minutes, and was knocked off by another raft; swung round and came out safe.

Sun. 29. Clear; very smoky; warm. Started from Coxestown at 5; passed Harrisburg ¼ to 8. Stopped at the White House, got a pilot for 7 dollars. Landed at Marietta at 5. Tremendous crowd of rafts. The whole landing for about 4 miles in length is landed from 15 to 20 rafts deep.

The White House was a stopping place to pick up a pilot to run to Marietta. This short but dangerous run went through Conewago Falls. The White House was located below Highspire where Olmstead Airfield is today. It had a long sluggish landing which made a good place to tie up. When the landing at Marietta was full, rafts were kept at the White House until they could be moved down to Marietta. Such rafts were said to be "not run in yet" (Mitchell 36).

Mon. 30. Cloudy; very smoky; temperate. Raining a little in the evening. Staid at Marietta. Several acres of rafts broke loose this afternoon; got them all stopped. The boys started home this morning.

May 1855

Tue. 1. Variable; warm; very smoky; raining a little last night & this morning. Staid at Marietta. Water getting low.

Wed. 2. Variable; warm; staid at Marietta. Cannot sell the spars. Timber sell-ing from 4 to 7 cents. Boards selling well. Great many people going home and leaving their rafts.

On May 9, 1855, the *Raftsmen Journal* in Clearfield reprinted an article from the *Meriettam* saying the river "is literally crammed with rafts ... never before has such a quantity been here at one time ... it was principally all tim-ber." This was the problem with rafting, all the winter's work reached Mari-etta, Columbia, Wrightsville and Port Deposit within a two week period if the river had a good spring freshet.

Thu. 3. Raining showers all day; cool. Water still falling. Staid at Marietta. Small's large sawmill at Wrightsville burnt down this evening. Saw the light at Marietta. [Wrightsville is about four miles below Marietta on the western shore and across the river from Columbia.]
Fri. 4. Clear, very windy and cool. 45 rafts broke loose this forenoon, got them landed on the opposite side of the river, the wind blowing that way. Went to Columbia to a circus. No rafts coming in today on account of wind.
Sat. 5. Clear; windy; temperate. Sold the spars to Churchman for 400 dollars. Came to Harrisburg in the evening.

Churchman was F. G. and G. Churchman of Wilmington, Delaware. Churchman would buy the spars at Marietta and have a crew run them down the Susquehanna Gorge from Columbia to Peach Bottom and through the Susquehanna Canal to Port Deposit, where they would be towed to the ship-yards at Philadelphia by steamboat through the Chesapeake and Delaware Canal. George Churchman was a flamboyant fellow spending his money freely.

By 1855, lumber brokers had started moving up the river from Port Deposit to Columbia and Marietta to get better prices. Then they would hire crews to run the rafts down the river. Langdon received a very low price of $400.00 for his raft or $20.00 per spar, and once he paid off all his debts, he had very little left. Pilots cost him $56.00 and his crew of four for 24 days at $1.00 a day cost him another $96.00, plus paying for their train ride from Harrisburg to Altoona. He had to pay the spar master and the hauler also, but he gave no figures for these costs. In the beginning spar trees sold to rafters at $1.00 on the ground after felling. If they broke during felling the tree was cut into shingles and they were sold, but the rafter didn't pay for a broken tree (R.D. Tonkin 7).

Twenty years later in 1875, Churchman contracted Huntley on the Sin-nemahoning Creek to buy 100 spars at $25,000 or $250.00 per spar (Huntley 330), which was a good price because he ordered one hundred spars. Usually raftsmen sold spars to the brokers in Marietta or Port Deposit by the inch of diameter twelve feet above the butt (Tonkin, R.D. 8). Spars were trimmed so that the twelve feet above the butt all had the same diameter.

O. Lynn Frank said Tonkin told him they got $10.00 an inch. If we look at V. Tonkin's measurement of a spar raft in 1883 at Port Deposit, we see his twenty spars measured 594 inches, resulting in $5,940.00 or about $297.00 per spar. For the longest time I couldn't understand why Tonkin got $350.00 for spar number two which was 80 feet long and had a 35-inch diameter, and he only got $265.00 for spar number eleven that was 12 feet longer with a 26.5-inch diameter. That is $85.00 for a 12-foot shorter spar. If the broker-middleman didn't take into account the length of the spar when buying, then why was the length included in the measurement?

The measurement of the lengths and diameters of the spar may have been

Measurement of a spar raft at Port Deposit, April 30, 1883 (courtesy Tonkin Family).

for the broker's resale of the spar (Mitchell 48). A copy of the measurement slip provided the broker with an inventory of what spars he had for sale. Knowing where to go to get the right length and diameter spar insured getting a higher price for his goods.

R.D. Tonkin (220–21) stated that in 1879 his father paid $40.00 for a tree standing in the woods. This was a very low price since the trees were in a rocky area and no one thought you could fell the trees without breaking them. He paid the spar master $4.00 per tree to make them into spars. If the spar master broke a tree in felling or rejected the tree once down, Tonkin had to pay the $40.00 anyway. Trees could be found unsound once on the ground due to internal rot. He gave no cost figure for hauling the trees to the landing. Langdon's diary continued:

> Sun. 6. Clear; windy; temperate. Came from Harrisburg to Altoona by 8 oclock, got breakfast and came home.
> Tue. 8. Showers of rain and snow, cold. A Borrough was granted at the Cherry Tree on the 30 of April. Commenced rafting in boards. [The board raft would be his second raft to run down the river that spring.]
> Thu. 10. Clear; cool. Very hard frost this morning. Commenced clearing for myself. Went to the raising of the All Bright meeting house this afternoon.
> Sun. 13. Clear; warm. Went to Camelite [Campbellite] meeting at the Cherry Tree. The woods at the back of our place is on fire: on the land of A. B. Waller. It is deadening all the living trees as it goes.
> Tue. 15. Variable; very smoky; very windy and warm. Sawing some floor boards this afternoon.
> Thu. 17. Clear; cool; half a flood in the river this morning; a slight frost.
> Fri. 25. Clear; very smoky; warm. Went to the Lyceum last night.
> Sun. 27. Clear; very smoky; temperate. Went to the Cherry Tree to the funeral of Michael Forbes' child.
> Mon. 28. Clear; very smoky on account so much fires in the woods; warm. Hard frost this morning.
> Wed. 30. Clear most of the day. Clouded up towards evening, windy, smoky and warm. Edward King brought home the rafting boxes.

The rafting box came home 26 days later. Usually one young man was left to accompany the rafting box home by train, canal boat, wagon and stage coach. The rafting box contained the essential equipment needed in running a raft.

> Thu. 31. Cloudy; raining some the afternoon; temperate. Received a letter from Stephen Langdon, Alleghany City, stating that grandmother Langdon died on the 20th inst. Performed at the Lyceum by delivering an original oration. Drained out the dam and caught a great many fish.

> June 1855
> Thu. 7. Raining very hard all day and all last night. Water very high and some rafts running. River this aft-noon bank full.
> Fri. 8. Variable; showery; temperate. Started with one board raft. Water high. Smith's dam very bad. Tore out a runner below the shute. Landed and fixed up, and staid all night in the cabin.

The runner was a keel of a platform. It would have been very interesting had Langdon described how this was fixed. Tearing out a runner of a keel meant breaking off the heads of the three grubs run through the keel. Each platform had three keel boards on its bottom, so perhaps breaking out one wasn't fatal.

> Sat. 9. Cloudy; raining a little the afternoon; temperate. Ran from Atchison's to Curwensville dam. Detained over 3 hours by a jamb below Spenser's dam. There were several rafts piled up together. We landed at Goose Island and walked down to the jamb.
> Sun. 10. Cloudy; showery; raining all last night. Thunder this afternoon. Temperate. Water high and running fast. Coupled the board raft of 7 platforms (one 12 ft. long) with Goss' half raft of small timber 110 ft. long. Finished coupling by 12 oclock. The water being very high we lay there all the afternoon. Engaged Richard Ellis to run to Green's dam for 2 dollars per day.

The board raft was about 120 feet long and Gross' timber raft would have been lashed side-by-side to make a very small fleet, about 42 feet wide and 110 to 120 feet long.

> Mon. 11. Variable. Very windy; sprinkling a little rain; cool. Ran from Curwensville to Shaw's dam; landed for high water, and lay there all day. Very few rafts on the river this flood.
> Tue. 12. Variable; cool; very foggy in the morning. Started from Shaw's dam at 7; ran to the foot of Buttermilk [Falls] by ¼ to 6 and landed. Another raft came in and struck us and stoved us a good deal. Got it fixed up by dark. 5 hands coming through the mountains & going all the way.
> Wed. 13. Variable cool; foggy in the morning. Sprinkling rain in the afternoon. Started from the foot of Buttermilk ¼ to 7, landed in Lockhaven dam at dusk.
> Thu. 14. Variable; cool the forenoon; windy part of the day. Started from Lockhaven ¼ to 4; landed in Muncy dam just above the shute ½ past 8.
> Fri. 15. Clear most of the day; windy part of the day; temperate. Started from Muncy at 4; landed at Lewisburg to try to sell at 10. Was offered 10 dollars. Ran on; landed at the Northumberland bridge for wind; staid about an hour, and ran down to the shute by 7.
> Sat. 16. Cloudy; temperate. A terrible storm of thunder and lightning, wind and rain in the afternoon. The wind blew a perfect hurricane for a few minutes. The greatest storm that ever was known in the neighborhood of Harrisburg. Thunder, lightning and rain in the evening. Started from Shamokin at ½ past 4. Got a pilot at Shamokin to run to Coxestown for 12 dollars on account of our pilot being sick. Ran to Bargers and knocked off 5 sticks of Goss' half raft, on the pilot rock, about 12 oclock. Landed just below, and the pilot went down to Montgomerie's Island and caught the sticks. We then ran the raft down to the Island and put them in by dark.

The pilot rock was just below Liverpool. Yates' charts indicated that the rafts needed to be close to the western shore, running only 25 to 30 rods off shore, which was 230 feet to 460 feet. Yates does not call it The Pilot, but says "rocks coming out into the river." This place is just above the most dangerous part of the river between the Shamokin Dam and Greens Dam.

Sun. 17. Raining nearly all day; windy and cold. Raining all last night. Started from Montgomerie's Island at 5; landed at Coxestown at 11. Landed on account of bad weather. Lay there all the afternoon.

This day's run took them by Girty's Notch and past sunfish (a rock at the notch), Muskrat Hole and Lazy Man's Gap, then across the river to the chute at Greens Dam, apparently no problem for Langdon's raft.

Mon. 18. Cloudy; temperate. Sold the raft; 7 platforms long (one of them a 12 foot platform) 15 courses deep and a thousand ft. of pannel on top for 290 dollars in the water: to Adam Islington.
Tue. 19. Raining all day; cold. Walked down to Harrisburg, 5 miles, and bought goods of John Rhodes.
Wed. 20. Cloudy; temperate. Started at Harrisburg at 3 in the cars. Arrived in Altoona at 8; walked home before sundown.
Wed. 27. Clear most of the day; warm. Hoeing corn all day; the first day the ground has been dry enough for the season.
Thu. 28. Variable; Very warm; lightning in the evening. A very heavy thunder shower commencing at 3 oclock this morning and causin almost a flood in the river. Went this morning to chop in the clearing and cut my foot. George brought the goods & rafting box from Wilmore & also a barrel of flour, price $11.50 at Jefferson.

This was the end of the 1855 rafting season when his younger brother brought the rafting box home. His life settled down to running the sawmill, working on the farm, working as a carpenter, and participating in giving lectures and debates at the lyceum. He never said what his essays and debates were about.

July 1855

Tue. 10. The mill going some, most every day.
Tue. 17. Mill going part of the day.
Thu. 19. Performed at the Lyceum by reading an Essay.
Tue. 24. I commenced working weatherboards for the Allbright meetinghouse near Brillharts this afternoon. Going to weatherboard it for $1.75 per square and board myself.

August 1855

Fri. 3. Performed at the Lyceum last night by debating.
Thu. 16. Went to the Lyceum but there were very few there on account of the rain; the house was not called to order. Received some programmes for the exhibition which is to take place on the 21st of September.

He must have gotten his assignment to give his lecture five weeks later on the 21st of September. He gave the lecture to a full house with standing room outside.

Fri. 31. People have commenced making timber, and a great deal is to be made next winter notwithstanding the great quantity made last winter & the low price in the spring.

White pine was not cut until much later because at this time of the year there was too much sap which would stain the wood and reduce its price.

September 1855

Sat. 1. Emma Tufling and myself were married this evening. [William Langdon's life would change forever. He no longer piloted rafts, but worked as a carpenter.]

Fri. 21. Cloudy; temperate — raining in the evening. Performed at the exhibition by delivering an oration. The church was crowded full, & a great many out side. [This was the lecture he agreed to give back on August 16.]

October 1855

Sat. 6. Was working all week for Robert Hughes in the Tan-house at the Cherry Tree, laying a floor, putting up a partition &C. [This was a big project for Langdon.]

Fri. 12. Finished working at the tan-house. Made one dollar & quarter per day for 11 days. [A dollar a day was very good wages; that is why he noted it in his diary.]

Tue. 16. Commenced working at the Millwrighting for James Brothers; for one dollar per day and found; at a sawmill building for Kinports & Douglas, near Garmon's grist mill. Finished raising the mill this forenoon. [It seems there was nothing William Langdon couldn't do as a carpenter.]

Sat. 20. Hazy — warm. Wild geese flying [a sure sign along the Susquehanna River that fall is here].

December 1855

Mon. 31. Clear most of the day; cold. Snow 5 or 6 inches deep; good sleighing. People commenced hauling timber on this place today. Very little timber hauled to the river yet.

This was his last entry in his diary for 1855. He talked about other people making timber and hauling it but said nothing about himself doing any. He was a married man now with a family on the way and maybe running rafts was too dangerous for a family man. There is no proof that he ever piloted a raft again.

George Langdon, William's younger brother, was killed during the Civil War. He rests in the Cherry Tree Cemetery.

8

Tales of the West Branch

This collection of short stories illustrates some of the adversities the rafts-men faced daily. Getting stuck on a rock was a problem that had several solutions. William McGovern wrote three articles explaining how raftsmen ate on their rafts and about the dangers of rafting. Alfred Koozer tells us what it was like to get caught in a spring snow storm at night. An article in the Clearfield *Raftsman's Journal* explains what a down river town was like in rafting season. Another section gives the history of Cherry Tree Joe, the West Branch's Paul Bunyan. Bertha Conrad tells us how a group of young ladies made the trip down river in April of 1893. John S. Beck explains how a green horn rafter learned the hard way. A final entry explains how Gallows Harbor got its name.

Getting Stuck on a Rock

Getting stuck on a rock was a common occurrence for raftsmen; however, spar rafts that weighed about 110 tons and moved at four miles an hour would bump over most rocks in the river. In the State Museum of Pennsylvania's *Video of the Last Raft, 1938*, the camera focused on the square timbers on the rear platform as the raft passed over a submerged rock. The sticks appear to expand and explode as the rock hits the underside of the raft. Then, as if by magic, the sticks shrink back into place as if nothing had happened, demonstrating the elasticity and resiliency of constructing a raft in this manner.

If a raft did stick, it was prudent to get it off as quickly as possible, because most rafting was done on receding floods, and the longer the raft stuck on a sand bar or rock, the more likely the raft wouldn't be able to get off it until the next flood.

When Langdon's raft stuck it was only one platform long or about 93 feet and weighed about 55 tons. There were several ways of getting the raft off the rock. One was to cut the lash pole and let the separated sides of the platform slip downstream and away from the rock. The other was to cut the lash pole so that two spars would swing out into the main current, which would help pull the rest of the raft off the rock. Evidently Langdon had tried one of these methods and it hadn't worked. Langdon was helped by a "Good Samaritan" raft crew when they came alongside and snubbed to Langdon's raft and pulled him free. This was not an unusual act since the raftsmen were often neighbors or relatives or future relatives.

Billy Byers (oral history 2) tells an interesting story about a raft stuck on a rock. One day he was riding a raft down river when they came upon a raft stuck on a rock. The Kitchen brothers—Dave, Andy and Len—were on the stranded raft. They were "Smiling George" Kitchen's sons. When Dave Kitchen saw him coming, he hollered, "Got a broad axe?" (A broadaxe weighed about seven pounds, had a short handle and a 13 inch blade for hewing trees into square timbers.)

Billy Byers replied that he had. "Throw it to me," Dave Kitchen replied. Billy Byers knew the Kitchen brothers often tossed axes to each other so, as Billy Byers's raft passed by the Kitchen's raft, he tossed the axe overhand. The axe spun through the air and Dave Kitchen reached out and caught the axe by the handle with one hand. That night Byers got his axe back when the Kitchen raft tied up at the same landing as his raft.

Rafting Grub

Landon said nothing about feeding the crew during a voyage, but William McGovern in his article "Rafting on the West Branch, a Fateful Trip Recalled," tells us how it was done in 1881. His article was published in 1938.

> Each crew had their own method of living. They did not differ very much, but were nearly all after the same plan. Some done their own baking, while others had bread baked at home, when not too far away. However, most of the men preferred hot biscuit each meal. Invalids and breakfast foods were very much out of place. The general plan was, implicitly and frugality, but enough for everyone to eat. As underfed men, meant under work, and hot tempers.
>
> On one camping trip, I remember very well. We left the supply store with 2 barrels flour, 4 barrels Mess Pork 200 lb. each. ½ barrel N.O. syrup, plenty of black tea. Coffee was not used then. You had neither the means to brown it, or grind it in large amounts. Coffee came at that time, in its green state. A few years afterward Arbuckles came in. The dishes consisted of tin pie plates, tin cups, iron handled knives and forks, tin spoons.
>
> Condensed Milk had not come into use at this time, and today there are many things that can be bought for the table, that at that time were not ready for instant use. Had we been able to get the variety of prepared foods, our work in cooking would have been very simple and very light. But the old time cook had never heard of a can opener. Mess pork was our principal meat. Par boiled, to take out the excess salt, and then slightly browned for the table, it was fine. We used no butter, but had plenty of sorghum for our biscuits. Tea in a tin cup, if sweetened with brown sugar or molasses it turned somewhat blacker than the original. Very little sugar was used, as there were neither pies or cakes baked.
>
> We were always kept well supplied with potatoes, cabbage, turnips and tomatoes. Each meal we had Yankee Biscuits. We used soda and cream of tartar, as baking powder had not come into general use at that time. The start was made

with dried rising, mixed with flour and warm water into a dough. Set near the stove to raise, and at meal time poured out on the dough board and made into a dough, then cut out for biscuit, put into pans and baked in a good oven with a quick fire.

They, when baked right, were very light and wholesome. To set the next batch, warm water was put into the dough that was left, stirred flour into it until the proper consistency was reached, set behind the stove to get moderate heat and this method could be kept up for some time until it was necessary for fresh raising.

Danger at Shamokin Dam

Many raftsmen said the chute at Shamokin Dam was very dangerous. William J. McGovern in his article "A Rafting Trip on the West Branch One Hundred Twenty Years Ago" describes the problem when the crew was caught in the slack water of the dam with a strong wind blowing out of the northwest. Blue Hill rises up about four hundred feet above the slack water of the dam along its western shore, blocking the wind from the northwest. However, just as the rafts approached the chute along the western shore they were subject to the wind coming down the valley along what is today Route 15. This valley causes a venturi effect, increasing the wind's speed. The rafts were run during a rafting flood or when the river was three to four feet higher than normal. This was high enough for water to be spilling over the dam, and thus the slack water had currents in it that would draw the raft over the crest of the dam if it got too near. The chute at Shamokin Dam was very narrow and along the western shore. McGovern was on a fleet (two rafts and both were 300 feet long, so his fleet was 56 feet wide and 300 feet long) which had to be uncoupled before they could take it through the narrow chute at Shamokin Dam. The wind was blowing his fleet away from the western shore and the chute. This occurred in the spring of 1881.

McGovern picked up his story as his raft came out from behind Blue Hill.

Going through Shamokin Dam we had a very strong wind blowing against us, and pushing the fleet toward the opposite shore from the chute. The wind was quartering and up the stream; so while we were moving very slow we were being pushed away from the side we needed.

Being strong-armed for this, we pulled and pulled and every time I pulled I thought "well this will be my last" but I would catch my wind again going back and still continued on, until the pilot saw we could not help ourselves and gave the order to pull with the wind, as we had not far to reach the opposite shore. There was nothing to tie to but a telegraph pole. I went out with the rope. Fortunately the raft was almost stopped and the man helping tie was fagged out same as I. We laid in the shanty all that night and the next morning we had the steam boat, what was owned by the Canal Co., tow us out to near the opposite shore; and the wind having fallen, we had no trouble to navigate the chute. The Shamokin Dam was said to have a breast height of 18 feet. [The dam was 2783 feet long across the river and was 9.5 feet high (Snyder, Canals 111)].

But finally we went through the long chute. And having now Down River Pilots we were set for anything that was in front of us. I do not remember at this length of time where we tied up at night.

A few years before our trip, two men by name of Flynn and Pyles undertook to run a raft without a shanty on it—that was very much easier to handle against a wind and starting very light handed in the Shamokin Dam to run the chute, through miscalculation or wind went over the dam. The raft going to pieces. Pyles lost his life. Likely killed or badly hurt amongst the floating loose timber. Flynn was rescued by men from the shore who had boats.

It being Sunday the crew that manned the Steamboat were off duty. It was the duty of this boat to help rafts in trouble on week days. These men took a chance and lost, their timber scattered for miles down the river. I have this information from the survivor many years afterward.

A Tragedy at Millers Landing

William Langdon passed Millers Landing in an uneventful trip, but years later in the early 1880s, William McGovern reports in his article "Rafting on the West Branch, a Fateful Trip Recalled" of running past Wood Rock and Millers Landing across the river from the mouth of Moshannon Creek with different results. "One oak and pine raft had been giving us lots of trouble from the White Break to the Wood Rock; at the Wood Rock he had trouble, lost a few sticks. We had poled him around our raft as his raft run somewhat faster than the one we were on. Night was coming on and very high water to work against, so we consulted together and decided to tie up, just above and opposite the mouth of Moshannon Creek. We done so and found our crippled raft just in the act of landing. We ran a short distance ahead and tied to a large tree. The raft now behind us was having some trouble as we could see from the excited state of the men in getting landed."

The oak and pine raft had caught up to McGovern's raft above Wood Rock, so using poles to push the two rafts apart, they let the oak and pine raft pass them. Then when the oak and pine raft hit Wood Rock, McGovern's rafts passed the oak and pine raft. Wood Rock was a very dangerous place in the river where many rafts were stoved. Mitchell (14) describes the rock as the only big rock in mid-stream above Columbia. At the time of a rafting flood it was 8 to 10 feet out of the water. It got its name because during bigger floods wood would get caught on the top of the rock. McGovern continues:

> After securing our raft and seeing everything was safe, we started up to see what the trouble was with our neighbor. We found a very bad accident had happened. One of the crew, and a green man, had fallen into the river, caused by an undermined sand bank giving away. He was helping carry "slack" of rope to snub the raft, and was on the raft waiting for the raft to come closer to the bank, when he misjudged the distance, jumped for the bank when it being partly washed under, gave way and he fell between the raft and bank. He was not seen again by anyone. As the raft slowly swinging to shore covered up any trace of him. We all

hunted, below the raft thinking the current would carry him down to our raft. But although we all hunted, Merrill [McGovern's friend] and myself until dark, we never saw him again.

More than a month after, the body was found near Birch Point many miles below the mouth of the Moshannon. Very singular it was, my companion and I were destined to visit his grave some years afterward. The next morning after a short delay we parted crews and most of the men in the other crew I never saw again. We left our mountain hand off at the foot of Buttermilk Falls, where but for our troubles the day before he should have arrived a day earlier.

A mountain hand was a raftsman who helped take one raft to below Buttermilk Falls where the two rafts were coupled together. From there on, one crew of six men would take the raft down the river and the mountain hands walked back home.

Some years afterward, my friend Merrill and I, were employed not many miles from Birch Point, and on a bright Sunday morning we started to visit the grave of the unfortunate young man to whom fate dealt such a harsh fate. With the help of a native along the river, we found his grave. Close to the river, and at the foot of one of Centre County's high mountains. The grave was on a small flat, and had a very neat wicker fence around it, very tastefully made and contained some broken jars that at one time no doubt, had been filled with flowers.

Our guide informed us that his mother and a young wife had built the fence, and brought the flowers, perhaps many miles. In our time wild flowers grew in profusion about his resting place, and on the mountain side thousands of bees and birds were visiting them. Some years afterward in the vicinity of his grave, I made an attempt to find it again. But it could not be found. Even the spot looked different. Flowers were again blooming; bees and birds were in profusion, and the waters sang the same old song of nature. And a pang of sadness caught me that I could not resist for the untimely end of the raftsman and his hopes.

Man, despite all his errors, being led by a higher hand, reaches some happier goal at last.

Caught in a Spring Snowstorm

Buttermilk Falls is about three miles below Karthaus and just above the village of Cataract. It was customary to run both rafts through the falls separately before lashing them together to form a fleet. Large operations like McGovern's used two crews to get below the falls before sending one crew home.

The falls are riffles about a mile long with huge gray rocks along the shore that if hit would tear the raft apart. Coming out of the falls there is a sharp right turn in the river of about 90 degrees. It is because of these problems most pilots waited until after passing the falls to fleet up.

Small operations such as the Koozers' which was a six man crew, would start at first light and run one raft below the falls and tie it fast. Then they would walk back up the river, getting home after dark. The next day they would take the second raft down and lash it to the first raft before going down the river.

Alfred Koozer's oral history is much like all the oral histories, where the events are not told in the order in which they happened. I have taken the liberty to put his tale in story form.

This happened on Alfred Koozer's first trip down the river when he was 14 years old. His father, Courtis Bell Koozer, was the pilot and he decided to stop at Karthaus with the first raft. This would save them about six miles or an hour and a half walking home that evening. The walk back from Karthaus was about 25 miles or a little over five hours. The day had been wet and cold, so it sounded like a good idea.

The next day they brought the second raft to Karthaus and fleeted up. It was mid afternoon when they were ready and the pilot decided to run to Briar Bottom. It was snowing and getting colder. The pilot thought the river could be much lower the next day, so he decided to run to Briar Bottom, the first landing below Buttermilk Falls. Briar Bottom was about 13 miles down river and the pilot thought they could get there in about three hours and fifteen minutes, or just before dark. Alfred's father had become impatient while rafting-in at Frazier's Rock below Clearfield. Three days before they finished building their two rafts, other rafts started going down the river — he was afraid they would take too long, the rafting flood would recede and they would have to wait for another freshet, if one came that year.

The crew consisted of six men: Alfred's father, the pilot, Old Max Taylor, the steersman, a big man by the name of Smith, another younger man who Koozer didn't identify, Roy Shirey, who was a little older that Alfred, and Alfred, whom everyone called "The Kid" because he was the youngest crew member. Every rafting crew had a Kid. The Kid was the steersman's assistant and the raft's snubber when landing.

Going through the falls, the fleet accelerated to three times the normal speed they had made on the river before reaching the falls. It was at this point that a spring snowstorm hit — you couldn't see your hand in front of your face. Alfred didn't know how they gauged the turn coming out of the falls, but they made it. His father, on the front of the fleet, guided them by standing on the front of the raft and watching the current in the water. Knowing how the river turned one way and then the other, he would have them row the fleet back and forth across the river to get to the inside of each turn. The current near the shore goes slower because of the friction between the water and the shoreline. If the fleet is kept out in the faster current, the current will carry the fleet around the turn. However, if the fleet is on the wrong side, or outside of the turn, the current will push the fleet into the bank, stoving the vessel.

The snowstorm lessened, but darkness came on early. Alfred's father stuck a cant hook down between the logs and hung a lantern on the top so he could watch the current. (Cant hooks were also called peavey or cant dog. They were about six feet long with a metal point and a pivotal hook to catch and turn the log.) At night the footing on the fleet became very dangerous since it was made of round logs with the bark peeled off. This type fleet moved logs down the river to other sawmills where they were made into board or timber for bridge building. They had laid boards on top of the wet, slippery logs to walk on, but in the dark it was easy to miss a board and have your foot go down between the logs.

Alfred's father consulted with Old Max and they decided they were approaching Briar Bottom. They moved the fleet close to the right bank and the Kid got the snubbing line ready to go ashore. Smith volunteered to take the line ashore and find a snubbing tree, the Kid would help him with the line. Old Max said to Alfred, "Whatever you do, don't get caught up in snubbing line and get yourself killed." Alfred hadn't thought about that.

He and Smith removed the sweep from the right raft so it wouldn't get broken in the landing. Old Max manned the sweep on the left raft, ready to press the fleet into the shore to slow it for snubbing. Alfred and Smith picked up the snubbing line and moved closer to the fleet's edge. Smith said, "Don't jump, wait until you can step ashore."

Then, before they were ready, the front end stoved into the river bank, sending everyone flying forward. If Alfred hadn't been holding onto the snubbing line, he felt he would have been tossed into the river. The river was completely dark, the jar of the stoving had knocked the lantern into the river and they had no light aboard.

It was several seconds before the crew knew what was happening — the rear of the fleet had caught the current and the fleet cartwheeled down the river. The front was becoming the rear and the rear was becoming the front.

From the front end he heard them shouting, "Bring the snubbing line forward! Bring the snubbing line forward!" Alfred hustled to untie the snubbing line from the lash pole and as he did he heard the front end sliding back into the water.

As the front end pulled off the bank, the back end stuck on a sunken bar and the fleet continued to cartwheel until the front end was going down the river first. It took a few minutes for everyone to regain their composure, and then Old Max moved forward to talk with Alfred's father.

He and Smith replaced the right sweep and they manned the two rear sweeps until Old Max returned. "We are going to try to land at Cook's Run, that should be coming up in about an hour and a half."

Alfred pulled his scarf up around his neck and his hat down over his ears and rubbed his hands together in the mittens his mother had knitted for him, trying to keep warm. His feet had been wet for two days and he didn't know when they would get dry.

It seemed like forever before they passed the mouth of the Sinnemahoning Creek on the left. In the darkness they were almost passed it before they realized where they were. Old Max said, "We need to row over to the left bank to land at Cook's Run." With him and Old Max on one sweep and Smith on the other, they started to move their sweeps back and forth across the deck, moving their end crab-like toward the left bank. It was very dark now with no stars, making it hard to see the shoreline.

Before they got to Cooks Run his father, Roy, and the other man started calling out for someone to come out to help. It wasn't long before a lantern light was seen coming out across the rafts already tied up there. Both ends tried to row toward the light. After several strokes Alfred realized they were too far out in the stream to make the landing. The man with the lantern shouted, "You're way out in the middle of the stream, you'll never get here." There was a long pause in their rowing as the man on shore shouted, "Maybe you can make Halls Island down near Renovo?"

When he saw his father coming back to talk to Old Max, he knew they were in trouble. His father said to Old Max, "We can't take the chance of hitting the bridge piers." They were talking about the bridge at Renovo which had eight piers. The Kid knew bridge piers were dreaded by all raftsmen.

Old Max replied after some talk, "We could run her hard ashore and stop her. There's a place above Shintown, about a mile above the bridge." After some thought his father said, "That's our last chance."

Old Max said, "We can put the two young guys ashore to snub, you take Smith with you to help, the Kid and I can manage the rear sweeps." Old Max said to Alfred, "When we hit, hold onto the oar handle to keep yourself from being knocked overboard."

His father and Old Max walked across the fleet to Smith. Both men had spoken very solemnly, and the Kid knew they were worried. Smith and his father walked forward, leaving Old Max to man the other sweep. Alfred could see Old Max, and he could make out forms on the front of the raft, but he couldn't see the shoreline.

As they rounded a bend in the river to the right, they moved the fleet over to the left. Old Max kept the rear end out further in the river so the front end would run up on shore.

It was then that Old Max shouted, "Hang onto the oar!"

Alfred felt the jolt as the raft's front end ran up onto the shore, and like Old Max had warned him, he held onto the oar's handle as he was jerked forward. The raft timbers creaked as they absorbed the shock. Then he heard his father scream like he had never heard him before. Old Max shouted to Alfred, "Pull your sweep aboard."

Alfred went to the place where the sweep rested on the head block and with all his young strength lifted the sweep up off the head block, bringing the pin, with him and then moved forward bringing the sweep aboard, protecting the sweep. If it broke, there was no way to control their fleet.

When he stood up, Old Max said, "Come on, let's see what happened—

be careful." They made their way forward to see Alfred's father sitting on a log on the deck, moaning. "What happened?" Old Max asked.

"When the raft hit the shore the timbers parted and he slipped down between them into the water. I just got to him before they closed or the logs would have crushed him." Smith. said.

Alfred looked around and Roy and the other man were not on the fleet, but he could hear the timber creaking as they were being pulled back into the river. From the river bank he heard Roy shout, "We can't find a tree big enough!" Roy's voice faded into the darkness and Alfred, Old Max, Smith and his father drifted down stream toward the bridge at Renovo. Alfred knew his father couldn't help, and the three of them were not enough to guide the fleet in the darkness. The four men were quietly contemplating their predicament.

It was then that Old Max turned to Alfred and whispered as if the other two couldn't hear, "When we hit the bridge pier, the rafts will stop on that pier and then swing sideways until we hit a second and maybe a third pier. When we hit the other piers, the rafts will be held in the river's current and water will start to flow over the upstream side of the rafts, forcing it to the bottom of the river creating a dam. The water will break up the rafts and all of us will go into the river. When we hit a pier, move carefully towards that spot where the raft is up against the pier, and be prepared to grab onto a log, for that is the last piece of the raft to go under. Hang onto the log until it takes you to shore." Old Max paused as if he had an after thought, "Don't think about anyone but yourself — save yourself. We'll take care of ourselves." Then he was quiet as if waiting for death.

Alfred glanced around looking for the bridge and its piers; the river was too dark to see anything. Alfred remembered they were only a mile above the bridge — it would only take fifteen minutes. Both his feet were wet and cold — soon he would be wet and cold all over. He wanted to turn to his father and say, I love you, but he didn't want the men to think he was scared or was afraid of death. Even his father stopped moaning and was waiting for the inevitable.

Along the north side of the river the Philadelphia and Erie Railroad tracks connected the Great Lakes with the East Coast. A train was making its way down the tracks toward Renovo, the railroad repair town. The headlight on the engine cut through the snow and darkness. Alfred watched, thinking it might be the last thing he would ever see.

As the train passed them, something struck him as being wrong. The trees between him and the headlight weren't moving — if he was moving, then the trees should look like they were moving also. The distance between the trees that were close and those that were farther away did not change.

"I think we're stopped!" he exclaimed. "I'll check the front end." he said, starting to move forward.

"No, you don't," Old Max said, grabbing him by the arm, "It could be all broken up and you would fall into the river. Move over to the side of the raft and put your hand into the water. If you feel a current — we're stopped."

Alfred moved to the side of the raft, pulled off his mitten and put his hand into the water. "We're stopped," he cried in relief. "We're stopped." It was as if new life was given to the four men on the raft.

About that time they heard Roy's voice coming from the shore, he and the other man had come down the railroad tracks looking for them. Alfred turned toward the shore and shouted back, "We're over here! Stuck in the river!"

Roy found a farmer along the river that had a boat and Roy shouted that the farmer would be coming out to get them.

While the men waited for the farmer and his boat, they began to sing "Home Sweet Home." Alfred's feet didn't feel as cold as they had. Once the crew came ashore the farmer's wife cooked them a big meal of fried ham and eggs. That night Roy and Alfred slept together in the same bed, Roy would jump with his nightmares and wake Alfred. Once back to sleep Alfred would jump and wake Roy. This went on all night. The next day they found their raft beached on the upriver point of Halls Island, and by noon they had their rafts coupled and headed down the river to Lock Haven, safely past the Renovo bridge with its eight piers.

However, passing under the bridge they had to contend with the Renovo boys dropping stones from the bridge, trying to hit the raftsmen.

Alfred Koozer would make one more trip down the West Branch of the Susquehanna River before taking a safer job in lumbering.

A Rafting Town in Season

Marietta, Pennsylvania, to which William Langdon ran his spars, was but one of several destinations for raftsmen on the Susquehanna. Columbia, Harrisburg, and even Port Deposit, at the head of tidewater in Maryland, received their share of rafts. All were to some degree possessed of the wide-open character of Marietta, so graphically described below in a letter to S. B. Row, editor of the *Raftsman's Journal*, and published in that Clearfield newspaper on May 27, 1857. The description gives some credence to one writer's complaint that rafting "kept half the population of Clearfield County drunk down the river through the better part of the year." Certainly, the raftsman's life in Marietta seems to have been anything but dull.

The letter appeared as follows in the *Raftsman's Journal* in 1857.

Marietta, May 19. 1857.S. B. Row, Esq.— Dear Sir:

Thinking that perhaps some news from this place might be of some interest to the readers of the Journal, and having nothing else to amuse myself with, I proceed to devote this evening to their entertainment.

This is the latter part of spring and yet the air is cold and raw, so much so that ones fingers ache while walking the streets, in case he has no gloves to cover them, which article you know most Raftsmen disdain to wear at this season of the year.

The rain which commenced falling sometime during the night, still continues to descend with violence. Much trouble is anticipated in holding the lumber at this place should it continue much longer. The banks are low and sandy with but few trees, which render the holding of much lumber during a high freshet quite a difficult matter.

There is a large quantity of timber in market, of which there is very little changing hands at present, owing I suppose to the unfavorable state of the weather. The price has heretofore been rather favorable to holders, but this week it has fallen off to some extent, yet, I think, if owners were not so anxious to get home to their farms and families, the prices would still continue good. The prices last week ranged from 8 to 11¾ cents per foot for pine; some oak sold for 19 cents, but this week it ranges from 9 to 10 cents, still I think the timber is all needed, and those who are able to hold on to it for a time, will be apt to realize a fair price.

Boards are selling at Middletown and this place, at from 9 to 18 dollars, according to quality. Shingles, from 10 to 14 dollars. Expenses attending rafting this spring are almost double what they were formerly. This is owing to a series of floods, only one of which was suitable to raft on yet. They were all used, and mostly to the Raftsmans' disadvantage. The timber is all here now, except a few scattered rafts which were stoved in the mountains, and even those have a fair prospect of joining their mates ere long.

Mr. Editor, did you ever visit Marietta for a week during the rafting season? If not, you have lost one of the best opportunities of studying human nature you will have. It is quite amusing to loiter around Front Street during the day and observe the modus operandi of fleecing the more ignorant part of the watermen out of their hard earned money. At every alternate door you will observe a small board stuck out with the notice that within the dirty walls cakes and beer are sold. Some of them, and the fewest number too, bear the look of respectable shops; the balance are attended by one or more young females of a rather suspicious character. The hotels on front street are crowded to overflowing and free fights are plenty beyond conception. The bad whiskey drank here during the season of rafting would of itself float half the lumber to Peachbottom, or perhaps into the Bay. There are several fancy jewelry shops in operation, in which is sold any amount of brass in the shape of breast-pins, eardrops, lockets and watches, to the unsuspecting backwoodsmen and warranted by disreputable rascal, to be pure gold, and in which the poor buyer thinks he sees quite a speculation. Then there are three or four Patent Medicine venders mounted on chairs and door steps, rendering the streets hideous with their songs and gulls, to come and buy or test the virtues of their nostrums. And then, such a combination of talent, and curiosity as is offered to the people of Marietta for the low price of 12½ cents is astonishing. Last week we had Mr. Edwards and Lady, the celebrated ballad singers, and the Ethiopean serenaders, and this week a person lecturing on phrenology (a system of character analysis based upon the belief that certain faculties and personality traits are indicated by the configuration of the skull) at the Town Hall, and the Mammoth Lady from Missouri, said to weigh 550 pounds. She is certainly a scrouger, but I do not think she would weigh that much, yet it is hard to tell without seeing her weighed. To-day a cock-fight passed off in an old tobacco dry-house near town, on which I suppose there was about three dollars staked. After pushing them at one another some few times, Bob's chicken turned tail to and run, which terminated the contest. So you see that the good people of this place and those sojourning here have many ways of amusing themselves, to which the Clearfield people are almost strangers.

I must say for the Donegal House, where I am stopping for the time, that it is a first class house kept by Lewis Houseal, Esq., than whom there is no more gentlemanly landlord this side of Philadelphia. I would advise all uprivermen who contemplate stopping for any length of time, to give this house a trial, for those who love good substantial dinners and clean beds will find both these luxuries here.

Begging your pardon for so "much ado about nothing,"

I remain yours,

W.S.W.

About 1860 lumber brokers came to Lock Haven seeking better prices, reducing the competition from other brokers in the lower river. This suited many raftsmen who no longer had to make the trip down the river. Also, log drives to the booms in Williamsport and Lock Haven created an end of the trail environment like the cattle drivers found in Abilene and Dodge City. When this happened, Lock Haven became the new "Babylon of the Endless Mountains."

Cherry Tree Joe

This article uses information from George Swetnam's article, Joseph Dudley Tonkin's book, and O. Lynn Frank's book, *The Early Settlement and Water Transportation Era*.

Cherry Tree Joe is still very much a legend along the "Little Ditch," as the West Branch of the Susquehanna River is known above Clearfield to the town of Cherry Tree. Several old raftsmen referred to him in their oral histories with Sam King during the early 1960s. Swetnam's article stated:

> More than a dozen years ago, while writing "Pittsylvania Country," I became aware that the Pittsburgh district had three major folk heroes, one principally associated with each of its three rivers. But while a great deal had been published on Mike Fink, the Ohio River keelboatman, and Joe Magarac, the Monongahela Valley steelman, there was almost nothing in print on "Cherry Tree" Joe McCreery.
>
> Cherry Tree Joe, Pennsylvania's Paul Bunyan, was the basis of all the legends that had been told for many years through the lumber industry from Maine to Washington. This was long before an advertising campaign crystallized around the Wisconsin figure of Paul Bunyan. But while books aplenty had been written about Bunyan, the only thing I could find in print about McCreery was a ballad with a few lines of introduction, printed in J. Dudley Tonkin's "The Last Raft," from a broadside and copied in "Pennsylvania Songs and Legends."
>
> Inquiry among folklorists, historians and "old residenters" brought little help. There were plenty of tales about Cherry Tree Joe, but little unity of tradition. While there was a general feeling that McCreery, like Mike Fink, was a real person, no two people seemed to agree on whether he was from Cherry Tree, on French Creek in Venango County, or from Cherry Tree in Indiana County, on the West Branch of the Susquehanna. There was dispute — but not enough to

indicate a very healthy interest — as to whether he rafted on the Allegheny, Clarion, Kiskiminetas or West Branch.

Crowded by a deadline, I had to forgo any serious research, including the chance to visit either Cherry Tree. In desperation I simply laid out the problem and told a few of the stories:

He was a giant of a man, his size varying from a mere six and a half, or seven feet in some stories, to such a figure as could wear a raft on each foot and skate down the river. He was supposed to have a cabin somewhere back in the woods, where he kept moose for milk cows and a panther for a house-cat. His wife cooked on a griddle six feet square, and used a barrel of flour every morning to make flapjacks.

Cherry Tree Joe was crafty, too. One year he didn't have any white pine to raft down to Pittsburgh, so he sawed up a lot of knotty hemlock, and rafted it down, instead. That was the first hemlock anyone had tried to sell in the town, and he told the dealer it was "knot-pine." By the time he was back in town again the dealer had found out his mistake (hemlock wasn't worth over half as much as pine) and was hopping mad.

Cherry Tree Joe wasn't ruffled at all. "Don't you remember?" he said. "The first thing I told you when you asked about that raft was: 'It's not pine.'"

There were other stories, too. He was so strong he could shoulder five bushels of shot, but when he tried to carry the load on a bet, he mired up to his knees in flint rock. He was so tough that when he spit on the ground, it would bounce.

When a raft would get tied up on a rock, snag or dam, instead of using dynamite, rivermen would just call for Cherry Tree Joe. But one time the result was unexpected, to say the least.

That was a bad jam, and the whole raft was made of birch logs. While he studied just how to get the matter straightened out, Joe pulled out his knife and began whittling. Before he realized what had happened, he had whittled the whole raft into toothpicks.

Joe's eyes were so sharp, the legends went, that he could take his rafts down the roughest river in pitch darkness. He never needed to carry lights or a foghorn, for when he sang or whistled he could be heard three miles. He didn't have many enemies, but for those few it made their hair fall out just to think about him.

Not long after the book was published, I was delighted to receive a letter from a woman in the area north of Pittsburgh, who mentioned that she was a descendant of Cherry Tree Joe. Scenting a chance to gather some authentic information about him, I dashed off a letter to her, carefully explaining the problem of the two towns named Cherry Tree, and the four rivers, and asked which was correct.

Within three days, back came the return envelope, with my letter enclosed. Written across the bottom in the hand of my correspondent was the statement: "Yes sir: You have the right Cherry Tree Joe McCreery." Except for the name, not a word more.

Pending an opportunity to get to visit the lady and explain my problems more convincingly, I filed the correspondence so carefully that in more than a decade I have never been able to find a trace of it! It was not until the autumn of 1955 that I found opportunity to press the search further, when I was drawn to Cherry Tree, in Indiana County, by the final meeting of the old Raftsmen's Association, whose few remaining members were dissolving the group.

After a monument had been dedicated to the raftsmen, and the service feelingly concluded with a paraphrase from Cherry Tree Joe ballad:

The cheery hail of "Land! Tie up! To be heard no more, forever, upon these rivers."

I found time to make some inquiries about the folk hero. I discovered at once that I had found the right Cherry Tree.

Especially among the older raftsmen and townsfolk, many of whom could remember McCreery, there was no difficulty in getting information on either the man or the legend, although not all the statements about the man proved correct.

Perhaps most helpful was R. Dudley Tonkin, veteran Cherry Tree lumberman, who clearly recalled knowing Joe McCreery. He and others took me to the town cemetery, and showed me the folk hero's grave, where the stone revealed that he died on Nov. 23, 1895, "past 90 years of age."

Cherry Tree Joe, I learned, was born in 1805, near Muncy, Pa. For a man whose legend was to grow so fast he became a folk hero in his own lifetime, it seems appropriate that he should have been born in Lycoming County, where they used to say that the land was so rich that if you dropped a shingle nail on the ground at night, it would grow into a railroad spike before morning!

Joe came to Indiana County with his parents, Hugh and Nancy McCreery, when he was about 13 years old. The area around Cherry Tree was pretty wild then, and he got plenty of exercise helping his father clear their land.

Cherry Tree wasn't a town then, and had no post office, but it was already a well-known place, and had been for years.

The Indians used to call it "Canoe Place," because it was the farthest canoes could go up the West Branch at normal water. Perhaps because of this, a large wild cherry tree which grew there was made one of the principal markers of the land line drawn in 1768 under a treaty with the British, by which settlers could move (legally) into the area west of the Allegheny Mountains.

Some of the world's finest timber grew on the hills along the West Branch, the Allegheny, and smaller rivers that drain parts of Indiana County. Forests of white pine provided the hundred-foot masts for clipper ships built at Philadelphia, Pittsburgh and New Orleans, and red and white oak and black walnut their beams, planking and trim.

Although a recent history of Indiana County says the first raft down the upper West Branch was run in 1827, it is probable that Joe may have begun his rafting career with older men by the time he was 15. Rafts were run down the Upper Allegheny and Clarion by 1805, at which time Philadelphia provided a much better market for timber than either Pittsburgh or New Orleans, to which those rivers ran.

Joe McCreery was big and husky as a youth, but he was agile and quick, too, as a logger had need to be, if he wanted to live long. Rain or shine, hot or cold, you had to be out when time and water enough for a drive came. And when a log turned under your feet it might be a question of jump quick or be crushed to death, instead of merely risking a bath in icy water. Rafts of planks, squared timber and logs were run down the West Branch at a fairly early period, and log driving became common after 1846. Most of the early lumber for rafts was out of the old up and down "thundergust" sawmills, so called because they were on small streams where every thundershower was utilized for waterpower.

Like many good athletes, Joe McCreery loved to show off, according to the tradition in his home town. He'd make a log spin, just to show how well he could handle it, or skin a cat on a quarter line over churning water after the raft journey had ended at Lock Haven or Columbia.

According to Mr. Tonkin, who probably knows more about West Branch lumbering than any other living man, and has written an excellent book on the subject, Cherry Tree Joe was at times more of a showman than a worker, though he could perform prodigious feats of strength when he wished.

"Cherry Tree Joe died when I was about 15 years old," he said. "I recall him as a man of something over six feet — maybe six foot three — weighing 200 pounds, with a beard all over his face. But they used to say he was 'a great hunter,' which was one way of saying he dodged work when he could. Still, he's become a sort of patron saint of the lumber industry."

In 1861 Cherry Tree Joe joined the 11th Pennsylvania Volunteer Calvary, although he was 56, serving till the following March, when he was discharged after losing a leg. This may have been in an accident, as the regimental history fails to mention a battle in which this would have been likely to happen, though there were some clashes and pursuits. After losing his leg he became short tempered, and was often called "Contrary Joe."

Even before Mr. Tonkin was born, Cherry Tree Joe was already a living legend, as is evidenced by the fact that the ballad about him was published in the "Cherry Tree Clipper," about 1880, according to an account in the "Cherry Tree Record," its successor, published five years before his death. It was credited to "Henry Wilson," about whom even Mr. Tonkin has been able to find out nothing, but who might have been the lawyer of that name who flourished in the region around Lock Haven during Civil War days. An undated broadside printed at Spangler, Pa., whose appearance might indicate it was printed about 1890, also contains the attribution to Wilson, but shows many minor variants of text.

Joseph Dudley Tonkin and O. Lynn Frank claimed Henry Wilson had been a one time resident of Cherry Tree. The poem contains too many names of men from the Cherry Tree area to have been written by someone from Lock Haven, over eighty miles away through the mountains.

Swetnam states that local tradition says the song was composed about 1840. Both Swetnam and O. Lynn Frank, however, indicate that it would have been impossible to write the poem before April 1870, when the General Assembly of Pennsylvania appropriated three thousand dollars to remove obstructions to navigation on the Susquehanna River above the Clinton County line in Clearfield County. For it was the way the three thousand dollars were spent that inspired the writing of the poem "Cherry Tree Joe." The expenditure of the funds was to be under the direction of E. B. Camp, Robert McKage, James B. Graham and John Patton.

Chest Falls, about two miles downriver below the little town of Mahaffey, Clearfield County, was the most dangerous place in Clearfield County. Many rafts had stoved there and the falls had claimed the lives of several raftsmen. In Frank's book (42 to 47) he shows ten pictures of how to get a raft through Rocky Bend and Chest Falls. On this part of the river the raftsmen only ran pup rafts, which were usually less that 170 feet long and 26 feet wide, weighing about 100 tons.

As the river approaches Rocky Bend it is flowing in a northeast direction, and as it enters Rocky Bend the river makes a right turn of 90 degrees to head southeast. The raftsmen had to stick to the inside of the turn to prevent being washed up on the beach on the outside of the turn. Next, the river makes a 180 degree turn to the left, heading to the northwest. The raftsmen had to row their raft across the river to the left side to make this turn, all the time avoiding the turbulent water and white caps that indicated big submerged rocks. Immediately after completing this turn they had to row their raft back to the right side of the river to make the next turn to enter Chest Falls. This turn was 135 degrees to the right, and the river narrowed, causing many rafts to be thrown to the outside of the turn. These three turns are all within six tenths of a mile. Once out of the falls the river flows east.

Entering Chest Falls was the most dangerous part of the trip: On the left side was a huge table like rock sticking out of the water, even during rafting floods when the water is three feet above normal. The raftsmen did not call this rock "table rock" but it looked like a table top sticking out of the water. The rock is about 20 feet across. This rock was off the left shore and blocked the left half of the river. The pilot had to have his raft pass this rock within one foot, so that his crew could move his raft farther to the left to miss a rock point entering into the river on the right, just below the table rock. Remember, these raftsmen were wearing heavy woolen clothing and most couldn't swim. When their raft stoved on a rock it came to an immediate stop, often throwing the raftsmen overboard and into the icy water.

E. B. Camp and Robert McKage decided that the money should be spent to improve navigation through the bend and falls. A dam was proposed to be built that would submerge the large rocks with a chute that would carry the rafts safely past the large table rock and rocky point below it. Contrary Joe McCeery, 65 years old with a pegleg, proposed what he claimed a less expensive plan — he would dynamite the rocks out of Chest Falls. Having a persuasive manner, Joe not only convinced Camp and McKage that his method would be cheaper, but they put him in charge of the dynamiting. Not knowing a thing about using dynamite did not keep Joe from accepting the job.

"On the way out to Chest Falls," Mr. R. Dudley Tonkin related, "they stopped at John Patchin's store, and talked his son Jack out of a gallon of whiskey."

When the whiskey and the dynamite were all gone, Joe had blown the bird dirt off most of the large rocks in Chest Falls, but the hazards remained. Local legend has it that Joe lit the dynamite fuse and tossed one stick at a time at a rock. For dynamite to be effective cracking a rock, the dynamite must be packed in clay against the rock so that the explosion shatters the rock. Undeterred by what local people said about his efforts, Joe bragged that he had cleared the falls of all obstructions, and to prove it he would run a raft through the falls to show them.

Early the following spring after the ice went out, Joe built a raft and was the first to run Chest Falls. Joe's raft hit table rock, broke up and ended up on the river bank, proving the local people were right. This incident caused Henry Wilson of Cherry Tree to write the poem "Cherry Tree Joe," and the eight verses were made into a ballad. Swetnam reported:

The falls were as big a hazard as ever, and everybody blamed Cherry Tree Joe whenever a raft wrecked there.

Even while he was alive, there were all kinds of stories told about Cherry Tree Joe.

One was that in the big flood in the spring of 1845 he had run a raft right over the famed cherry tree at his home town, which is near where Indiana, Cambria and Clearfield Counties join. Another, that he single-handedly broke a 10-mile log jam at Buttermilk Falls, and that at the famed Gerry's Rocks (of song and story) he once lifted a timber raft clear, set it down in safe water, and jumped aboard.

There's also a story that one day he was racing rafts with his friend, Bob McKeage, down Clearfield Creek, and it looked as if Bob might get ahead. Joe reached out and pulled up a hundred-foot white pine by the roots and stuck it in the channel in front of Bob's raft. That ended the race as far as Bob was concerned, but he never held any grudge over it, and the two are buried within a few feet of one another in a cemetery high on a hill above Cherry Tree.

There were stories about his return trips from rafting, too.

Once, so his fellow-raftsmen said, he called John L. Sullivan's bluff in Dwyer's Hotel at Renovo, and slapped the champion's wrist. At John Eisel's tavern at Snowshoe, where he had stopped for a drink ("Water's only for women and babies," he used to say.) he picked up a broad-axe and whacked off the tail of an organ grinder's monkey. The animal jumped up on the bar, and he and Joe bombarded one another with bottles till the place was a shambles.

Joe did some logging and rafting on other rivers, too, including the Clarion, Allegheny and Kiski, according to report. It was apparently while rafting on the Kiski that he married Eleanor R. Banks of Blairsville. That was in 1834, when he was 29, although legends say he was always a great ladies' man.

They had eight children, all boys, including John O. McCreery (the name is often spelled McCreary, also) of Pittsburgh; Morgan, of Ebensburg; Bill, Aquila, Banks, Wallace and Alfred, of Cherry Tree, and Joshua, who was killed in the Civil War. An 1890 newspaper story said he had six grandchildren, 24 great-grandchildren, and 23 great-great-grandchildren.

Despite his somewhat catch-as-catch-can habits, Cherry Tree Joe (the real man) was a lifelong Methodist, and incidentally, a Democrat.

He had always sworn he would die with his boots on, but it wasn't destined to be that way. His health had been failing, and he died quietly at home.

But neither he nor his boots were forgotten. For years, whenever the old raftsmen would meet, they always carried Joe's boots to the reunion, and hung them up as a memorial to him.

Dudley Tonkin relates, too, that the Cherry Tree Joe legend and ballad were once so well known, that when he walked into a hotel in the little mountain town of Jellieo, Tenn., during World War I, he got a surprise.

Jellieo, population about 1500, was a lumber town, and when the clerk looked at the register, she gave Mr. Tonkin a big smile.

"Oh," she said, "so you're from Cherry Tree, Joe McCreery's town!"

I published much of this matter in a newspaper story soon after the visit, quoting from the song, in hopes of finding someone who knew it in folk transmission. One reason was a nagging desire to know more about its tune. Many people say it was sung to "Yankee Doodle," and recent broadsides and some Indiana Countians say the tune was "Blue-Tail Fly." But neither would fit the words.

To my delight, a few days after publication of the story I received a letter from a woman in southern Washington County, who wrote that she had been much interested in the story. According to her letter, she was a great-granddaughter of Cherry Tree Joe, and remembered the song well.

"My mother's dad was Bill McCreery, and Joe was her grandfather, she wrote. "My dad knew the song about Joe, and often sang it. I learned the song and tune from him.

"Cherry Tree Joe died at Grandfather's place when I was about six years old. I remember him well. Mother named one of my brothers for him, and he made a swing in Grandfather's yard, and when he was there, nobody but little Joe could get to swing on it."

Here was the opportunity I had sought for finding the song in folk transmission. Taking no chances, I filed the letter so carefully that — once again — I have never been able to find it.

I did remember, however, that the letter came from the small coal-mining town of Marianna, and made a trip there, in hopes of finding someone who would be able to supply the name. It was in vain.

For almost six years I made inquiries and combed what I call my brain for the name. And last October, when I passed near Marianna in returning home from a visit to Morgantown, W. Va., I suddenly recalled that the name was Mrs. Jasper Estep. But there remained the fear that had nagged at me for all those years: She had been born more than 75 years ago. Suppose she had died in the meantime, or become incompetent?

A check at the post office revealed that Mrs. Estep was still active, and lived beside the Methodist Church, only a few blocks away.

She not only remembered the song, but sang it to a tune quite different from "Yankee Doodle" or "Blue-Tail Fly," or for that matter, any other that I could recall.

"I remember how my great-grandfather used to sing that song about himself," she said. "He never seemed to mind the things it said about him.

"He used to tell us about the wolves that came to his father's farm in the early days. Sometimes they would leap against the cabin door until it seemed they would break it in.

"Many a time a panther followed him home. One time he stayed a little too late in town, and had to light matches to keep a panther off as he came home. The last one gave out just as he got there, but he had called, and they had the door open, and he jumped in. The panther followed him right to the door."

(Since the demise of the panthers in Western Pennsylvania was a little early for the use of friction matches, Cherry Tree Joe may have drawn the long bow now and then, as is not uncommon with "old residenters.")

Ladies on the River

Many old time raftsmen, interviewed by Samuel A. King while taking their oral histories, said they never remembered women being on rafts on the West

Branch of the Susquehanna River. However, the *Raftsman's Journal* in Clearfield,
Pennsylvania, of April 1893, had an article telling of a group of young ladies who
made the trip from Mahaffey to Lock Haven, Pennsylvania, aboard a raft, accom-
panied by a crew of men. With the *Journal* article was an excerpt from the April
1893 diary of Bertha Conrad of Houtzdale, Pennsylvania. Conrad was a passenger.

Conrad's diary refers to several reference points along the river, such as
Hoyt's Dam, Goose and Plum Islands, and Gallows Harbor. The raftsmen
named and used these points in their navigation. Many names have colorful
histories. Above Lumber City there is one mile of straight water, but before
entering the straight water, the raft must first get around Spencers Rocks. About
a mile and a half below Hoyt's Dam the river flows in an easterly direction,
then suddenly turns sharply to the left and runs northwest for a thousand feet,
then it comes around to the right until it's heading south. Remember, their rafts
were usually about 150 feet long. At this point it was necessary to get the raft
over to the right side of the river to avoid Spencers Rocks jutting out into the
river from the left bank. Going by Spencers Rocks the river narrows, the current increases and the river turns back to the left, to the east again, all in about
2,000 feet. Once by the rocks the crews on both ends of the raft had to pull
hard to the left to keep the current from shooting their raft up on the right
bank and stranding them. A raft so stranded would often have to be chopped
apart before it could be returned to the water. Raftsmen who successfully made
it beyond this point and found another crew aground up on the bank would
bleat out BA, BA, BA, BA, like sheep, harassing the misfortunate crew. Therefore, the area was known as the Sheep Pen (Frank, History 10).

Below are the entries from Bertha Conrad's diary, followed by the author's
notes which help explain her comments.

> Monday April 17, 1893. Had a postal from Maggie. The rafting party started
> this morning and will be in Clearfield tomorrow, so I'll go to Clearfield on the
> seven o'clock train.

Margaret Conrad was Bertha Conrad's sister who was visiting with the
McGees. Bertha Conrad was coming from Houtzdale about 15 miles south of
Clearfield. Conrad was a 31 year old Houtzdale school teacher.

> Tuesday 18. Am in Clearfield and Mr. Shaw has found out the raft did not
> start yesterday. There is a jam at Hoyt's Dam. Took the 12:15 train and went to
> Mahaffey. Walked up to Uncle Jimmie's [James McGee's]. Charley Goodfellow
> came this evening. [The town of Mahaffey is about six and one half miles above
> Hoyt's Dam and about 20 miles up river from Clearfield.]
> Wednesday 19. Charley G. and I went to Mahaffey for a train but couldn't get
> one. So Charley got a rig and drove Virge Gallagher and me to Hoyt's. There was
> the raft. I stayed, and he took Virge back to Mahaffey. It is raining tonight.

Hoyt's Dam was 1.3 miles down river from Bells Landing where the road
and railroad tracks were very close to the river. Dr. J. P. Hoyt built a bridge
across the river and a high dam in the river to run his sawmill and a gristmill.

The dangerous Chest Falls is halfway between the village of Mahaffey and Hoyt's Dam, and it would have been very interesting to read Bertha's comments about running the falls.

> Thursday 20. It rained and blew all day. It is not very pleasant on the river. Cleared up a while this afternoon, so Ag and I were on the swing. Rained very hard this evening. We leave tomorrow. [Ag was her cousin Agnes McGee. Log-jams like this one that held them up for four days were not uncommon.]
>
> Friday 21. The boys got up at three o'clock. The raft on the [Hoyt's] dam went over without any help. They ran and caught it at Goose Island [one mile below the dam] — broken in two. The next one stuck on a big rock [probably Sloans Rocks, about one-half mile below the dam], another one on a bar. It was very exciting. Finally they got them all off and came back for us. We stayed on the raft and came over Hoyt's Dam and tied up at Goose Island. While the boys fixed the rafts, the girls got dinner. Reached Curwensville at 7:30 (P.M.).

It is doubtful that the men would send the rafts through the chute without manning them, especially since the women rode through the chute. Evidently, McGee's crew made it past the Sheep Pen okay.

> Saturday 22. The run from Curwensville to Clearfield. Here we stopped and ran around in a snowstorm. Mrs. Mahaffey and [a] little boy joined the party. Then on to Plum Island [one half mile below Shawville]. I cooked dinner and supper. Afterwards we went to a house up on a hill and tried to dance; Agnes McGee was mad about it.

The *Raftsman's Journal* reported, "Under a resolution, passed before the girls were allowed to leave their mothers, dancing and card playing were not a feature of the trip." Gretchen Hiller, Maggie Conrad's daughter, said the young women had agreed to the above resolution, but when their first chance to break the resolution came, they took it.

> Sunday 23. Jim Mahaffey came this morning. They had lashed two pups [rafts] together and had gotten started but got stuck on a bar. We passed them and stopped. Tom [Thomas McGee] and Bert [James Breth] went back to help them. It took until four o'clock to get it off. We went to Gallas [Gallows] Harbor and stayed all night.

Benjamin Knepp was the proprietor of the Gallows Harbor Hotel where the young ladies could get a warm bed and board for 25 cents a night, and the men could enjoy a glass of whiskey for five cents (Correspondence with Benjamin Knepp's great-great-grandson, James Knepp.).

> Monday 24. Run all day. Stopped at Cataract and lashed together. I wrote a postal to Mom [Mrs. David Conrad]. Stopped at Renovo all night. Had visitors — Mr. Harris, Miss Harris, Miss Kane (the banker's daughter), and another gentleman. A young lady reporter came down for items. I gave her one. The girls all went to town. The day had been just perfect.

Cataract is below Buttermilk Falls, a riffle where they could lash both full rafts side-by-side to make a fleet. The raft was as long as a football field and over one-third as wide, but only required a crew of six men.

Tuesday 25. We had a lovely time and reached our journey's end [Lock Haven] at half-past two. Had two pictures taken and then went up to see Normal [she meant Central State Normal School, today's Lock Haven University] and stayed for supper. Later brought the girls down to see the cabin. We ran for the train to see the Liberty Bell but missed it.

The Pennsylvania Railroad was taking the Liberty Bell along the route between Erie and Philadelphia. The display train caused great excitement, but another timber raft in town did not make the newspapers.

Wednesday 26. Went to town both morning and afternoon. Ag [Agnes] and Mollie [McGee] both got hats. The Winslows and Dopp [McGee] spent the day at Stover's [in Blanchard]. Charley, Maggie, and Edith went to the train to meet them and got squashed. Had a gay time tonight.

Thursday 27. Got up at four o'clock, packed and made the 8:42 train at Beach Creek. There were fourteen of us to Philipsburg. Maggie and I left the train and came home. The rest went on to Mahaffey. And so ended the Rafting Expedition. We left Tom [Thomas McGee, Jr., owner of raft] in Lock Haven. He had not yet sold his raft. Had two pictures taken when we were leaving the raft.

Raftsmen had to take the trolley to Mill Hall to catch the train home since the "River Line" between Karthaus and Clearfield didn't open until July 1902 (Scott, Clearfield). I searched the *Renovo Record* and the five Lock Haven newspapers of the time for articles about their raft, but found none.

The article in the *Raftsman's Journal* on Wednesday, April 26, 1893, read:

Down the Susquehanna

A Merry Lot of Ladies and Gentlemen from Up the River Take a Pleasure Trip

On Saturday morning, about 9 o'clock, a raft pulled into the "Lick," this place, upon which was erected a regular Saratoga cottage decked with bunting and from which floated the stars and stripes. [A lick was the gravel bar that usually formed where a stream or creek ran into the river. It got its name because the deer and other wild animals came there to drink. Also, the small puddles of water that formed there had a higher salt content than the fresh water in the stream or river.] As soon as the rope tightened and the fleet swung safely to shore, there emerged from the cottage a number of well dressed ladies and gentlemen, who spent a couple of hours in making a tour of the town and calling on friends. Their stop here was in the midst of a severe snow squall, which deprived them of sightseeing. A Journal reporter, in company with Dr. F. G. Bennett, one of the number, visited the raft and took a peep at the register of the cottage, from which he copied the following names of cabin passengers.... [At this point the newspaper listed everyone on the raft.]

The cottage was handsomely arranged, the provisions looked good and the ladies seemed to be directing the cooking in a way that gave promise of their future usefulness. Under a resolution, passed before the girls were allowed to leave their mothers, dancing and card playing was not a feature of the trip. Good books, musical instruments, crocheting, etc., occupied their time when the weather would not permit of them occupying a place on the outside of the house viewing the rugged mountains and scenery generally. We understand that the fleet reached Lock Haven on Monday without accident, and although the weather was very cold, all enjoyed themselves in the highest degree.

My First Rafting Trip

John S. Beck left a wonderful firsthand account describing his first trip down the Big Pine Creek on a board raft. He was born in Lycoming County, Pennsylvania, December 19, 1849, and died in April 30, 1946. As a young man he worked in the woods about five years. At age 22 he and his brother hired on to work for Wesley Childs, a lumberman who was taking timber from land along Cedar Run, about three and a half miles from where that stream empties into Big Pine Creek. Big Pine Creek runs through the Pine Creek Gorge to join the West Branch of the Susquehanna River west of Jersey Shore. Pennsylvania has many creeks named Pine Creek. Cedar Run is about four miles below Blackwell at the bottom of the gorge.

John Beck worked in the sawmill until all the lumber was cut for the 12 rafts, over a million board feet. The two mills cutting lumber must have been steam driven mills, because water driven mills only cut about 1,000 feet a day.

The following is taken from Beck's paper:

The sawing was finished in December 1873, and at once work started on building the rafts, or "rafting-in," as it was called. There was lots of lumbering going on in the Big Pine Creek Valley, and our twelve rafts were not the only ones to go downstream that year.

A lumber raft was made of a series of platforms or lumber piles, fastened together end to end, with a joint, so that this long chain of platforms could go around the curves in the stream and over the spillways [chutes] of the various dams in the creek and river. There were often twenty platforms in one raft, so it might be three hundred and fifty feet from one end to the other. There was an oar at each end of the raft to guide it. The pilot and two helpers were on the front end and the steersman with two helpers was on the back end. The steersman had more control over guiding the raft than did the pilot. [This was because rafts traveled faster than the water and thus the steersman could guide the raft with his oar like a rudder.]

The pilot and steersman were specialists in this work, and were brought in by the man who had purchased the lumber. It was their job to oversee the building of the rafts and the floating of them to their destination.

To me, the building of the platforms, was an interesting experience. The lumber was stacked in great piles along Big Pine Creek, and early in January 1874 the work of rafting-in began. Each platform would contain about six thousand, one hundred feet of lumber, and often twenty platforms would make up one raft. These platforms had to be built in the water, for if they had been built on the dry land, it would have been impossible to move them into the water. Old timers at rafting-in seldom got wet; new hands often got more than their feet wet.

Once, a platform of lumber that extended several hundred feet upstream was

Opposite: Party ready to leave their raft, April 1898. Bertha Conrad is the tall woman in the group of four behind the canoe. Maggie Conrad is the woman at far left, according to her daughter, Gretchen Hiller. Note the three square timbers below the water line. They are the result of rafting-in belly down (courtesy Clearfield County Historical Society, Clearfield, Pennsylvania, and the Hiller Family).

to be moved down to go into a certain place in the raft. Mr. Childs thought the men should get some ropes to hold and control its floating downstream, but the pilot said they would not need the ropes, and got onto the platform with a long pole. He pushed the platform into the current, and guided the front end until it came to a stop against the bank of the stream. The back of the platform was pushed ahead by the current to make a half turn. By the time the platform had made its half turn, the pilot had run to what had been the back end, but which now was the front end, and guided it into the bank, thus starting another half turn. Several half turns soon brought the platform to its desired place in the raft.

We fellows standing on the bank of the stream did not at first understand what the pilot had in mind; when the platform first started to turn, one of the green horns jumped into the water and yelled, "I'll hold it!" The pilot saw what the man was trying to do, and called, "Let her swing!" By this time the man was up to his neck in the water, in the middle of the stream, but managed to crawl onto the platform. High and dry on the bank of the stream, we were at first scared for our friend in the water, but when we saw he was safe on the platform, our anxiety changed into laughter. He had to take a considerable amount of kidding for thinking he alone could hold back six thousand board feet of lumber in that swift current.

In building a platform, a large number of selected two-inch planks were marked to have two-inch holes bored in them, and through these holes, pins would be placed to hold the platform together. One of the men was given the hand auger to bore the holes; he had never done any work like that, and was not making out too well. Now, I had worked one summer at the carpenter trade, so I asked the fellow to let me try a couple while he caught his breath. Mr. Childs came along about that time, and when he saw I was making out all right, told me to keep on at it, and took the other fellow off to do some really hard work.

While the rafts were being built, the pilot was looking over the men on the job, and wondering where he could get a crew to run his rafts. He asked the different men if they had ever snubbed a raft, and when he found that no one there had, he went to Childs and asked about getting a crew, as he had not found anyone with any experience in stopping a raft. I overheard Childs tell him not to worry about a crew, as either one of the Beck boys could stop a raft any place he asked them to. I thought to myself, "Mr. Childs, you don't know how little I know about stopping a raft."

Early in March the twelve rafts were finished and tied up in Big Pine Creek, awaiting the spring flood when they could be floated down to the river and tied up in Larry's Creek Eddy. [Larry's Creek Eddy was where the Pine Creek drained into the West Branch of the Susquehanna River.] From there two rafts would be tied together, side by side, and floated down the river to their destination.

The flood in Pine Creek would not last long, so it was necessary to get the rafts out of there as soon as possible. It was our plan to take one out every day until we had them all down the river. As the distance from Cedar Run to Larry's Creek Eddy was about twenty miles, we would make that run in four or five hours and have the rest of the day to walk back to Cedar Run, to be ready for our next trip the next day. I think that walking was about the hardest work I ever did. Some of the men weren't able to make it in one day, even though they did stop at the various hotels for refreshments.

Finally came the day when the melting snows and rains had raised Big Pine Creek to flood stage; at daylight the six of us got onto our raft, waved to our friends, and were on our way to the river.

To me, on my first trip on a raft, it was very exciting. I was on the front end of the raft helping to handle the oar, and my place was the one nearest the end of the raft. Next to me was one of my friends, Martin Fable, and at the end of the oar was the pilot. Up there at the very end of the raft I had a funny feeling. I was nervous and just a little bit afraid. The current was swift, and the water was cold when once in a while a bit of spray was thrown in my face. I had heard of accidents happening to rafts, of men being thrown off into the water. I wondered what chance one would have of getting out if something like that did happen. Many times that first half hour, I almost wished myself back at the camp. At many places the stream had run over its banks, and as I looked out over that large piece of water, I wondered how the pilot could know where the channel was located, and what was to keep us from running onto the flat bottom land, where there would not be enough water to float our raft.

At other places the banks of the stream were high and we had a narrow channel, where the water seemed to be much swifter. There were bends and turns to be made; I thought, "What if we can't make one of those turns; what if the front end gets fast in the bank and the back end starts to swing around, and we are jammed in the channel?" These and many more thoughts bothered me, till I was wondering why I ever consented to go as part of the crew.

As the current carried us along and nothing happened, I soon got over my nervousness. Once in a while we would make a stroke with our oar, but really there was very little to do.

A short distance above Waterville, a man named Stoddard had a saw mill, with a dam across Pine Creek (this is just over half way to the Larry's Creek Eddy). We would have to go over this dam with our raft. When I thought of that, I again had nervous chills. These dams were built with a flat platform as a spillway [chute], and made so the rafts could ride over the dam on the spillway. The drop from the spillway was about five feet to the level of the water below the dam.

As our raft entered the backed up water of the dam, it seemed as though we almost came to a stop: but slowly we moved forward toward the spillway. As we came nearer, we were caught in the suction of the vast amount of water pouring through the spillway, and it seemed to greatly increase our speed. Suddenly we were hanging in mid air.

Then it seemed the front end of the raft took a nose dive into the whirling, roaring water below the dam. I felt as though I was there all alone and wondered what to do. But not for long. Things happened awfully quick. The oar blade caught in the water and whipped the oar from our grasp, swinging it around with a force we could not stop. The pilot and Fabel managed to get away from it by squatting on the raft, and letting it pass over their heads. But I had no place to go to get away from it. I would have been pushed off the raft into the water, had I not jumped over the oar as it came towards me. As it was, my feet were caught by it, and I was thrown flat on the raft. We all were all right but felt we had a close call.

We got our oar back in place and found the blade had been broken off, so that our front end of the raft was out of control. We were being carried rapidly down stream, and it was necessary to tie up the raft to repair the broken oar.

The pilot looked at me, and said, "John, how about you getting off to snub the raft? I said "All right," and made my way as fast as I could to the last platform, and told the crew back there what had happened and that I was to snub the raft. Now I had never stopped a raft by snubbing, but I had seen it done. I knew I had to get ashore and hitch a good strong rope around a large tree. Then I'd have to let out the slack on the rope slowly enough so that the raft would not be stopped too suddenly.

There was a large coil of two inch rope on the last platform, with one end tightly fastened to the cross braces. I asked the steersman if he could get the end of the raft close to the bank, so I could jump off where there was a large tree a short distance ahead of us. He said "All right," and with a few strokes with his oar soon had the end of the raft close to the bank of the stream.

I took the rope and played out about fifty feet or slack, got the rest of the coil on my shoulder, and when the raft came close to the bank, jumped off the raft right at the tree I had selected. I ran around the tree clock-wise, and threw my coil of rope over that part of the rope that was stretched from the raft to the tree. Then pulling my coil of rope back under the part stretched from the raft to the tree, I had a half hitch, or snub, on the raft. Then giving out my slack on the rope very slowly, I soon had the raft coming to a stop. [Usually two or more wraps around the tree were taken before the snubber pulled on his end to tighten the wraps around the tree, thus the friction caused the rope on the tree's trunk to stop the raft.]

When the raft was stopped, I called to the steersman for instructions. He had sent his two helpers forward to help with the repairing of the oar blade, and said I should just hold the raft as it was. Soon the two men returned, reporting everything was all right, and they were ready to go on. By this time the back end of the raft had swung out into the middle of the stream, so it would have been rather hard for me to get back on the raft. The steersman called to me, "Let go the rope, John! We'll go on without you. You can go back to camp and be ready to start out tomorrow."

I watched the raft disappear around a bend in the stream, then decided to go up to the dam and watch the other rafts come over the spillway. I had just gotten there when a raft came over the dam. It too, had the oar blade caught in the swirling water and the oar pulled from the grasp of the men holding it. One man was pushed off the side of the raft and was helped back on by the pilot. The man who had occupied the position I had on our raft, was pushed off the front end of the raft, and rolled out from under the second platform, where he was seized by the pilot and pulled onto the raft. The two men who had been in the water were in no condition for any work, and in fact there was nothing they could do, as their oar blade, too, was broken, and their raft going down stream, out of control. It only went a short distance when the front end caught on a gravel bar, and the back end of the raft began to swing around. The stream was too narrow for it to make a complete turn, and it finally came to a stop directly across the channel.

There was a rowboat near by, and I got it to row over to get the two men who were soaking wet, but not being used to rowing, I was unable to get across the swift current. Another man came to my aid and said if we could get the boat upstream a ways, he might get across. He finally did, and the two men were taken to Stoddard's camp where they were given dry clothes and a chance to get warm. Aside from the ducking, they were none the worse for their experience.

By this time another raft put in its appearance on the crest of the dam. When the pilot saw the raft across the channel he decided to break it in two, and clear the stream. He sent his two helpers to the back of the raft to help the crew there hold the raft from turning. When his front platform hit the raft that was across the channel, instead of breaking it in two, it started to slide over the first one. It went forward until it was about half way over, and then stopped. It reminded me of a big snake crawling over a log. This time there were no broken oars or duckings.

Soon after this, another raft came over the dam and headed for the mix up. I can well remember the look of surprise on the face of the pilot. He was a tall man with a high black hat pushed back on his head. He made the same decision as did the other pilot that he would knock those two rafts out of the channel. He sent two of his men back to help hold the raft from turning, but he had no better luck. His raft started to slide over the one that was across the stream, but only got about half way. Now there were three rafts with about three hundred and sixty thousand feet of lumber in one awful mixup.

By that time I decided there was enough lumber jammed in that narrow channel. I ran upstream as fast as I could to warn the crews of the other rafts coming down that the channel was blocked. I got the crews of the next two rafts coming along to tie up. They told me there were no more rafts coming, so I went downstream to the dam to see how they were getting along with clearing the channel. They had cut the raft that was across the channel and had gotten part of it away and tied. Soon the other part was floated clear and tied to some trees along the bank. The other rafts were now free to go on their way.

I walked back to Cedar Run and had a great story to tell the boys at the supper table that night. In taking our eleven other rafts down Pine Creek, we had no further mishaps. After this when going over Stoddard's dam we actually sat on our oar to keep the blade out of the water. The rides downstream in the early morning were a pleasant experience, but the walking back became very tiresome.

I have often thought of that first ride I had on the raft, of our mishap at the dam, and of the two men who were old hands at rafting, but who nearly lost their lives. I guess I was born lucky, for in looking back, I can recall a number of what seemed like close calls, but I have never had a serious injury.

Gallows Harbor: How It Got Its Name

Some people think Gallows Harbor got its name when runaway slaves were caught and hung there, but those who captured slaves returned them to their owners in order to get the reward. Alex Livingstone made a trip down the river in 1844, and he said that places on the river were known then by such names as Gallows Harbor, Big Sink and Little Sink, but he was never informed of the origin of the names (Mitchell 14).

The most plausible explanation was given by Luther Dunlop. He said that during the rafting season there were so many rafts tied up together that they were afraid the first raft's line would break. The first raft was tied to a tree or a ring cemented into a bed rock. Outboard rafts tied to inboard rafts and all rafts hung on the first raft's snubbing line. In this manner the river could almost be covered with rafts. The pilot of the first raft thought that his rope would break if another raft tied up, so when another raft tried to land he ran out over the rafts shouting, "Don't hitch on, all the rafts will go adrift! If you do, I'll knock your brains out!" The pilot swung his rafting axe as he ran.

The snubber from the approaching raft ignored the pilot and tied to the group of rafts. While he was bent over making it fast, the pilot hit him with his rafting axe and killed him. The raftsmen spending the night there selected a judge and jury and tried the pilot. He was found guilty and hung from a tree. The next morning the raftsmen tied loose and ran down the river (Dunlop, oral history 11).

James Raffarty told of a similar incident with a much better outcome. Raffarty and his friend Coyle, both about 18, were left in a place he called Dead Man's Curve to guard six rafts, while his father and the rest of the crew went back upriver. They were told that they shouldn't let any rafts tie up to their six rafts. The water was rising and they used a second line to hold the first raft. Their rafts had snubbing posts built into the outside timbers, which were used to couple rafts into fleets. These snubbing posts were three inch holes bored in the timber — the holes were made square and square hickory pins were driven down into the timbers. This kept the pins from turning in their holes when snubbing lines put stress on them. This made an inviting place for approaching rafts to snub.

It was getting dark when a raft rounded the curve and pulled toward their six rafts. A big redheaded man on the raft picked up a coil of snubbing line and came to the edge of his raft. James estimated that the man was about twice the size of him or Coyle. James hollered at the men on the raft not to land — but they kept on coming. Coyle had a pole axe over his shoulder but made no threatening move with it. A lump welled up in James' throat as he thought what his father would do to him if the redheaded stranger hitched fast and pulled their six rafts downstream.

The redhead ignored the two young men by acting as if they weren't there, and when his raft slid alongside of the Rafferty's rafts, he stepped onto their rafts and hitched to a snubbing post on their raft. As his rope started to tighten the redhead turned his back to them and walked away. Rafferty was frozen with fear, but Coyle swung his pole axe and cut the redhead's snubbing line. When the redhead heard the chop he turned to see what happened. His raft was slipping downstream away from the Rafferty's rafts. He had two choices: he could come back and beat up the two young men, but if he did he would miss his raft going downstream and he would be stranded, maybe never catch up with his raft. Or, he could get back on his raft and cuss out the two young men for outsmarting him.

Both Rafferty and Coyle were relieved to see the man going down the river shaking his fist at them (Rafferty, oral history 9).

9

Log Driving

Log driving techniques were developed in Maine and Canada and brought to the Susquehanna Watershed in the 1840s. At first logs were driven down a river and put into log ponds at sawmills all along the watershed. In 1851, however, a huge boom was constructed on the south side of the West Branch at Williamsport, which took up half the river and extended over nine miles upstream. The logs were trapped in the boom and then moved to the 35 sawmills north of the river in Williamsport to be sawed into boards, before being shipped by rail and canal boats all over the country. Log driving existed until the early 1900s. During the last part of the 1800s and early 1900s log driving was replaced by narrow gauge railroads that ran into the mountains where streams were not available to drive logs. Also, transportable steam driven sawmills became available and replaced the larger Williamsport mills.

A Log Drive to Williamsport in 1868

When I contacted Samuel A. King asking to use his oral histories, he not only gave me permission to use them in my work, but he insisted that I include the information from the article he wrote for the *Quarterly Journal of the Pennsylvania Historical Association,* April 1962, "A Log Drive to Williamsport in 1868." This article can be downloaded from the Pennsylvania Historical Association website. King was an assistant professor of history at the DuBois Campus of Pennsylvania State University. His information is combined with R. D. Tonkin's and G. W. Huntley's. King drew heavily from both sources.

The DuBois-Woodward Drive of 1868, managed by John DuBois and Hiram Woodward, commenced on March 19, 1868, when the first of about 178,000 logs were driven down the Bennetts Branch to Driftwood, then down the Sinnemahoning Creek to Keating, and hence by the West Branch of the Susquehanna River to the boom at Williamsport. This was a total distance of about 100 miles in 62 days. The 178,000 logs, bearing 17 different brands, would make 44.5 million board feet of timber. Each owner had his own brand so he would get credit at the sawmills. The DuBois branding hammer imprinted a bull's eye of two rings, and the Woodward brand was a broad axe with the letter "W" inside. These brands were registered in the

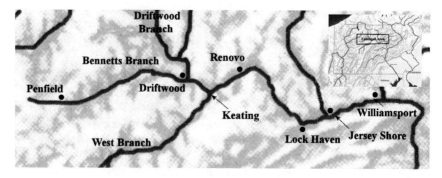

The 1868 DuBois-Woodward log drive to Williamsport.

county courthouses where the owners lived, and were used at the sawmills to give credit to an owner when his logs were used. The owners did not get credit for their logs until a sawmill used their logs. Sometimes this was a year or more after the logs were put into the boom. The boom operators charged a fee for storing the logs until they were moved to the sawmills. If the boom broke — as it did on May 31, 1889, when 6 to 10 inches of rain fell over Pennsylvania causing the Johnstown Flood and breaking the boom at Williamsport, releasing about half of the trapped logs — the log owners, not the boom operators, took the loss. Owners had to borrow from banks to pay the jobbers who then paid the men. If the owners didn't have the money to pay the jobbers, the woodhicks didn't get paid. Unpaid woodhicks, not understanding the whole process, often would retaliate by setting the log owner's landing afire, putting some owners out of business.

None of this would have been possible if many men, who called themselves woodhicks, hadn't started early in the fall of 1867 to fell and skid the logs to the water's edge. Then they waited for the snow in the mountains to melt and the ice to go out to provide the freshet, so the logs could be flushed downstream. All streams, creeks and rivers in the Susquehanna Watershed are very shallow and require about a 3 foot flood to run logs and rafts downstream.

This was not a single event on the watershed that spring, as this large drive ran into another large drive coming down the West Branch at Keating. More logs came from the Driftwood Branch and the First Fork into the Sinnemahoning, while others went down the Pine Creek to the West Branch at Jersey Shore. This drive was only one of the drives conducted that year, but was typical of all drives from the early 1850s until 1909 (King, *Log Drive* 151).

John Dubois and Hiram Woodward

As one of the wealthiest lumbermen on the West Branch, John DuBois had started the practice of driving logs when he helped to organize the Susquehanna Boom Company. Major James H. Perkins proposed a boom in the river to catch and hold the logs until the sawmills in Williamsport could use them. John, his brother Matthias, and a business partner, Elias S. Lowe, owned controlling interest in the company, which was incorporated on March 26, 1846. The boom went into operation at Williamsport in March of 1851 (Taber, *Williamsport* 25). The town of DuBois, just west of the Bennetts Branch of the Sinnemahoning, was named for him when he established his large sawmill there.

John DuBois had purchased 30,000 acres of timberland in Clearfield County along Bennetts Branch in the summer of 1842. Never popular with his Williamsport competitors, hard-headed and somewhat tight-fisted, he relished the "dog-eat-dog" competition of the Victorian age. He maintained a reputation for fairness but not for favors; he upheld the letter of his business obligations and expected others to do the same. His relentless energy, his systematic thinking and his unfettered self-confidence and initiative were maintained to his deathbed, although he expressed regrets for his bachelorhood and late in life permitted himself to become a church member (King 154–155).

DuBois' partner in the drive was Hiram Woodward, who first came from Luzerne County to Penfield to work as a jobber. He and John DuBois cleared the Bennetts Branch of obstructions and in 1855 made the first drive from that stream to Williamsport. In later years DuBois boasted that two veteran loggers from the state of Maine had failed to get their logs out that spring because they did not peel them. He also claimed to have made this drive to Williamsport in 9 days, a personal record that was never exceeded (King, *Log Drive* 155). The Alfred Ames video, *From the Stump to Ship,* shows that even in the 1930s the log drivers in Maine did not peel their logs. Woodward had studied at Wyoming Seminary before devoting his life to the woods. Short of stature, strong of physique, Woodward was famed throughout the northwoods as a champion wrestler.

To manage a log drive with a payroll of 60 to 100 men was a risky obligation, but the partnership of the wealthy lumberman and the hard-hitting jobber made an ideal combination for this epic venture.

The Woodhicks

There have been speculations as to why the men who worked in the woods preferred the term woodhick over lumberjack, but no good explanation has ever been given. Along the Susquehanna Watershed "lumberjack" was never used. A log driver was a woodhick who had felled the trees and moved them to the water's edge. When the drive began he became a log driver, helping to drive the logs downstream into the boom.

The log driver was much like the cowboys who made the "long drive" from Texas to Abilene or Dodge City in the days of the old Southwest. There was much in common between the work of these two widely separated groups. Both were responsible for the safe delivery of branded property over long distances, which required weeks and even months to perform. Both were subjected to theft along the way: the cattlemen from rustlers and the loggers from "Algerians." Both drives were perilous and exhausting, demanding physical endurance and spiritual fortitude. Both provided for feeding their hands along the way: the cattle drive with a chuck wagon and the river drive with an ark. Both ended their journey with a bacchanalian celebration in a railroad stockyard or a down-river community where the men were paid. Though the cowboys have been celebrated in song, legend, and drama, the Pennsylvania loggers have been nearly forgotten.

This is the saga of one such drive that was made in the spring of 1868 (King, 151).

The Raftsmen and Log Drivers' Relationship

To understand the relationship between the raftsmen and the log drivers, one must remember two things: The log drivers came down from Maine and Canada and were known as Down Easterners and foreigners by the local raftsmen, and the second thing is, that fighting was a form of recreation. Also, the Down Easterners ate dried cod and pea soup, where the locals ate pork and beans. Both could not be fed in one camp (King's Oral Histories).

The Pennsylvania Public Highway Law of 1771 established the rivers as an open thoroughfare for arks, boats and rafts. By the 1840s, when the log drivers started driving logs, raftsmen had been using the river for 70 years, protected by the law. In fact, when the state built the canal system in the early 1830s, it had to abide by its own law and provide a chute at the feeder dams that would allow ark and raft traffic to continue to use the river. Not knowing how to build chutes for 10 foot high dams, the state men built most of their chutes too short, which caused arks and rafts to wreck coming out of the chute. Almost all of the chutes at the feeder dams had to be rebuilt. This was the work environment for the raftsmen.

The whole West Branch Watershed was an excellent source for 90 foot spars and 40 to 80 foot long square timbers, and thousands of these rafts came down the West Branch annually.

Before the boom was built in Williamsport in 1851, the log drivers drove logs down the river like they did in Maine. They cut their logs sixteen feet long, left the bark on them and rolled them into the river after the ice went out. Crews were used to prevent log jams along the river as the main body of logs floated downstream. Another crew followed, putting the stranded logs back into the river; this was called sacking the rear. Downstream, at the sawmills in Williamsport, a third crew in boats steered the loose logs into the mill log ponds. This crew worked around the clock using torches to spot the logs at night until the sacking crew arrived.

This method left many logs stranded along the river that were taken up by the finder and held as his property. The owners lost much valuable lumber this way, because sudden floods and ice flows would sometimes carry away large amounts of timber and strand it all along the river. As the lumber business increased, laws were passed to protect the lumbermen from losing their timber and provided methods to salvage it. These loose, un-peeled logs jammed the river and pushed rafts over dams or into bridge piers and rocks.

When the boom was installed in 1851, a sheer boom was used to catch the floating logs. The boom consisted of log piers made into cribs and filled with boulders. These piers were erected on the river bottom during periods of low water, and spaced 50 feet apart in a line down the middle of the river. The north side of the river was left open for navigation, while the south was used for catching and holding logs. Between the piers, floating timbers coupled to the piers and each other acted like a fence to keep the sawlogs confined in the boom until they could be sorted out by "boom-rats" and distributed to the different mill ponds (J.D. Tonkin 76–77).

A sheer boom was used to herd the floating logs into the boom. It was made of logs chained together that extended upriver on an angle of about 45 degrees, herding the floating logs into the boom like cattle into a corral. This blocked the river and prevented rafts from moving downstream to market. When the raftsmen complained, the sheer boom operators only wanted to open the boom every ten days (Taber, *Williamsport* 24). This too was resolved in court; raftsmen couldn't be held up that long.

The leading raftsmen along the West Branch arranged for a protest meeting in Clearfield on March 17, 1855, which was well attended. They adopted a resolution declaring the "boom method of lumbering not only impeded navigation, but if continued, would destroy the square timber and spar business, rendering the forests valueless and depriving the people of a means of livelihood."

The raftsmen became the aggressors by "ironing the logs." The raftsmen drove metal objects into the sawlogs, thus damaging the saws at the mills. The log driver's solution was to peel the bark off the logs so they could spot the iron. Peeled logs didn't jam as often, were easier to skid, and worms didn't get under the bark. The log drivers benefited from this move.

However, on March 30, 1857, along Clearfield Creek, a group of raftsmen attacked several log drivers, firing a few shots. Three days later 47 raftsmen were arrested for rioting and several log drivers were arrested for obstructing the stream. Eight prominent raftsmen were fined and five prominent log drivers were found guilty of obstructing the stream, due to unpeeled logs. Thus ended the loggers' and raftsmens' war. Afterward the two parties worked together (R.D. Tonkin 24–26).

Sawlog owners began branding their logs with log stamps. Each owner had his own brand which was registered in his county courthouse. The brands then were fixed to a five pound sledge hammer by a blacksmith and all logs were stamped on each end, leaving a brand on each log. Rafts, timbers and spars were also branded in case the raft stoved and lost a stick or two. Branded logs that got away were salvaged by people living along the river and sold back to the owners for a nominal fee. These people were not "Algerians."

On the 1868 drive and other early drives, the partners DuBois and Woodward braved the passionate objections of the valley folk. Woodward later recalled that they were arrested fourteen times in one day by local officials who were friendly with the raftsmen. At Caledonia (about one third the way down the Bennetts Branch from Penfield to Driftwood) a strong cable was stretched across the waterway to stop them. When the kitchen ark on which they were accompanying the drive neared the danger spot, John DuBois waited, poised with an axe to cut the barrier in two. As the raft slid under the cable, DuBois swung and missed! Quickly he leaped over the rope, turned and luckily severed it before the shanty, with women inside, was swept overboard (King, *Log Drive* 155–156).

Log Rustlers

There were, however, some timber thieves who violated the law by sawing off both ends of the logs and putting their own brand on the logs before returning the logs to the river. The rebranded logs were then driven into the boom at Williamsport or Lock Haven, where the thieves were given credit for the logs.

This rebranding was usually done at night. These thieves were named after the pirates of Algeria — "Algerians." They worked largely in Clinton County along the West Branch, which ran the whole length of the county. Clinton County started six miles below Driftwood and ran to Jersey Shore. When the "Algerians" were brought to court, they would claim there was no criminal intent because they believed they had acted within the law. But if it could be shown they had violated the law, they were ready and willing to pay for the timber. The juries, who were composed of Lock Haven rivermen whose neighbors were the perpetrators, were inclined to acquit when it had been shown that the prosecutor had been offered the value of the timber. Consequently, it became the custom for "Algerians," when caught in Clinton County, to go to the timber owner and offer to settle. If he refused, the jury would invariably acquit the thieves and the timber owner got nothing. If the "Algerian" did not get caught, he was just so much ahead in the game. If the timber owner did not accept pay, he was just so much out in the end. The success of the "Algerian" seemed to depend on whether he got caught (Huntley 483). Even today to be called an "Algerian" by a upriver man can bring on a fight.

In 1875, when Bill Huntley put in 100 spars for George Churchman, he ran some of his rafts down the Sinnemahoning to Keating. Another raft coming down the West Branch hit one of his pup rafts and broke it loose, sending it down the river and breaking it up. Huntley followed and caught all the stranded spars. He had the ten spars tied together and his men returned to Keating to raft-in the other 90 spars into 4½ rafts. When Huntley's men got back to the broken raft, the "Algerians" had stolen six of the spars and had a sawmill in Lock Haven saw them into ship decking.

The "Algerians" settled the matter by paying Huntley for the spars (Huntley 354). There is no record of how much Huntley settled for, but the "Algerians" had to be surprised when he insisted on getting $250.00 for each spar, or $1,500.00 for the six.

The Camps

Tonkin stated that outside walls of camp buildings were made of hemlock logs chinked with slabs and plastered inside and out with clay. Floor joists were small round hemlock trees flattened on top with a broad axe. The gabled ends, floors and roofs were made of boards cut on a muley saw. He describes a camp for about 70 woodhicks at Elk Lick on the West Branch that was quite elaborate for its day. Clear spring water was piped into the kitchen and washroom by gravity flow. A small stream was made into a flume which ran under the kitchen and washroom and served as a sewer.

The camp was composed of five separate buildings: the kitchen and dining room, lobby and sleeping quarters, stable, blacksmith, and office and commissary. The kitchen and dining room was the most important because 4 meals a day were prepared for about 70 men. Breakfasts and the evening meals were served in the dark, but the morning lunches and afternoon lunches were served in the field where the men worked. If a man worked hard 12 hours a day in the cold he needed 4 meals a day. Camps that employed Canadians and men from Maine served codfish and pea soup, but the local boys demanded beans and pork. Therefore the camp either employed local or "furriners" since both would not eat the other's food. When a camp owner's son decided that the men were eating too much and cut back on the food, most of the men quit and moved onto camps that were better run.

The Elk Lick kitchen and dining room building was 24 feet wide and 50 feet long with the dining room 36 feet long, seating 70 men. The kitchen had a 10 plate stove for cooking and plenty of room for washing dishes. The cook and the cookee (the cook's helper) lived separate from the men in a small room off the kitchen. The lobby and sleeping quarters were about the same as the kitchen and dining area. Two decks of bunks were built along the outside walls with each bed 5½ feet wide and 7 feet long and sides 6 inches high. This box-like bed held straw for a mattress for two men. Three pests inhabited these beds with the men: lice (head lice), gray backs (body lice or cooties), and bedbugs. Cotton ticks filled with loose oat straw and a pillow made of the same helped relieve the problem. Most camps had several large pots for washing clothing and bedding on Sundays to get rid of all forms of life. These buildings were lit at night by kerosene lamps and heated with potbelly stoves.

The stable held 8 pairs of horses and was 30 feet by 48 feet. Feed troughs were along the outside walls with horses facing outward, making cleaning the stables easier. The blacksmith shop was 24 by 30 feet and filled with his forge and tools. The blacksmith made horse shoes and had to put a toe iron on the shoe and turn the rear ends up to form a calk, so that the horse would have good footage in stones, ruts and mud. In the winter the calks were made sharp to hold in ice and frozen ground. He repaired and made all the tools and chains used in logging. Also, the saw sharpener often worked in the blacksmith shop.

The office and commissary usually had more windows and was a busy place keeping records and paying bills. Smaller operations had only one structure, the loft being used as a dormitory and the downstairs being divided into a lobby and cook room (R.D. Tonkin 61–64).

Camp DuBois had separate buildings for eating, sleeping, and business. Judging the amount of board feet put in by Camp DuBois there were most likely only about 28 woodhicks. The stock account included a large quantity of ox shoes and horseshoes, indicating that an equal number of animals were used. The user always ground his own axe at night by the flickering light (King 158). If a local watering hole was within walking distance it was often visited after they washed their clothing on Sundays.

Camp Dubois Opens

The bookkeeper opened Camp DuBois on August 14, 1867, bringing his daughter to cook for the few hands who were preparing for the cutting season (King 158). It would be late September before the pine bark became loose enough to peel. Both pine and hemlock logs were peeled to make them smooth enough to float over obstructions in the water and to prevent the bark from discoloring the wood (Huntley 259). Early in September the bookkeeper's wife and another daughter arrived to help with the cooking. His wife was paid $4.00 a week and her daughters each received $3.00 as helpers.

The foods consumed at the camp were: Rio coffee, tea at $1.10 a pound, New Orleans molasses, mackerel, trout, dried apples, firkens of butter (a firken was a small wooden vessel or tub for butter, equal to a quarter of a barrel, about 24 pounds) cabbage, beans, bacon, salt pork, cheese, beets, potatoes, onions, and crackers. Local farmers supplied many of the provisions; others were bought at St. Marys, and a few shipped by rail from Erie. The "tote wagon" was kept busy all winter making the 20 mile trip north to St. Marys.

Records show that Bill Long, "King Hunter of the Alleghenies," provided fresh venison during the winter months. He had learned his hunting skills from the Senecas and had served as a guide for John DuBois when he first cruised the timber of Clearfield County. The old hunter watched with a heavy heart as the giant trees, all of which were standing when William Penn started the colony, were felled and peeled (King 159). (A timber cruiser was a man who estimated the board feet that could be taken off a tract of land.)

The Jobber

The actual cutting of the timber was contracted for by a jobber who agreed to fell, cut, peel, and deliver into the slide between a minimum and a maximum amount of board feet at a fixed price per thousand. DuBois paid $2.25 per thousand. If the logs were to be pulled to the creek or banked at a landing, additional fees were paid. King presents a jobber-owner agreement where the owner agreed to pay the jobber $4.50 per thousand board feet of white pine to deliver 2 to 5 million board feet each year to Trout Run. These logs had to be 12 inches or over at the top (small) end (160–161).

Felling and Skidding

Most of the trees felled were white pine, a few were hemlock and poplar. There was indication that spars and square timbers may have been already cut, like some groves along the West Branch. Logs averaged 24 inches in diameter with a few 39 to 41 inches in diameter at the top end. Tall trees were subject to much shaking by the wind, causing cracks on the butt end, making from 5 to 8 feet of the butt unsound.

Many slides were built of two hardwood logs laid side-by-side on cross-members and hewn out inside to form a V-shaped trough. The slide brought logs from the top of the mountain down 400 feet to Bennetts Branch to a land-

Log slide near DuBois (courtesy Clearfield County Historical Society, Clearfield, Pennsylvania).

This a stacked sawlog landing. The logs can be released into the stream by knocking out the two holding up the stack. They roll down the bank into the stream, then when the splash dam is knocked, the rush of the splash flushes the logs downstream into the river (courtesy Clearfield County Historical Society, Clearfield, Pennsylvania).

ing. The *Harrisburg Patriot and Union*, March 18, 1868, stated that the winter of 1867–1868 had more snow than usual, which would provide plenty of water for the spring drive (King 161).

Parties Along the Sinnemahoning Creeks

During the long winter the woodhicks worked six days a week and had Sundays off. The older men went home to their families. Some of the men spent Sundays in a local barroom such as Ambrose Campbell and Len Chives at Blackwell, either watching a fight or participating in a fight. When they could, the young single guys went to a party to meet girls. Mountain hotels and sometimes private homes made extra money by sponsoring parties. Being along the Philadelphia and Erie Railroad running along the Driftwood Branch of the Sinnemahoning Creek had its advantages, for oysters were brought up by train from the Chesapeake Bay and served at all night dances for fifty cents a plate (Huntley 355). The museum in St. Michaels, Maryland, has 32 gallon wooden barrels that were used for packing the oysters in ice in the metal buckets.

Some weekends there was other entertainment. Once Mary Earl invited some young people of Driftwood to a dancing party. Three sledloads of young folks came, riding on straw in wagon boxes mounted on sleds, while they were wrapped up with bearskin robes. At midnight they ate supper at the Alpine House in Sterling Run, after which they danced in Earl's Hall, located just across the street. The teams were well blanketed and stabled at the Alpine House barn until the dancers were ready to return home. Some young men of the lumber camps claimed they were disappointed because only Driftwood folks were invited. They hung around the barroom of the Alpine House that night and "tanked up" on liquor. At five o'clock in the morning the sleds were made ready for the young folks to return when the disappointed men invaded the hall. They were exceedingly drunk and boisterous, causing the dancers to run out of the hall and get into the sleds.

Edler's Orchestra came with the party and had furnished the music. Jake Woodley, who played the snare drum, was a member of the orchestra. He was very proud of his beautiful drum, which he had won in a contest. After running out of the hall with his girl, he went back to get his drum, which was left on the rostrum where the orchestra had been playing. Having ascended the rostrum, he saw five drunken men closing in on him, shouting in guttural voices: "Eat him raw; eat him raw!" As one of them attempted to ascend the rostrum, Jake would knock him down with a chair until three men lay helpless in a heap. Taking his drum in one hand and a chair in the other, Jake got down off the rostrum and laid low the other two men. Then he went out and got into the sled which was waiting for him, and soon the turbulent party was on its way. Directly someone struck up "We Won't Go Home Until Morning" and everybody joined in the singing, which turned their fear into cheer, until they arrived at Driftwood about daylight (Huntley 402–403). Sterling Run is about ten miles up the Driftwood Branch above the village of Driftwood.

How the Number of Logs Was Estimated

Logs were scaled or measured for the number of board feet in each log in the woods. The scaler used a huge caliber to measure the diameter of the smaller end of each log. On the caliber were usually three scales, one each for 16, 14 and 12 foot logs. By reading the appropriate scale for the length of the log measured, he read off the estimated board feet the log would produce.

The Scribner Log Rule, developed around 1846, is a good example of a diagram rule. It was created by drawing the cross sections of one inch boards within circles representing the end view of logs. A space of one quarter inch was left between the boards to account for saw kerf. The Scribner Rule does not have an allowance for log taper and typically underestimates logs, particularly if the length is long.

These measurements were given to DuBois' bookkeeper, who used them to calculate the log drive charges. King stated that the DuBois logs averaged 4 per 1,000 feet; scaled with the Scribner rule, this was considered exceptionally good timber (King 164).

How a Drive Was Organized

About the same time King's article appeared in the Pennsylvania Historical Association's journal in 1962, he had started taking oral histories from woodhicks. The transcripts of King's interviews describes four divisions of labor. The first group was the "jam busters," as some called themselves. They were stationed at bridge piers and prominent rocks where logs were known to pile up, causing jams if they were not pushed back into the current. Pikes were long wooden poles, up to 15 feet, with sharp metal points on one end to stick into logs to push them back into the current. Bateaux were used to move men with their pikes to strategic locations. Some times the jam busters had to work from the bateaux or the bateauxman would hold the boat near to the pile of logs ready to retrieve the jam busters while they worked on top of the log pile breaking it up. The jam busters had to move along with the main body of logs. The river and creeks flow about 4 miles per hour during flood stage, so if a log were pushed into the Bennett's Branch at Bark Camp Run where the log drive started, it would only take about 25 hours to reach Williamsport. However, during the first 20 days of the drive they added 17 brands of logs during the first 23 miles of the drive. During this time one man could be standing on top of a rock from dawn to dusk every day for 20 days before they would move him to another place.

The second and third groups "sacked the rear" by moving the logs that were stranded along the river bank back into the water. From the interviews it appears that the men worked ahead of the horse teams. If the men couldn't move a log, the teams would drag it back into the deep water. If the teams worked ahead of the men and they misjudged a log that the men could move, the log was lost to the drive. The men had many unique ways of returning the logs to deep water, one was called "Jack Belling" a log. Jack Bell had come down from Maine and he showed the men how to move a heavy log. Six men using cant-hooks were placed along a log, three on either side with two at the front end, two in the middle and two at the rear. Each man stuck the pointed part of his cant-hook into the top of the log and the hook part of his tool into the bottom of the log. Then all six men lifted the log and carried it into the deep water to send it on its way down river.

The fourth group consisted of the kitchen-bunk ark and two arks to bed the horses (King's Oral Histories).

The Drive Begins

On March 12 and 13 it rained and on the 14th the ice went out. In Harrisburg the Susquehanna River raised 17½ feet and at Williamsport the boom was hung. On Thursday, March 19, the foreman of the drive had the splash dam opened and 4,076,000 board feet were knocked from the landing into the river. The drivers would lose track of the days, for one would be like the next and they would work seven days a week until the drive was done. Above Penfield, where the DuBois Camp was located, the Bennetts Branch is narrow enough to jump across in summer and even with the splash a jam formed. It took the rest of the day to break the jam.

A rider was dispatched to other camps to tell them to break their landings. A half mile down river 550,000 board feet came out of Mountain Run, today called Moshannon Run. By the second evening the drive was one mile down river at Penfield, where they ate their supper at the Woodward Camp. Day 3 and 4 the Woodward crew added their logs to the drive, 12,244,000 board feet (about 49,000 logs). It is here where the logs of D. B. Taylor joined the drive with 348,000 board feet, making a total of 4 brands in the drive. The drive now employed over 100 men and 8 teams hauling logs back into the river's main current.

Some of the logs pushed into the current on the first day were already in the boom at Williamsport. However, the current and the surface tension on the water formed a crest or crown in the center of the current and most of the heavy logs found their way to the waters edge. If the splash was receding, the logs were left stranded. It is this process of returning the logs to the current, or sacking the rear, that is the most difficult, requiring the log drivers to sometimes enter the cold water up to their armpits.

J. H. Koozer had begun building a logging ark at Penfield in early February. Joseph Koozer was the grandfather of Alfred Koozer, the young man who was caught in the snow storm going through Buttermilk Falls (see Chapter 8). Huntley stated that the typical Bennetts Branch ark was 20 feet wide and 60 feet long (Huntley 243).

The ark had a new stove, costing $51.00, used to feed over 50 drivers four times a day. The ark joined the drive as it passed Penfield. Its commissary was stocked with large quantities of chewing tobacco, blue soldier's trousers and gloves, and a supply of rubber boots. These log drivers did not wear the calked leather boots of a later period.

At Tyler's Flats the 5th brand joined the drive with 2,000,000 board feet. These logs were cut by David Tyler and branded with his name in capital letters. The Clearfield *Raftsman's Journal*, March 25, 1868, reported a cold snap toward the end of this week that made the work more difficult. Ice formed along the edges of the stream and the men sacking the rear had to break the ice before wading into the frigid water. When the ark arrived at Tyler's Flats on March 27, seven men decided to quit and drew their wages.

Hiram Woodward broke Webb's landing near the Elk County line, and the logs of Brown, Earley and Company bobbed out of Cherry Run at the present village of Force. This was the 6th brand and they were less than 4 miles into the drive with over 100,000 logs.

As the water fell below rafting stage, the ark lingered in the Slab Town dam near Weedville (4.7 miles into the drive). Sixty-four men were needed up Kersey Run to help E. B. England and A. Pardee, who were falling behind schedule, bringing down the 7th and 8th brands with 3,000,000 board feet. Kersey Run also brought a 9th brand with 3,600,000 board feet belonging to Bowman Perkins, a 10th brand with 657,000 board feet belonging to John S. Fisher, and an 11th brand of 927,000 board feet belonging to Finney and Barrows.

While the drive was "hung up" at Slab Town, John DuBois made a hurried trip to St. Marys to obtain more cash. His checks on this drive were written on the West Branch Bank of Williamsport and were all for $400, apparently an amount that was secretly known only by the cashier in Williamsport. A charge of 1 percent was made in St. Marys for cashing checks (King 165).

Three inches of snow fell Saturday, April 4, and the air continued cold over the weekend. On Monday most of the snow melted, but on Tuesday, four more inches came down and quickly thawed (*Raftsman's Journal* April 8). As the level of the water rose again the drive moved to Lindemuth's dam at Caledonia, where 94 wet and ravenous drivers were fed at Joseph Miliner's. Seven inches more snow on Thursday soon disappeared and the Bennetts Branch was running "bank full" (*Raftsman's Journal* April 15).

William Dunn's brand (the 12th) of 260,000 board feet joined the drive at Caledonia, 6.3 miles into the drive (King 162–166).

Lindemuth's dam, at Caledonia, was the main splash on the 100 mile trip to Williamsport before the construction of the Corporation Dam at Doctor's Rock (near Benezette) in 1871 (Huntley 471). An artificial flood crest carried the logs to Driftwood, where they reached the deeper waters of the Sinnemahoning.

After the Corporation Dam, or as it was often called "The Big Dam," was built in 1871, builders could create a splash that would cause a two-foot flood on the Sinnemahoning that would last for two hours. Driftwood, where the Bennetts Branch flowed into the Sinnemahoning, was 15 miles below the Big Dam and Keating was 30 miles below the Big Dam. The Big Dam had three gates; the biggest was a 28 foot wide bear trap gate to let rafts through the dam. The other two were 22 feet wide, one a bear trap gate and the other a barn door gate. The barn door gate was built just like a barn door with cross beams to hold the doors shut. When they wanted to open the gate they chopped the cross beams and the water behind the doors forced the doors open. Bear traps had gates that fell down behind the bear when he entered a log box, and the gate, being longer that the original opening, sealed the bear inside. The more the bear pushed against the gate the tighter it got. Bear trap gates worked much the same; the gate was dropped and the water behind the gate pushed it tightly into the dam foundation. However, getting the gate up with the weight of all the water pushing against it required lots of force to lift the gate. For this reason big chains were fastened to the lower part of the gate and the gate was ratcheted up using water power (Huntley 471).

At Benezette, 9.7 miles into the drive, logs came from the south from Laurel Run, which drained what is today the Parker Dam area, and the 13th brand with 5,466,000 board feet of Peck and Barnard. In later years a logger recalled that the force of this water was so great that the men quit the river when the Laurel Run logs zoomed into Bennetts Branch and some of the sticks shot across to dry ground on the other side.

From the north, Trout Run drained a vast area, and with all the fury of runaway horses came 4,351,000 board feet with the 14th and 15th brands of St. John and Rothrock, and St. John, Jones and Moore.

The Benezette blacksmith, Tim Gulfory, worked long hours to shoe the horses and repair hand pikes. The Widow Winslow furnished lodging for some of the men and Mrs. Ogle sold hay to feed the teams. As the logs moved on down the river, everyone in the valley turned out to witness the annual pageant of the river solid with moving logs. Like watching the ice go out, local folks never tired of seeing the log drives.

After all the logs had left Lindemuth's dam, John DuBois saddled his black mare and rode off to Driftwood for more cash to buy provisions. Everywhere along the route food was purchased from the inhabitants: David Horning provided 150 cabbages at 8 cents a head, Thomas Hewitt 45 bushels of corn and a barrel of sauerkraut, and "Cracker" Hicks a barrel of flour and another of pork. Most of the supplies came from St. Marys, although some were ordered from Williamsport (King 167).

At the 14 mile mark the logs rounded the bend in the stream and flowed by Grant. After the Civil War, General Kane, who had formed the Pennsylvania Bucktails unit, invited the great general of the Civil War Ulysses S. Grant to come to Pennsylvania to do some fishing. This is the spot where they went fishing, the only problem was, it wasn't fishing season and they didn't have fishing licences. It is also the spot where General Grant was arrested for fishing without a licence and fishing out of season.

At Dent Run, 4 miles above Driftwood and 6 miles below Benezette, a log jam formed. People along the river walked for miles to watch the drivers working to find the key. Once the jam was broken, 4 men were sent up Mix Run (at the 17.5 miles mark), future birthplace of the movie star Tom Mix (January 6, 1880), to help Brown and Early bring down 300,000 feet of pine. Now the drive had 174,440 logs packed into the narrow Bennetts Branch.

With the logs at Driftwood flowing into the wider Sinnemahoning Creek, John DuBois decided to go ahead to Williamsport. He was 59 years old at this time and could confidently rely on his partner to bring the drive safely into the boom. He sold his horse and saddle and boarded the Philadelphia and Erie train at Sinnemahoning.

At Driftwood (19.5 miles into the drive), where the two main branches of the Sinnemahoning converge, 16 men were discharged on April 19, the 37th day of the drive, because the deeper water required less labor. Few hands drew money at Driftwood, because there was little time to celebrate. When the drive reached the village of Sinnemahoning, 3.5 miles downstream, the last logs joined the drive. Barrow and Bickford's brand (the 17th brand), with an ampersand in a circle, had been stamped on 810,000 board feet of logs cut in the valley of First Fork.

Now the total number of logs in the drive was about 178,000 consisting of 44,430,000 board feet. At Keating, pronounced "Kat-ing" by the men, the Sinnemahoning drive tangled into the rear of the West Branch drive under the supervision of Emery. When the leading logs drifted into the other drive on April 24, the two crews doubtless worked together, as was done in future years. Nothing is contained in the ark ledger to describe the next week, in which the combined drives passed Westport, Renovo, and North Bend. Rafts also floated through the drive in increasing numbers, but many of them, estimated at between 400 to 500, were still expected at Harrisburg on April 24 (King 167 to 168).

Tragedy on the River

Just above Lock Haven two men found themselves stranded on a bar without the assistance of the bateaux and tried to ride a large log to shore. When they got into deep water where their pikes wouldn't reach the bottom the log rolled and threw them into the water. Henry Wesser, about 21, could not swim and sank out of sight. His body was recovered about 45 minutes later (May 22, 1868, Lock Haven *Clinton Republican* and the *Raftsman's Journal*, May 27, 1868). His death occurred on Friday May 1.

Wesser was a member of the Roaring Creek Lodge of Good Templars at Dunning, Luzerne County, and the Lock Haven members of this order attended his funeral and buried him in the Old Cemetery there. John DuBois personally paid for the funeral expenses and gave the deceased's wages for 35½ days to his brother Jacob, who was also employed on the drive.

Some of the men had already arrived in Lock Haven, rivermen's Babylon, before the accident, where they renewed their acquaintances with John Barleycorn and some popular Jezebel (Hanlon 88). On April 28 and 29, 26 of the old hands asked for cash, ranging from $5.00 to $25.00 (King 168 to169).

On to Williamsport

Lock Haven had a boom extending 3 miles west and north of town that could hold 100 million board feet, but these logs were going to Williamsport, 18 miles downstream. Sheer poles fended them into the navigable side of the river, under the towpath bridge over the slack water of the canal feeder dam and then through the chute, which was close to 700 feet long. Mules and horses pulled canal boats from West Branch Canal on the south side across the river to the Bald Eagle Canal on the north side by walking on the towpath on the bridge. A piece of wood was used that slid along the handrail and held the towline, making it easier for the mules.

Thirteen miles down stream below Lock Haven at Jersey Shore many logs became stranded on a bar. Thirteen men and two teams were left behind to sack the logs. As they approached the boom at Williamsport fewer men were needed, so 30 men were paid off on May 7 and 8 at the rate of $4 per day for 42 days. Each was given a ticket to return to the Sinnemahoning on the Philadelphia and Erie Railroad. DuBois and Woodward purchased the tickets at $2.80 each.

About the middle of May, the last loggers were discharged. Generally these men had followed the drive from the beginning. The foreman was paid for 62½ days, the bookkeeper for 52 and 20 others were also given settlements. Eight regular teamsters, in addition to two more who had worked a short time at the conclusion of the drive, were also dismissed.

The water was too low to return the arks to Penfield, so the teamsters proceeded slowly homeward with their animals. During the summer when the water was higher, teams of horses were dispatched to Williamsport to bring the arks home, because it was cheaper to tow the arks back up the river than to build a new one each year. The canal towpath could be used by the teams until they got above Lock Haven and then the teams would enter the water along the river's edge and men on the raft with poles kept the arks in deeper water.

A total of 44,430,000 board feet of timber was brought to Williamsport in this combined drive from Bennetts Valley. These figures represent 27 per-

This jam occurred April 21, 1874. The wooden bridge ran from Lock Haven north to Lockport. Notice the towpath alongside used by mules to tow canal boats across the Susquehanna River (courtesy Clearfield County Historical Society, Clearfield, Pennsylvania).

cent of the 165,338,389 board feet charged boomage that year in 1868 (Meginness 361). It was said that Clearfield County white pine averaged 20,000 board feet per acre, so the DuBois-Woodward drive consumed the virgin growth on 2,221 acres.

Jobbers and lumbermen whose logs were safely in the boom were billed according to the distance their logs had traveled by DuBois and Woodward. Logs brought from the vicinity of Penfield were charged $1.00 per 1,000. From Trout, Laurel and Mix Runs, the charge was 45 cents per 1,000. Logs from the Sinnemahoning were charged 25 cents per 1,000. DuBois and Woodward charged themselves 25 cents per 1,000. Or, Hiram Woodward saved $9,183.00 on the delivery of his own logs and John DuBois a smaller sum $3,057.00 (King 169–171).

The logs that traveled 100 miles were charged 1 cent a mile to drive 1,000 board feet to Williamsport ($1.00 per 1,000 board feet for about 100 miles). Logs traveling 87.5 miles were charged 55 cents a mile per 1,000 board feet (40 cents per 1000, for 87.5 miles), and those traveling 78 miles were charged 32 cents a mile (25 cents per 1,000, for 78 miles) per 1,000 board feet.

The reason the first logs owners paid so much was that the Bennetts Branch above Penfield is very narrow, making the log driving much more difficult than downstream in the main branch of the Sinnemahoning and West Branch. Also, it took 37½ days to travel to Driftwood. Only 19½ miles into the drive, that's 60 percent of the time spent traveling the first 20 percent of the way.

This was not the first year DuBois and Woodward ran a drive to Williamsport, and everyone benefited by combining the 17 brands into one drive.

Williamsport boom. Notice the line of cribs along the right side of the boom logs (courtesy Pennsylvania State Archives, Harrisburg).

West Branch Log Drives

The West Branch had started harvesting its timber after 1827 with the appearance of board rafts on the river, and two years later the Chesapeake and Delaware Canal was opened between the Chesapeake Bay and the Delaware Bay. West Branch lumber began reaching Philadelphia, and lumbermen in that city took notice and quickly moved to the West Branch to make their fortunes.

By 1836 square timber and spar rafts started going down river, and when the boom in Williamsport was opened in 1851, sawlogs were driven down the river. This brought jobbers who were usually Scots-Irish or a few English and watermen who had the knowledge of how to use the streams and rivers to move logs to the West Branch. The watermen were usually French-Canadians who came from Maine and Canada.

At first the jobber was contracted to take the logs from the stump to the boom. This, however, proved wasteful when several log drives mingled together on the river, causing a duplication of effort. The West Branch did not have one man with the experience of John DuBois who had helped build the boom and knew log driving. However, they did see the advantage of having larger drives under one control, where jobbers and owners shared the costs. Big drive bosses often helped local jobbers get their logs to the West Branch in time to be included in the drive to Williamsport.

Many of the men interviewed by King had worked the West Branch rather than Bennetts Branch and Sinnemahoning Creek, but it didn't appear the two areas did anything differently. The work of the drive was divided into four groups. The jam busters worked ahead of the logs, the second group sacked the rear, the third group were the horse teams that pulled the heaviest and stranded logs back into the river, and the fourth group were the arks (King's Oral Histories).

Log drivers usually wore woolen clothing with bright colored socks, stagged trousers (cut off about eight inches), and Cutter Wisconsin calked boots (this was in the 1880s and '90s).

As logging progressed,

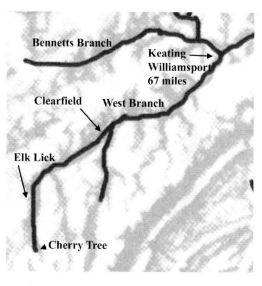

Headwaters of the West Branch of the Susquehanna River.

Log jam near McGees Mills, 15 miles down river from Cherry Tree. To get the size of the problem see the four men walking across the jam (courtesy Clearfield County Historical Society, Clearfield, Pennsylvania).

land along the West Branch of the Susquehanna River which had been designated as a public highway was cleared and farmed. Trees farther from the rivers were harvested and small creeks were needed to move the saw logs to the river for driving down river to the sawmills. These creeks often flowed through the farmland where the landowner could charge exorbitant fees or block the use of the stream altogether. This situation threatened the logging industry and a movement was organized in Williamsport to change the situation. Lawyers from Harrisburg were hired to present the problem to the Pennsylvania Assembly.

On March 28, 1871, the assembly approved "An Act to Allow the Improvement of Creeks and Rivulets," 100 years after declaring the West Branch of the Susquehanna a public highway. According to the act, a person or persons could enter into an agreement where improvements could be made to the stream so as to facilitate the movements of sawlogs down the stream from where the trees grew to the public highway. Improvements included building dams at the head of the stream used to flush logs down the stream, building cribs and piers to hold logs until the drive, cleaning out rocks, bars, driftwood and trees, and widening and deepening the channel.

Improvement companies were formed and registered in the county courthouse, where they stated the length in miles and both ends of their improvement. By doing this they agreed to pay for all damage to buildings and land caused by flooding and logs. Court appointed assessors evaluated the damages. If logs were stored on land not belonging to the lumber owners, a "bankage" fee of 10 cents per 1,000 board feet was paid to the land owner. The improvement company had the exclusive right to use the stream for driving logs and could assess fees to other logging companies who were not part of the improvement company who wanted to use the stream.

These splash dams were also used to create artificial floods on the public highways for rafts that didn't have enough water to get down river to deeper water. A knock (release) from a splash dam cost between $5.00 and $10.00. The charge to knock a dam was more than some raftsmen wanted to pay, so they would send one of their own up a stream to steal a splash by knocking the dam at night. This caused dam owners to post guards on splash dams.

Cherry Tree is on the West Branch of the Susquehanna River at the southwest corner of Clearfield County. The Susquehanna River had been designated a public highway up to Cherry Tree, but beyond, the Act to Allow the Improvement of Creeks and Rivulets, passed in 1871, applied.

Here the river is wide and shallow, and logs began to jam the river shut. Throughout the night more logs added to the jam. Both logs and rafts were prevented from running down river. The up river dam was closed to fill up for a splash the next day. The dam would be knocked at one o'clock the following day when the dam would be full with water running over the dam's breast.

At one o'clock the next day all the men, women and children from the town of Cherry Tree gathered along the river bank to witness the spectacle. Log drivers mingled with the people waiting for the water, ready to assist the returning of logs to the river once the jam went out.

Just after one the river began rising, spreading over gardens and back yards as the crowd cheered, "she hauls." The jam began to rise up as if ready to explode, then it settled down as the crowd cried out "she hung."

Now the jam was tighter than ever. A jam tightens down after each time it moves or dynamite is exploded to break it and it doesn't go out. The log drivers tried to find the key log which would break the jam, but failed. Then the senior partners of the log drive conferred again; the solution, more water.

All upstream dams were closed in order to fill up. A time table was worked out so that the most upstream dam was opened first. Then as the water rushed down stream the next dam was open as the splash reached its slack water. Dams on side runs were opened so that their splash would join the large splash on the river.

The same crowd assembled on the second day and just after one o'clock the huge splash came down the river. Trees along the river's bank bent their heads downstream, pig and chicken pens moved to new locations, outhouses moved downstream with yard fences. The jam went out. Quickly the log drivers began returning the stranded logs to the river.

Tonkin gives details about cutting the Elk Lick track, which was cut from 1884 to 1888. This track was one mile below Cush Creek or 11 miles below Cherry Tree and about 172 miles from the boom at Williamsport.

The track was next to the son of the Spar King's property. John Patchin (the Spar King) was the man who had brought the rafting of spars and timbers to the West Branch. He had picked out the best stand of trees for himself and his son.

By this time cutting was done to get the most money for the trees. The cutters went into the property and cut the spars and square timbers first, because they sold for the most money. Then the sawlog cutters cut everything else that was standing. The sawlogs were driven to Williamsport for $3.50 per 1,000 board feet or 2 cents a mile for 1,000 board feet, twice the cost of the DuBois-Woodward drive. The DuBois-Woodward drive had a total of 44,430,000 board feet where the Elk Lick drive only had about 10,000,000 board feet, about 23 percent of the DuBois drive. Economy of scale may have increased Elk Lick costs per board foot, as it was about 20 years later and the middle third of the drive (from Clearfield to Keating) went through a very desolate area. There were miles where supplies couldn't be easily furnished, whereas the Dubois-Woodward drive had roads running along the water's edge all the way.

During the sawlog harvesting jobbers often set up competitions to increase productivity. Who could saw the greatest number of logs in one day produced many teams of two men willing to set the camp record. Bark peeling and tree felling also were seen as competitive events.

There were many parties along the West Branch like the one described at the Alpine House in Sterling Run. Because of the slow mode of travel, parties lasted the whole night with a big breakfast before heading home at daybreak. Trains did not run up the West Branch like they did the Sinnemahoning Creek and therefore no oysters were served. The long ride home in a sled, bundled under bear hides, provided an excellent opportunity for young couples to get to know each other (R. Dudley Tonkin 35–85).

10

Woodhicks

This set of anecdotes brings to life events in the woodhicks' daily work. As said in the previous chapter, narrow gauge railroads and transportable steam driven sawmills replaced the log drives early in the twentieth century. If the reader is interested, information can be found in the series *Logging Railroad Era of Lumbering in Pennsylvania* published by Taber, Kline and Casler.

Jam Breakers

As with the DuBois-Woodward log drive coming out of the Sinnemahoning Creek into the West Branch, and the Emery log drive coming down the West Branch, meeting at Keating could mean disaster, since the log drives out of the West Branch were usually as big or bigger than those out of the Sinnemahoning Creek. Three hundred and fifty thousand logs were a lot of logs in the river and it is understandable how jams could occur very quickly. It was inevitable that log drives from both streams would meet at Keating — they both started as soon as the ice went out.

Kahler's oral history (10–12) of Ambrose Campbell is a wonderful story of jam breakers. The author has taken the liberty to combine Kahler's report with research to tell the event in story form.

Log jams were a nightmare and a panic to lumbering; to some it meant loss and destruction, or heavy damage claims. No time could be lost with them, as they always grew worse and never better. (There would be other drives coming down the river later and running into the jam making it bigger and harder to break.) Very few men knew how to unscramble them, once they got started, so that such a party became well known in the field and were regarded highly. They were the "Jam Busters." It was very dangerous work, to say the least. It always meant taking a chance on your life, so it brought high rewards, if you could call it that, for the price was generally one hundred dollars, plus travel, board, find and all the whiskey you wanted. That is upon the condition that you broke the jam and then lived to collect your money. Yet there were some who did really do it, which created them fame among lumbermen.

Log jams were usually started by a key log getting stuck, which in turn stopped others and thus caused the jamming. The other logs built up and piled

This log jam occurred 26 miles down river from Renovo in the slack water of the Lock Haven Canal Feeder Dam on April 21, 1874. It was caused by a large number of rafts breaking loose and lodging against the bridge piers (Mitchell 17). Sawlogs formed a second jam, which appears to be four or five feet higher than the jam in the foreground. This second jam, with water dammed up behind it, caused increased danger to the jam breakers. To the right a canal boat loaded with boards is trapped. In the center a boy sits on a peaked roof, most likely what is left of a raft shanty (courtesy Clearfield County Historical Society, Clearfield, Pennsylvania).

behind them, while a dam formed and built up water pressure. It was a terrible menace to all from the very first and it grew rapidly worse all the time. Every means and method was used as soon as possible, and word sent out to Jam Breakers right away, and to get there fast.

Renovo, or the area that is now Renovo, was like every other mountain village until 1862, when the Philadelphia and Erie Railroad company ran its first train to the area. The Philadelphia and Erie line was to compete with the financially successful Erie Canal in New York State. The area was selected as the site for the company's railroad shop, and the name Renovo, which means "I renew" in Latin, was selected as the name of the village. Renovo soon grew into a busy railroad town with even an opera house. Kahler did not say what year this happened, but it is very descriptive of town life along the river in log driving season.

One year just such an event took place at Renovo. For four days the men ran across the jam picking at logs with no success. Daily more logs joined the jam, backing the water up higher and higher. Chicken coops, small farm buildings, and outhouses were carried downstream into the jam. Worst of all for the Pennsylvania Railroad, its tracks for the Philadelphia and Erie line were washing out, threatening their connection between the Great Lakes and the Eastern United States. Dynamite was used, but the logs only settled in tighter. What was needed was a man known as a "jam buster," not the jam buster used by the log-driver to prevent a jam, but a man who could walk across the jam and find the one "key log" that if turned loose would release all the energy held back by the dammed up water and break the jam. The "Pennsy," as the Pennsylvania Railroad was known, sent out offers to find a jam buster to break the jam.

Finally two young men were found at Cammal, the little village along Pine Creek just below Blackwell. They were Abner Campbell and his older brother Ambrose, or Brose. When they learned of the five hundred dollar reward for breaking the jam, the brothers jumped on two horses and rode down Pine Creek to Jersey Shore, where the Pennsy had a locomotive steamed up and ready to rush the brothers forty miles up the West Branch of the Susquehanna to Renovo. With no cars attached to the engine but the tender, the locomotive raced westward over the track toward Lock Haven. The tracks between Jersey Shore and Lock Haven are very straight and the engineer had the locomotive going as fast as it would go. This was an emergency and the engineer was using that excuse to drive his engine at top speed. Brose watched the fireman shovel the boiler full, wondering how much the engine could take before it would blow up — something that was not unusual in that day. Looking out of the cabin he could see the fields and farm houses racing by; it had only been a couple of years earlier that people believed that if a man traveled faster than a horse could run, he wouldn't be able to breathe and would suffocate. Brose stuck his head out of the cabin and sucked in a big breath through his nose, just to test the theory that he could breathe — he wasn't suffocating. He didn't feel dizzy from lack of air, so he guessed that there was nothing to the old belief.

Going through Lock Haven the engineer slowed his locomotive, but blasted on the train's whistle, letting the townspeople know to get off the tracks. Many young children and their parents were there to wave to the train. Brose thought that someone must have told them about the jam at Renovo and they had come down to the tracks to see the Jam Busters go by. Brose waved back to the crowd hoping he wouldn't disappoint them.

At the western end of Lock Haven where Lock Haven University is today, the tracks turn north to follow the west side of the river. It is here that the engineer opened the throttle, blew the whistle and let his locomotive run at full speed again. They had hardly reached full speed when the engineer pulled back on the throttle and the train slowed again. They were about four miles above Lock Haven and the tracks ran northwest along the west side of the river. Coming around a left-hand curve Brose could see a trestle railroad bridge crossing the river to the other side. The engineer was slowing to cross the bridge. As the locomotive crossed the bridge it shook the trestles and Brose wondered if the bridge would collapse with the train on it.

The engineer tapped him on his shoulder and pointed down at the river bottom. Brose leaned forward cautiously, not wanting to get too near the open side of the cabin where his head could hit a trestle, and looked down where the engineer was pointing. Brose's eyes widened as he fixed on the river bottom. There lying on its side was another locomotive that had been going south when it jumped the tracks and landed in the river. Cold sweat formed on Brose's forehead as he watch the sunken engine as long as he could, wondering how many men had been killed in that accident. The rest of the trip Brose tried to concentrate on the problem ahead and ignore the train ride as the train followed the east side of the river north.

As their locomotive raced into Renovo the orange sun was starting to dip behind the green pine tree covered mountains, but the whole town was at the station to meet the two young men. The crowd consisted of two types of men. First there were the woodhicks, which Brose and Abner were very familiar with because they were part of this group. This group was easy to spot with their wet clothing, calked boots and stagged trousers, cut off about eight inches high, so they wouldn't step on the bottoms and stumble while working (Tonkin, R.D. 57). These young men had worked in the woods all winter long and had a wanderlust in their eyes, because they were only a day away from finishing their job, getting paid and blowing part of the money in the "Endless Mountains," Dodge City, Lock Haven. Like the famous cattle drives of the West, Lock Haven served as a place where a log-driver or raftsmen could let off emotional steam that had been building up for months. These unbathed men were very skeptical of foreigners coming into their area and showing them how to do something they had failed to do in four days.

The other group consisted of the railroad workers from the machine shops. They were dirty too, but their dirt was only one day old since at night they were home with their wives and children. They were eager to see the two jam busters and learn what these two men could do that the others couldn't.

The Pennsy officials met and briefed Brose and Abner on what had been tried, as the two men were offered a free meal and a room in the hotel. The officials warned them not to try to break the jam until the next morning because it was getting dark, but Brose insisted they at least look at their job so he could formulate a plan for the next day. The brothers each carried a lantern and their cant-hooks as they walked down the bank and out onto the log jam.

From the bank a crowd of townspeople and woodhicks watched them. Back and forth they ran over the logs, with the agility of a cat. It was apparent to everyone watching that Brose was the most knowledgeable, as he was pointing out the logs that might be the key log. Finally, Brose spotted what he thought was the key log, and he placed his lantern on top of it so as to mark it before returning to shore.

High on the mountain you could see the bright green pine trees in the setting sunlight, but down in the valley near the river it was dark — people were using lanterns to see.

When he got to the river bank, Brose told the official that he had found the key log and that he was going to try and break it that evening. The town official pleaded with him to wait until morning, but Brose insisted that he could do it that evening. The Pennsy men brought him dynamite, but he refused it, saying, "I'd rather take a chance on my life with a log, than to be blown to pieces with that damned stuff, I'm afraid of it, and I know more about logs." Then he announced to the crowd, "Build me up some fires along the bank, as we'll need lots of light to try to get back to shore."

The two brothers walked back over the jam to the key log, Abner with his lantern and cant hook and Brose with his cant hook. When they reached the key log, Brose removed his lantern and used his cant-hook to test the log. As he turned what he thought was the right log the whole log jam began to shake and make creaking noises, indicating he had the key log.

He said to Abner, "This is it." Shaking Abner's hand, Brose instructed Abner to take the lantern and start toward the shore, and when he got about twenty yards from it, he should place one lantern where Brose could see it, and so he could run toward it. Then he should go up on the bank and swing the other lantern back and forth to signal he was ready. Brose said, "If I fail tonight, then you try it tomorrow." With the cant hook on the key log, Brose waited for Abner's signal.

The fires along the shore were growing brighter as he watched his younger brother make his way toward shore. Brose was left in the dark with his cant hook.

Halfway to shore Abner hung one lantern on his cant hook and proceeded to the bank. By then it was completely dark with only the one lantern looking like an orange speck where the river should be. A hush drew over the crowd as Abner began swinging his lantern back and forth, signaling Brose which way to run.

It started with a slow roar and increased in loudness. The mountains on both sides of the river echoed the noise — it sounded like every bowling-pin in the alley was being knocked down hundreds of times. The entire mass was grinding and groaning; logs were flying high into the air and a deafening roar was increasing. The orange light in the lantern went out — Ambrose was not seen. The crowd stood dumbfounded as the jam broke and the logs went out. Then the river returned to normal, but Brose didn't appear on shore. It was so quiet on shore you could hear the river water lapping at its shore.

The crowd using lanterns searched frantically for Brose's body along the banks. It seemed like forever to Abner, as he walked down along the river's bank looking for his brother. About a mile below town he heard some say, "He's over here." Abner rushed toward the voice — people were crowding around the man in the water hanging onto a log. Abner hardly recognized his brother's bruised and bleeding head lying on the log. His face was all black and blue — Abner couldn't tell if it was from the cold water or the logs had bruised him. Ambrose was conscious, but couldn't speak.

Before they could lift Brose out of the water another voice called out, "Let me through, I'm a doctor." The doctor took charge and had Brose lifted out of the water and onto a makeshift stretcher, which he was covered with blankets to warm him. Ambrose was carried up to the town and placed in the hotel provided by the Pennsy. Along the way he was cheered by the woodhicks and railroad men.

At the hotel heated laundry irons were wrapped in towels and placed under the blankets to warm him. Abner began to feel better when he realized Ambrose was sleeping.

The next morning the woodhicks and railroad men appeared at the hotel and carried both brothers on their shoulders to the bar. They wanted to hear Ambrose's story. After first given a stiff drink by the bartender, Ambrose was hoisted up on the bar, where he slowly drank his drink, while the bartenders quickly served the crowd. Someone shouted: "How do you feel?

Brose answered, "A little stiff and sore — nothing that will last."

"How did you survive?" was the next question.

"Well, the logs went out a lot quicker than I thought. I guess there was more water pressure on them than I had figured."

"What did you do to keep from being crushed?' another asked.

"Well, I knew if I stayed with the logs I'd be crushed, so I dove to the bottom and held onto a rock as long as I could. You can hear the logs banging around even though you're underwater. I just waited until everything got quiet up there." he said, looking up at the barroom ceiling.

"Then what?" an anxious woodhick asked.

"Well, I just popped to the surface and grabbed the nearest log. I knew that eventually the log would beach itself."

The crowd cheered and the two brothers were carried to the next bar, where Ambrose told his story to another set of woodhicks and railroad men. This time when he finished, the organizers of the log drives presented him with five hundred dollars.

At the third bar a Pennsy official presented each brother with five hundred dollars, much to the delight of the crowd. The official asked them to stay over for one week, for which they were paid at the rate of ten dollars a day and all other expenses and their return to their Pine Creek camp. After a cheer the brothers were carried off to a fourth bar so Ambrose could tell his story again. In each bar he and Abner were given another free drink before they could answer any questions.

When Ambrose had finished telling his story at the fourth bar a little railroad worker asked, "What was the scariest part of this whole thing?"

Ambrose thought for a moment, then looked up to ponder the ceiling. "The only time I was afraid, was during the train ride up here. I thought the engineer was going to roll us in the river and drown us."

The barroom broke out in laughter.

Woodhick Baseball

R.C. Ober (King, Ober's oral history) of Wyside along the Sinnemahoning Creek tells a story about playing baseball for the United States Leather Company from Sheffield. This story, like many of the oral histories, was not recorded in the order in which events took place so I took the liberty of telling it in a story format.

One of the largest companies in the country, the United States, Leather Company tanned about 600,000 hides a year. Since it took nine cords of hemlock bark to tan one hundred hides, the industry required 50,000 cords annually. Originally hemlock trees were cut down for their bark and the wood rotted in the forest. However, towards the end of the 1800s when pine became scarce and wire nails were produced that would hold in hemlock, the wood was harvested as a substitute for pine. The old square nails made by blacksmiths would not hold in hemlock. Tanneries quickly depleted "Pennsylvania's Black Forest" as the hemlock forest was called, because even on a sunny day the branches of the hemlock trees blocked out the sun's light.

Sheffield is located on the Philadelphia and Erie Railroad line, connecting it with the markets all over the country. In five years the tannery processed 350,000 buffalo hides (killed in the Midwest). Some of the skins contained bullets, and from these hides the company had extracted upward of two tons of lead (Casler 811).

In those days, baseball was the most popular sport and every community that had nine men had a baseball team. Large factory teams like United States Leather Company paid their good players more money and usually drew big crowds. Ober was getting twenty dollars a game and they gave him and his catcher a job working with their hemlock operation. Ober stated that he and his catcher were offered a job if they played baseball for the prestigious company.

He tells of one particular game with The Bellefonte Academy (an academy was a high school) that typified many games played in that day. Before the game Ober went up to the umpire and admired the stick pin the ump used to hold down his tie. Umpires dressed in their "Sunday Best" for a big game and this ump had on brown wool suit pants, with a matching vest over a white long sleeved shirt with French cuffs. He wore a red and gold silk tie tucked into his vest with a pearl stick pin through the tie.

Ober asked, "Is that a real pearl?"

"It sure is. I got it down in Philadelphia when I worked in the shipyards," the ump replied proudly.

Ober told the ump how much he liked the pin, trying to get the ump on his side so the ump would call his close pitches strikes. The game started with the Sheffield Team looking good, but the Bellefonte Team was holding its own. Going into the sixth inning the score was tied at one all.

The first Sheffield batter hit a single into center field. The second batter grounded out at first and the first runner end up on second base. Sheffield's third batter popped up to the third baseman and they held up the runner at second.

With two out, the Bellefonte fans began to breathe a little easier. That was until the fourth Sheffield batter, who was Ober's catcher, came up to the plate and hit the first pitch out of the park for a home run, making the game three to one, Sheffield.

The Bellefonte pitcher struck out the next Sheffield batter with what most of the Sheffield players thought was help from the umpire; two of his strikes looked like balls, the Sheffield batter complained bitterly, to no avail.

Then Ober came out to the mound to pitch the bottom half the sixth inning. His first pitch caught the inside lower corner of the plate and the umpire called, "Ball one!" Ober looked at the umpire, but said nothing. The batter tipped the next pitch into the stands; now it was one ball and one strike.

On the next pitch the curve ball almost got away from Ober and there was no doubt that it was a ball; making it two balls and one strike. The fourth pitch to the first batter was questionable, and the umpire called it a ball.

With three balls and one strike the batter let Ober's fifth pitch go by. Ober threw the ball right down the middle of the plate and the umpire called, "Ball four! Take your base." Ober's head jerked around at the ump and his face reddened. Ober argued with the ump, but the ump turned away and called, "Play ball!"

The second batter bunted the first pitch down the first base line and Ober picked it up and threw to third, keeping the runner from going to third. This left a man on first and second base with no outs.

The Bellefonte crowd came to its feet to cheer its team. The Bellefonte player on second base was known for his base stealing and the crowd began to chant, "Steal. Steal. Steal."

The man on second took a long lead off the base and Ober threw to the second baseman, checking the runner's lead. Ober's first pitch was straight down the middle of the plate and the batter swung at the ball but missed. The man on second sprinted for third base because Sheffield's catcher had dropped the pitch.

The catcher picked up the ball and fired it to the third baseman in plenty of time to catch the runner coming down from second base. As the Bellefonte player slid into third base, the umpire rushed toward the play. Sheffield's third baseman had clearly tagged the Bellefonte runner out three feet from the base.

But the ump shot out both hand palms down and called out at the top of his voice, "Safe!" Bellefonte fans cheered their approval.

Sheffield's third baseman voiced his disapproval and the Sheffield manager came out of the dugout to protest. Bellefonte fans began booing. Ober calmly walked back to the pitcher's mound and waited for the umpire to return behind the pitching plate to call the balls and strikes.

With both hands on his hips, Ober waited for the ump at the pitcher's plate and when the ump approached he tossed Ober the baseball and called, "Play Ball!" Ober caught the ball with his left hand and when the ump drew near enough, Ober's right hand came up off his hip and his fist caught the ump right in the face. The umpire grabbed Ober by his jersey and kicked him in the shins; a roar went up from the crowd. The two men fell to the ground and began rolling over in the infield with fists and arms chopping at their opponent and occasionally you could see a foot or knee flying. As a dust cloud rose around the pitcher's mound, the players from both teams converged in the infield and the fight become a brawl.

The Sheffield bat boy and the manager gathered up the bats and other equipment and put them in a bag.

The Bellefonte fans came out of the stands to join in the brawl. The Sheffield team started to move off the field, forming a circle much like muskoxen do when threatened and as if they had practiced this maneuver often. Then with the bat boy and manager leading, the whole team started to run off the field. The Bellefonte fans began pelting the retreating Sheffield baseball team with stones, as the Sheffield team raced down the town's street together. Some fans searched frantically for small rocks to throw after the retreating Sheffield team.

A group of young men in their late teens and early twenties who had expected a brawl had stockpiles in their pockets, the right size rocks for stoning their opponents. This group of young men took up the chase and followed the Sheffield team through the streets of the town and to the railroad station, tossing their stones.

At the railroad station the Sheffield team scrambled aboard a passenger train to seek the safety of the railroad company. It wasn't until the conductor showed up that the Bellefonte fans gave up the stoning and walked back to their ball field and the Sheffield Players began to relax.

The Sheffield manager looked at Ober and saw that his nose and face were bloody. "What happened to your nose?" Ober looked in the window, using it as a mirror, and mopped the blood away from his face. Then he pulled a pin-like object from his nose saying, "I guess the ump got the best of me, because his tie pin went through my nose and face." Ober stated that most baseball games had about a dozen fights and usually ended with a fight.

Bullies

Each logging camp and local area had one man who was the best fighter, and he was known as their bully. Bullies came in two general types which I will call black-hat and white-hat bullies. Black-hat bullies took pride in fighting, especially newcomers. You had to endure the bully's demands or fight him. You fought or got out of his territory; fear brought him respect. Black-hat bullies went out of their way to pick a fight, often into other bullies' territories. The "white-hat bully" was a popular big man who defended and looked after the smaller men in his realm, only fighting when it became necessary. Often one logging camp would pit its bully against another logging camp's bully, and the woodhicks would place bets on the outcome.

The Marquis of Queensberry Rules for boxing did not come into existence until 1867, and by then the woodhicks along the West Branch of the Susquehanna River had their own set of rules, which included punching, kicking, crushing, and stomping — anything went. The fight was over only when a participant shouted that he had enough. If a man got hurt, it was his fault for not giving up soon enough.

Professor Sam King, at the Penn State Center in DuBois, collected woodhick oral histories in the early 1960s. O. C. Ober lived in Wyside, where the First Fork flows into the Sinnemahoning Creek from the east. Ober told Professor King that when a woodhick left the mountains he had trouble winning a fight because of all the rules he had to abide by. Ober worked in the Philadelphia shipyards for five years and he could remember two things about fighting there. First, you could only use your fists, and second, he saw more fights there in one day than he had seen in a lifetime in the woods (Ober 4). O. C. Ober was the pitcher for the Sheffield baseball team.

Abe Bloom

In his oral history, Luther Dunlap of Olanta (a village about five miles south of Curwensville) told Professor King about Abraham Bloom, a white-hat bully (12). Again, this oral history was recorded with events out of order; I have put the events into a story.

Abe Bloom lived in Bloomington, a village about three miles south of Curwensville, and according to Dunlap, he was a giant of a man weighing between 260 and 280 pounds with no fat on him. One day a traveling show with a strong man came to Curwensville, and to draw a crowd, the show's barker hyped the strong man, saying how he could lift a barrel of water and drink from its bunghole. The strong man rolled the barrel up on his knees and drank out of the bunghole. Then the barker taunted the men in the crowd by saying, "If anyone thinks this barrel isn't full of water, come down and examine it."

Dunlap said, "Uncle Abe walked down and catches the barrel up like it was a jug and tasted it. Then he said, laughing, 'Yes, gentlemen, that's water.'" (A barrel for liquids usually held 32 gallons of water which, weighed 267 pounds.) The barker said in amazement, "If that's the kind of fellows you have around here, there's no use of our coming."

Abe enjoyed singing and one night at singing school a fellow by the name of Caldwell kept interrupting the instructor and singers, making it impossible for them to learn their songs. Abe informed Caldwell to be quiet, but Caldwell continued to speak up, disrupting the singing. Abe then picked the man up by the neck and his seat and tossed him out.

Abe Bloom (**courtesy Clearfield County Historical Society, Clearfield, Pennsylvania**).

Caldwell threatened Abe, saying he would bring a man who would fix him. Abe told Caldwell, "Bring anyone you like, I'll lick the two of you."

The next singing school night Caldwell fetched his friend Straw, and Straw asked Abe, "I understand that you said you could lick Caldwell or any of his backers?" Abe replied, "That's what I said. And I can knock enough straw out of you to bedden your oxen for a week." Then Abe turned to the woman with him, who was Dunlap's mother, and said, "Hold my coat, Minnie." There were just two hits, one when Abe hit Straw and the second when Straw hit the ground.

Abe's reputation spread throughout the West Branch of the Susquehanna River and when he went to Lock Haven, the Lock Haven bully, a black man, challenged him. Abe put the poor man in the hospital. One day a Native American (woodhicks did not use the politically correct terms that I use) walked up from Cambria County looking for the bully Abe Bloom.

Abe was about to hook a homemade plow up to a yoke of oxen. (Homemade plows were not as heavy as the later all-steel plows. The homemade plow had a metal blade and the rest was wood, but they weighed close to 200 pounds.) The Native American asked Abe, "Can you tell me where this big Abe Bloom lives?" Abe picked up the plow by the handle and pointed the other end at his home and said, "I live down there." The Native American turned around and walked home without confronting Abe.

Miles Dent

Huntley tells us of another white-hat bully, Miles Dent. Dent was an extraordinarily strong man standing six foot two inches tall, weighing two hundred pounds, with very large hands and wearing a size fourteen boot. He lived six miles up the Bennett's Branch (three miles above the Mix family, the one that produced the silent film cowboy star Tom Mix. This area, still known as Dents Run, is the site of Pennsylvania's elk herd).

From Huntley's book:

> Dent was a crew member on a spar raft piloted by Jake English. After Jake sold the raft in Lock Haven and before heading home, the boys decided to get some refreshments in a saloon near the train station. They fondly called this area the Barbary Coast. The boys often stopped at this barroom, but the bartender had never treated them to a free drink. When they asked him for one, he refused, saying that no respectable bartender would treat at his own bar. Miles went outside the saloon and picked up a railroad frog. (A railroad frog is the part of the railroad track where one track splits into two sets of tracks or lines, specifically where the right track of one line passes through the left track of the other line. This piece of track weighs about 600 pounds.) Miles carried the frog into the saloon and placed it on the bar, saying, "Come boys, let's go home." The bartender panicked and served up the free drinks. Before leaving Dent returned the frog to its original place.

> Tim Crone, a pugilistic Bully from Lock Haven, claimed to be the champion of the West Branch of the Susquehanna, and when he heard about Dent's exploits, traveled to Dents Run to challenge Dent. When Crone arrived, Dent was plowing with a yoke of oxen in the field across the creek from his home.

> Crone asked Dent, "Do you know where Miles Dent lives?"

> Dent took the plow by the handle, raised it, and pointed to his house, saying, "I live over there."

> Crone mumbled, "Thank you." Then walked away [461–63].

Miles Dent, 1884.

This story was probably attributed to every "white-hat bully" along both branches of the Susquehanna.

Ambrose Campbell and Len Childs

What happened when two white-hat bullies" met? Kahler's article tells of one such incident:

One Sunday two different logging crews met in the Blackwell Hotel, in the little village of Blackwell, on Pine Creek. [Blackwell is at the downstream end of the Pine Creek Gorge, or as most Pennsylvanians call it, the "Grand Canyon of Pennsylvania." Even today if you stop at the Blackwell Inn, they will entertain you with stories about fights during the logging days.] A natural amphitheater existed behind the village where they fought. They did not allow children to watch fights, but the children hid in the woods around the amphitheater where they could see.

Ambrose Campbell, the Jam Breaker at Renovo, was with one crew; his Uncle Billy had made a reputation as a "White-hat Bully," so Brose was just carrying on the family tradition. The other camp's Bully was Len Childs. On a Sunday afternoon both camps were wanting some entertainment.

Brose Campbell slid up to the bar and asked for a drink, and when he reached for it Len Childs picked it up and downed it. Brose requested another drink, which was set before him, and again Len repeated his act. Brose ordered another drink, and the men in the bar all stood back from the bar, for they realized too well what was going to take place. This time when Len took the glass to drink it, Brose's fist shot to his mouth, breaking the glass and cutting Len's mouth and face.

That was the start, as they tangled into each other. The bar was cleaned of all bottles, mirrors broken, the stove upset, the bar-rail torn off, windows all smashed out and most of the chairs broken. The pair then worked on each other on the outside and fought to exhaustion, but neither gave in. Neither was able to stand, but continued the battle from his knees. The crews made no move to stop them, until the men crawled near the other and kicked out with their feet and then lay sprawled upon the ground. Finally, both crews decided it had gone as far as it could, so each took their man with them, but before departure both Brose and Len vowed they would fight on next sight and meeting.

Their next meeting happened in the Sanbach House, in Wellsboro, Pa., two and a half years later. [Wellsboro is north of the Pine Creek Gorge near the New York border.] Both men were dressed in their best clothes; Len was boarding at the hotel, while Brose was in town on business. Both were in the bar having a drink, when they recognized each other. Each finished his own drink and then announced to those present at the bar that they had a fight to settle once and for all. They selected the stable yard, back of the hotel as the place, made it known that neither wanted any outside help or interference, and then took off their coats and went to it. They drew a big crowd, and again fought until both were exhausted and lay on the ground. It was rough and bloody for the both of them, and at last they agreed to call it a draw and shook hands. Then the two of them, with assistance, went into the hotel to wash and clean up. They became the best of friends, which I can personally vow for. About thirty years or more after that fight had taken place, I [Kahler] was visiting Brose at his home, when a man came to visit him too. Brose introduced Len Childs to me and they then related the incidents (15).

Big Bob Gowdy

Kahler recorded this story told by Joseph C. Budd, a small store proprietor on the Loyalsock Creek:

Big Bob Gowdy was the Bully of the Sock, a powerfully built fellow with great chest and heavy arm muscles like steel. He was what the woodsmen called a crusher. His method of fighting was to grab hold of a man and squeeze and crush in his chest, or break his back.

Another tactic was to rush at a man, then lower his head and crash in, knocking the breath out of the fellow and putting him to the ground, where he delighted to kick in the ribs and trample the man with his steel corks. [The woodhicks pronounced calk as cork. A calk is a downward projection on a horse shoe to prevent it from slipping. Golfers have calks on the bottom of their golf shoes. When kicked with calked boots the woodhicks called it "Feeding Them Leather."] Gowdy had a contemptible streak in him, and would pick on a man for no reason other than his own dislike.

I [Budd speaking] had a store at Slabtown [the village no longer exists] and sold supplies of all kinds to the lumber camps and the men along the creek. Gowdy had a job and a large account on my books at the time.

The veterinarian, a pleasant Englishman and very fine doctor, rode a dandy horse, with a saddle bag to carry his medicines and tools, and was proud of his horse. The very first time Gowdy saw him he took a dislike to the guy and told him to get out of the Loyalsock. Well, the little Doc paid no attention and went about his own business, for he was in great demand, since horses in the woods were very valuable and a good veterinarian was hard to find.

One day while Doc was in the store and his horse tied to the rail out in front, Gowdy spied the horse, came up and cut off the reins, slashed the bag and straps, hit the horse and sent it running down the creek road. Somebody caught the horse and brought it to the Doc. He was mad when he saw the damage, but he ignored the insult of Gowdy. It only added fuel to Gowd's hatred, and he called him all kinds of foul names at every chance. Another time he took a chestnut burr and put it under the horse's tail, and then jerked the tail down hard into it. The horse screamed and reared in pain, and later it got infected. Gowdy laughed at the Doc and did everything to irritate the fellow.

One day in early spring, the creek was high and the logs were on the drive, and men were busy on both sides of the stream. Gowdy and his crew were on one side and Doc was coming up the other side, when Gowdy spied him and started to yell across at him and call him vile names. Finally, having taken enough, he told Gowdy he was ready to put him in his place. He came up to the store and tied his horse to the rail and then announced that he was going to square accounts with Gowdy.

We tried to dissuade him from the attempt, as nobody thought he was equal to such a big man as Gowdy, but Doc walked down along the creek until he was opposite Gowdy. Doc shouted that he was prepared and ready to fight and settle the matter. Gowdy yelled back for him to come down to the bridge, but the little Doc told him to stay right where he was, as he was coming across to him. Before we realized what was happening, the Doc was in the icy stream filled with logs, making his way toward the other side. We tried to call him back, but he just kept going, and none of us thought he would ever make it. As he reached the other side and was trying to get out, Gowdy ran to him and gave him a kick in the face sending him in again. Every time he tried to get out Gowdy would kick or jump on his hands, but at last he finally got on the bank. He shouted his challenge at Gowdy and told him to fight like a man and not as a skunk that he was. Gowdy lowered his head and came charging at the little Doc, who suddenly jumped aside, which let the Bully go crashing his head against a tree. A big cheer went up on both sides of the stream for the Doc.

Gowdy changed his tactics, and again came rushing with head uplifted this time. Doc changed position too, and no tree was in line now, and Gowdy came fast at him. As they came together, Gowdy made a grab to take his famous squeeze hold, but he did not make it; for the Doc made a quick step aside and swung a mighty fist to his jaw which dazed the mighty Gowdy. Before he could recover the Vet followed with more, sending the man to the ground in a sprawl. With Gowdy upon the ground, the Doc now took over in woodhick fashion. He jumped and kicked Gowdy in the face, blood poured over it, and he proceeded to batter his head against a big stone and finally kicked in his ribs. Again and again the Bully shouted that he had enough, but the little doc told him to yell it louder. When the men on the opposite side confirmed that they could hear him there, Doc gave him the final kick and walked away; the man who defeated Gowdy. Nobody had ever known that the Doc could fight, or that he had taken fencing and boxing lessons back in England while a student at Oxford.

Bob Gowdy left the Sock as soon as he could, and on my account book he left a charge of more than twelve thousand dollars. This was a big blow to me and I thought it all lost, as Gowdy had left the area. Then one day, about six years later, who should walk into the store but Gowdy. He looked fine and came right up to me and said, "Mr. Budd, I come to pay off my bill to you, how much do I owe?" I took out the book and gave him the amount. He never looked at the book but said, "Budd, your figures are correct, but you forgot the interest at six percent for the time you waited."

"No, I do not want interest, I am glad to get the principle, we will let the interest go." Gowdy settled the amount in full and included the interest too.

I invited him to come over to the house and visit with us, but he declined. He told me he wanted to get away from the area as soon as he could, and that the only reason he returned was to pay off his debt to me. He had gone into Virginia after his beating, taken on a lumber operation and been successful in business. He always remembered his obligations and paid them, and even in the Loyal-sock, where he was licked, he did not want anyone to say that Bob Gowdy owed them money. He then departed and never returned to the Sock area (8).

Even "black-hat bullies" had honor sometimes.

11

The Mississippi Watershed

The movement west of the Alleghenies started after the French and Indian War, over Forbes' Road, which was built in 1758 from Carlisle, Pennsylvania, to present day Pittsburgh. Braddock's Road — built from Cumberland, Maryland, to within nine miles of Pittsburgh in 1755 — also brought settlers after the war. The Cumberland, or National, Road built in 1818 did the same. Pioneers wanting to go farther west built rafts to take the easy route down the Ohio. Olean, New York, on the Allegheny River also served as a jumping off point to the Midwest. When the Erie Canal opened in 1825, settlers wanting to go to the Midwest came west on the canal to Olean and down the Allegheny and Ohio rivers.

Unlike the Susquehanna Watershed, the Allegheny and Ohio Rivers are much deeper and could be used the year around. Traffic continues today on these rivers.

Early Roads West

Ringwalt gives an example of these rivers being used as public highways.

Movements on the Ohio, in which arks were used for the transportation of emigrating families, with all their live stock, I [Ringwalt] describe in an account of Major Stephen H. Long's expedition from Pittsburgh to the Rocky mountains, performed in 1819 and 1820. It says: "The little village of Olean, New York, on the Allegheny River, has been for many years a point of embarkation, where great numbers of families, migrating from the northern and eastern states, have exchanged their various methods of slow and laborious progression by land for the more convenient one of the navigation of the Ohio. From Olean, downward the Allegheny and Ohio bear along their currents fleets of rude arks laden with cattle, horses, household furniture, agricultural implements, and numerous families having all their possessions embarked on the same bottom, and floating onward toward that imaginary region of happiness and contentment, which, like the "town of the brave and generous spirits," the expected heaven of the aboriginal American, lies often "beyond the place where the sun goes down."

This method of transportation, though sometimes speedy and convenient, is attended with uncertainty and danger. A moderate wind, blowing up the river, produces such swells in some parts of the Ohio as to endanger the safety of the arks, and the heavy, unmanageable vessels are with difficulty so guided in their descent as to avoid the planters, sunken logs, and other concealed obstructions to the navigation of the Ohio. We have known many instances of boats of this kind so suddenly sunk as only to afford time for the escape of the persons on board (12).

The Allegheny and Ohio Rivers

Rafting on these rivers was best described by French in his article "Allegheny River Rafting."

Rafting lumber from Warren County, Pennsylvania began about 1800 and it reached its maximum in the decade, 1830 to 1840. The early history of Warren County abounds with very interesting incidents along the larger Allegheny.

After the purchase of Louisiana in 1804, the hardy lumbermen decided to extend their markets for pine beyond Pittsburgh, Wheeling, Cincinnati and Louisville and go, in fact, to New Orleans with pine and cherry lumber. So large boats were built in the winter of 1805 and 1806 at many mills. Seasoned lumber, of the best quality was loaded into the flat boats and they untied on April 1, 1806, for the run of two thousand miles.

It was in defiance of "All Fools' Day," but they sold both lumber and boats. Clear pine lumber sold for forty dollars per one thousand feet in New Orleans,

Allegheny River.

double the Pittsburgh price. For three years thereafter the mills of Warren County sent boats to New Orleans loaded with lumber, and the men returned on foot. Joseph Mead, Abraham Davis and John Watt took boats through in 1807, coming back via Philadelphia on coastal sailing ships.

The pilots and men returned by river boats or on foot, as best they could. The markets along the Ohio from Pittsburgh to St. Louis soon took all the lumber from the Allegheny mills, and the longer trips were gladly discontinued. It was in 1850 that there came the first lumber famine at Pittsburgh. Owing to the low price of lumber and an unfavorable winter for the forest work, few rafts of lumber and board timber went down the Allegheny on the spring freshets, but the November floods brought one hundred rafts that sold for more favorable prices than had previously prevailed. Clear (no knots) pine lumber sold readily for eighteen dollars, and common pine lumber for nine dollars per one thousand feet.

The renown of these prices stimulated lumbering on the Allegheny headwaters and the larger creeks. So the demand for lumber was supplied, and the railroads soon began to bring lumber from many sawmills. The board timber was hued on four sides, so there was only five inches of wane on each of the four corners. These rafts of round-square timber were sold by square feet to Pittsburgh sawmills.

Rafts of pine boards at headwater mills were made up of platforms, sixteen feet square and from eighteen to twenty-five courses thick, nine pins or "grubs" holding boards in place as rafted. Four or five platforms were coupled in tandem with three-feet "cribs" at each joint, making an elastic piece seventy-three feet or nine-two feet long for a four or five-platform piece, as the case might be, sixteen feet wide.

At Larrabee, or at Millgrove, four of these pieces were coupled into a Warren fleet, 32 feet wide, 149 and or 187 feet long. [Larrabee is not on the Pennsylvania or New York maps.]

Four Warren pieces or fleets were put together at Warren to make up a Pittsburgh fleet. (A Pittsburgh fleet was 64 feet wide and 299 to 374 feet long.) At Pittsburgh four or more Pittsburgh fleets were coupled to make an Ohio River fleet. (An Ohio fleet was 128 feet wide and 598 to 748 feet long.) These became very large, often covered more than two acres of surface containing about 1,500,000 feet of lumber at Cincinnati or at Louisville. They each had a hut for sheltering the men and for cooking their food, often running all night on the Ohio River. To find where the shore was on a very dark night, they would throw potatoes toward the shore. If they heard a splash they were far enough offshore, if they didn't, they would row their rafts further offshore. These men were of rugged bodies and daring minds. (The area around Roulette, Pennsylvania, is a very large potato growing area today.)

The Allegheny, Ohio and Mississippi Rivers were formed by wearing down through the Appalachian Plateau and the area behind the plateau. They were deeper than the Susquehanna River, with fewer riffles to hazard the rafts, especially if they ran such large rafts at night.

French's description of the oar or sweep was the same as used on all other rivers and creeks:

The oars or sweeps were used to guide a raft of lumber along the flood-tides, crooked streams, and over a dozen mill dams to the broader river below.

From the Allegheny, boats or scows, 30 feet long and 11 feet wide, carried loads of baled hay, butter, eggs and other farm produce to the oil fields of

Venango County (Oil City, Pennsylvania area) in the 60<ft>s, sold there and took oil in barrels to the refinery at Pittsburgh; then sold the scows to carry coal or goods down the Ohio. Mr. Westerman built five boats at Roulette, Pennsylvania, about 1870, 40 feet long and 12 feet wide, loaded them with lumber and shingles and started for Pittsburgh, but the boats were too long for the dams and broke up at Burtville, the first dam below Roulette about two miles.

Much of the pine timber of the western half of Potter County was cut in sawlogs and sent to mills at Millgrove and Weston's in log drives down the Allegheny River and Oswayo Creek into the State of New York. The lumber was shipped via the Genessee Valley Canal to Albany and New York City and other points on the Hudson River. (Potter County straddles the Eastern Continental Divide, with the western waters flowing into the Mississippi Watershed and the eastern waters flowing into the Chesapeake Bay Watershed.)

The first steamboat to steam up the river from Warren was in 1830. It was built in Pittsburgh by Archibald Tanner (Warren's first merchant) and David Dick and others of Meadville. The steamer, called the Allegheny, traveled to Olean, New York, returned and went out of commission. [This is another case of the river being different than the Susquehanna River.]

The late Major D. W. C. James furnished the incident of the Allegheny voyage. A story told by James Follett regarding the trip of the Allegheny from Warren, illustrates the lack of speed of steam boats on the river at that early day. While the steamer was passing the Indian reservation, some twenty odd miles above Warren, the famous chief, Cornplanter, paddled his canoe out to the vessel, and actually paddled his small craft up stream and around the Allegheny, the old chief giving a vigorous war whoop as he accomplished the proud feat.

Chief Cornplanter, alias John O'Bail, first took his young men to Clarion County, about 1795 to learn the method of lumbering. In 1796 he built a saw mill on Jenneseedaga Creek, later named Cornplanter Run, in Warren County, and rafted lumber down the Allegheny to Pittsburgh for many years. Tributary streams, such as Clarion, Tionesta, and Oswago contributed rafts each year to make up the fleets that descended the Allegheny River from 1796 to 1874.

We must mention the Hotel Boyer, on the Duquesne Way, on the Allegheny River bank near the "Point" at Pittsburgh, where the raftmen and lumbermen foregathered, traded, ate and drank together, after each trip.

Indians were good pilots, but had to be kept sober on the raft. "Bootleggers" along the river often boated out to the rafts and relieved the drouthy (dry) crews, dispensing bottles of "red-eye" from the long tops of the boots they wore.

The Mississippi River

Both Larson and Russell described rafting on the Mississippi River, and the raftsmen used the same methods as were used on the Allegheny and Ohio Rivers in the early part of the 1800s. Both books show pictures of large fleets of rafts (250 feet wide and 600 feet long) lashed together and being pushed down the river using paddle wheel steamboats to market.

It is understandable that things were done the same way in other lumbering areas because many of the men interviewed for oral histories in Pennsylvania had talked about going to West Virginia, the Carolinas and Louisiana.

Appendix: Ark and Raft Construction

In some way this was the most difficult section to write. Many of the old writers told about their adventures on the river, but not how arks and rafts were constructed. Usually a master spar maker supervised the manufacturing of the spars and only he understood how and why the rafts were constructed as they were. This was true of the squared timber, board and round log rafts, as well as the arks. Also, what they did know, they felt was common knowledge and therefore did not go into detail when describing their work.

A case in point is: how did the spar raft builder get ten spars, each about 30 inches in diameter, into a raft only 26 feet wide? No tree grows perfectly straight. The white pine comes close, but all 90 foot long spars had slight bends. When a spar was put into the water it would roll over on its side with the bowed part sticking out to one side. Ten of these bowed spars could not be put into a raft, as it would easily exceed 26 feet in width. The bowed part of each spar was different and they could not be fitted together like spoons.

There were several hints, such as belly down, mark the concave side and cut a tenon on the butt end, but they do not fully explain how it was done. Mitchell gave an excellent description of how square timber rafts were constructed, but even he fell short in explaining it. I turned to O. Lynn Frank, a retired forest ranger who had befriended many of the old woodhicks and raftsmen. His explanation is given below. Once I understood it seemed obvious.

In Chapter 2, a general description of how Michael Cryder may have built his ark was given; however, below are detailed instructions of how an ark was built. Each section below gives a detailed description as to how various tasks were performed.

Ark Construction

The best information on ark construction came from an article in the Bath *Plaindealer* newspaper dated March to May of 1887. This knowledge is combined with other information found during my research and personal correspondence with O. Lynn Frank of Clearfield, Pennsylvania.

Hulls for arks were constructed upside down, using three square timbers, usually of white pine, with two timbers 55 feet long and one 75 feet long. The

This ark, on the West Branch of the Susquehanna River in 1898, was used to house and feed log drivers during the log drives. Arks that moved flour and other farm products from New York and Pennsylvania to Baltimore, Maryland, looked very much like this one (courtesy Clearfield County Historical Society, Clearfield, Pennsylvania).

timbers were placed eight feet apart, with the center timber 20 feet longer than the two side timbers and protruding ten feet at each end. To make the end of the arks pointed, two timbers about 13 feet long were used to join the side timbers with the ends of the center timber. The timbers were mortised together and pinned with white oak or ash pins. This was done at both ends. The three timbers were placed down so that their midpoint would lay over a log, in order to have the bow and stern ends of the timbers bend earthward. When they turned the ark over, the calked seams between the bottom boards would then close tightly (French, Colcord 66). Next they pegged 16 foot pine planks, two inches thick and two to three feet wide, to the timbers with white oak or white ash pegs; no nails were ever used. Flax or wool, saturated with tar or pitch, was driven down between the planks with a wedge to caulk the seams. Then the waterproof hull was turned over onto skids near the water's edge, where it could be pushed into the water. This required the strength of many men, much like an old fashioned barn raising. These events usually became an occasion for a community party, often a hog roast with other eats washed down with plenty of whiskey. After the party was over, they mortised four to five foot long studs into the side timbers to form the frame for a shanty aboard the ark, to protect the cargo from the weather. They planked the sides of the shanty and added a rounded roof. Even on the West Branch when arks were no longer used to take produce to market, but to feed and house the log drivers and their horses during the long drives to the boom in Williamsport, the arks had rounded roofs. The roof was made of thin boards that were easy to bend across the rounded frame. To make sure the spring rains did not leak through the roof and down onto the wooden barrels of flour and cause them to swell up, losing their airtight seal, pitch was used to seal the roof. The airtight barrels enabled the Baltimore merchants to ship flour to the Caribbean and Europe without spoiling.

A pine plank false bottom was added to provide protection from bilge water for bulk grain storage and wooden barrels. The area between the two bottoms provided a pooling area for water seeping into the ark.

Arks were guided just like the rafts, with a sweep or oar at both ends to move it right or left in the current, but the current determined the ark's speed. An ark sweep was shorter that those on rafts and was mounted on stem posts, one on the bow and one on the stern. Room inside the shanty was left for the small crew. Arks were much easier to handle than rafts, because they were much smaller and were never fleeted up like rafts. It would take two men two weeks to build an ark, and the cost of labor and material was around $75.00. In Havre de Grace the ark owners recovered about half their construction costs by selling the ark for its lumber for about $30.00. The cost of labor was about a dollar a day. Fifty to sixty arks made the trip to Baltimore from Steuben County, New York, each year.

Arks are celebrated as the symbol of pioneer life in Stueben County, and in 1995 the residents constructed a Bicentennial Ark and floated it down the Susquehanna to Havre de Grace, Maryland. The ark was one third scale and required nearly 1,000 volunteer hours to construct. Compare this with two men building a full scale ark in only two weeks or a total of 360 hours (15 hours per day and six days a week). They had Sundays off except during the rafting and ark running seasons. There are two differences in the shanty between this scale ark and the real ones; it is out of proportion and the roof is peaked, not rounded. The hull is a very good representation of an ark.

Board Raft Construction

This description of constructing a board raft was in the Bath, New York, newspaper, the *Plaindealer*, of March 5, 1887. In New York State, the West Branch term of "rafting-in" for raft construction was never used. Also, this knowledge is combined with other information found during my research and personal correspondence with O. Lynn Frank of Clearfield, Pennsylvania.

The trees were felled as described below, and cut into 16 foot sections. The early carriages used to move the logs back and forth during sawing would only

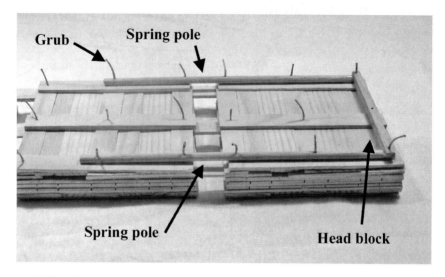

Model board raft with spring poles. Such poles were used to prevent wrecking when a raft went through chutes and riffles.

Board raft fleet on the Clarion River. Note there are no spring poles on these rafts and the head blocks are modified from the description. Coupling boards line the edge of each raft. Also, note the coupling between the two rafts and the sweeps. Note how the fleet snakes when rowing across the river. The raftsmen wore dark clothing to hide dirt and long frock coats to keep warm (courtesy O. Lynn Frank, Clearfield, Pennsylvania).

hold 16 foot logs. To build a board raft nine grubs were needed for each platform. The older men often made their living preparing grubs by digging out small oaks trees by the roots, or hickory saplings, about two inches in diameter and four feet long. With the bark peeled off the grubs, the roots were trimmed at the end, leaving a bulb about four inches in diameter.

To build a platform, three keel planks were selected. The keel planks, about three inches thick and any width over six inches, usually a foot or two, had three holes bored in each plank. One hole was in the middle and other holes at each end, about a foot from the ends. Each hole was four inches in diameter, two thirds of the way through the plank, and two inches in diameter the rest of the way. Three keel planks were placed next to a stream eight feet apart with the four inch side of the holes down. A grub was pushed up through each hole so that the bulb on the grub fit into the larger recessed hole on the bottom side of the plank. This helped prevent the bulb from being broken off when the keel planks hit a rock going down the river.

Three more coupling boards were bored with two inch holes (all the rest of the holes in the board raft platform were two inch holes) in the same manner as the keel planks. One coupling board was slipped over the three grubs at the front end of the keel planks. Another coupling board went over the three grubs at the rear end of the keel planks. The last coupling board, placed over the three grubs at the middle of the keel planks, made a strong 16 foot square frame. Boards of the same thickness filled the spaces between these three coupling boards until they laid down a very snug layer. A second set of three coupling boards drilled in the same manner were slipped over the grubs parallel to the keel boards, holding down the first layer. Then the platform was pushed into the water, where it received enough layers, each being transverse to the layer below, until the platform was about two feet thick. Building platforms was a wet job.

When constructing the next to the last layer, which ran in the same direction as the keel boards, the two outside coupling boards were moved back so that the hole in the front end of each board fit over the middle grub and the middle hole over the last grub. A last hole, about four feet behind the middle hole, was drilled so it would fit over the first set of grubs on the following platform, leaving about a two-foot gap between platforms. The next to last layer was filled in and the last layer was placed transverse on top of the coupling board layer. Three more coupling boards were laid down in the same direction as the keel planks and slipped over the grubs.

The grubs were drawn up tightly using a tool called a witch (waterman's lexicon) and the side of the grub was cut where it emerged from the last coupling board and a small wedge driven in to keep it in place. This made a staunch structure that would withstand any water and much pounding. A witch was a long handled stick which clamped onto the grub with a fulcrum near the grub, so that the long handle, when pushed down, would draw up the grub.

Ten to twelve of these platforms made a complete raft. There was always some space left between each platform to afford play and to permit the craft to bend slightly to accommodate itself to the breakers and keep it above the water.

Head blocks were made for each end of the raft to support the oars or sweeps, and to reinforce the ends of the rafts against digging into the water while running down riffles and chutes. They were made of oak, cut six inches wide, ten inches tall, and 16 feet long. Three holes were drilled in the head block so it would fit down over the three front grubs. Before sliding the head block over the grubs, a gain cut or mortice was made in each end of the head blocks on the under side. Next, a spring pole was cut, probably of hickory, five or six inches in diameter and close to 30 feet in length. On the bottom end of the spring pole a tenon was cut to fit into the mortice. With a hole drilled in the tenon, the tenon end of two spring poles were placed over the front corner grubs. Then the head block was slipped over the grubs, which wedged the whole apparatus down securely. The spring poles were pressed down on top of the coupling boards and the other end drilled and slipped over the outside grubs on the second platform and wedged down. This lifted up the front end of the platform, scow like, to enable it to ride over the swells and meet less resistance from the water. The rear platform was rigged with a similar head block and spring poles. If the spring poles were close to 30 feet long, they could be wedged down on the first and second grub on the second platform, making a very strong scow-like end.

These spring poles were not used on the board rafts on the West Branch, Clarion and Allegheny Rivers in Pennsylvania, as far as I could determine by researching and asking O. Lynn Frank. Also, William Fox did not mention spring poles in his construction of board rafts on the Allegheny. However, researching the Chemung Canal (Whitford), which opened in 1833, to siphon off the Susquehanna traffic to the Erie Canal, I found a reason for adding these spring poles. The canal required a feeder dam constructed below Elmira, 645 feet across the river, and four and one half feet high. Rafts and arks going down the river were a major part of the New York economy and provisions for these water craft to pass through dams were a necessity. By 1838 the steep decline of the Chemung Chute caused the water to erode the stream bed below the chute for a distance of 120 feet, and to a depth of from 12 to 20 feet. This caused the worn out chute to wreck board rafts by breaking off the front platforms and stoving the rafts. A spring pole would have strengthened the first two platforms and may have helped to prevent the wrecking of board rafts.

The reason for putting spring poles on the rear platform was that if a submerged rock or sand bar was hit with the front platforms, the current would catch the stern of the raft and twist the raft around, pulling it off the grounding, and the stern became the bow and vise versa.

In the center of each head block, a stout wooden pin was inserted, usually oak, two inches in diameter and sometimes over two feet in length, called the oar pin.

Each raft was supplied with several long, slender poles or saplings of elm or hickory 15 or 20 feet in length. The bulb on the butt end was made flat by shaving two sides, and it was perforated with a two inch hole, called a halyard, used in landing and tying up the raft. The perforated end was slipped over a grub, while the brush or small end was taken on shore and twisted around a tree or stump. It was fastened by means of hickory withes, of which a good supply was always on board for service. Withes were the four to six foot green ends of hickory branches that were almost as strong as steel cables. They were also used in making spar rafts, but don't try looking them up in your dictionary. Withes were also part of the watermen or raftsmen's lexicon on the Susquehanna River and its tributaries.

When ropes and cables became common and cheap, these halyards were dispensed with. Each raft was also supplied with a stout iron wood staddle five to six inches thick and 12 to 15 feet long called a "grouzer," which, in case of need was thrust down through the space between the platforms to ground (bottom of the river), to act as a drag, to check the headway of the raft and aid in landing. Grouser is also part of the watermen or raftsmen's lexicon.

Below the Chemung Canal Dam, east of Elmira, two of these rafts were lashed side by side with short coupling boards extending from a grub on one raft to a grub on the other, designated a fleet. Here one pilot and extra crew members returned upriver to get another set of rafts. One pilot and six crew members took the fleet down the river to Tioga Point, where the Chemung River enters the North Branch of the Susquehanna River in Pennsylvania. Here three crew members were sent home, and the pilot and crew of three took the fleet to market.

One cabin and one set of cooking utensils was sufficient for the fleet. The rafts were usually freighted with a small lot of choice boards, shingles and staves, sometimes other commodities. Occasionally the pilot and other persons going south would take their horses and carriage aboard to ride or drive back.

Muley saws (water powered saws) could cut about 1,000 board feet a day. Since a raft platform made of one inch boards and 24 layers (making the platform about two feet thick) contained 6,144 board feet, each platform represented one week's sawing by a watermill. A raft with 12 platforms probably represented a winter's work for one sawmill. Each fleet of board rafts that were two platforms wide and 12 platforms long weighed at least 442,368 pounds or over 221 tons. Green white pine weighed 36 pounds per cubic foot. A fleet was about 34 feet wide and about 215 feet long.

Manufacturing Sticks

The information for this section came from many sources. Most of the boys along the river grew up on farms, learned to chop by clearing land, and were good axemen by the time they were 17. Quite a large amount of timber was also made by the owners who lived on the farms (McGovern, *Rafting Trips*). Most of these men took great pride in their chopping, and whether chopping down a tree or hewing the side of a square timber stick, it was impossible to tell where one chop ended and another chop started. The finished chop looked like it had been cut with a planer and sanded smooth. Today hewers earn good money making decorative rafters for homes.

In the woodhick's parlance a stick was a spar, square timber or a round log that would be put into a raft and run down the river to market (Mitchell 21). All three of these were selected, marked and felled the same way. The spar was made by a master spar maker; they required the greater skill because they were made from the largest trees. Square timber and round logs were usually made by a woodhick skilled in felling trees and a hewer to make the tree into stick.

Spars were used to make ship masts, booms and yards, and square timbers were used in the building of bridges and dams, and for the support structure in ships, barns, large buildings, docks and warehouses. Round logs were sold to sawmills to be sawed into boards.

First the owner of the raft needed to determine how many sticks he would need. If he were going to make a spar raft he would need 20 spars for each raft. Each raft would consist of two platforms with ten spars each. Square timber rafts were usually planned to be three hundred feet long with five platforms, one each of 40, 50, 60, 70 and 80 feet long. A timber raft of this size usually took from 65 to 80 sticks. Round log rafts were made to take sticks down the river to sawmills, and rafts made of round logs contained any number of sticks.

The number of trees selected for felling always included several extra trees to compensate for breakage in felling, defects in the tree and loss in transportation. In 1874, George W. Huntley (330) from the Sinnemahoning Creek had a contract to deliver 100 spars to Marietta. He selected 111 trees to be felled. Luckily he did, for the Algerians (lumber thieves) stole six, he broke the biggest one and the remaining four were sawed into boards (Huntley 354). William McGovern told about making a square timber raft in 1880. They selected 100 trees to be felled and used the best 70 sticks to make their raft (McGovern, Rafting Trips).

When selecting trees for making sticks, all trees were appraised the same — some like spar trees, more critical than others. First, was the tree tall enough to make a spar? A good spar was 90 feet long, or longer with an 18 inch diameter at the top. In the primeval forest the pine tree's first branches were often 80 to 90 feet above the ground. Second, was the tree straight enough to make a spar? Trees are not absolutely straight (R.D. Tonkin 89). All trees have a little curve or bow in their trunks (Mitchell 23). The master spar maker would determine if the curve was acceptable. The bow can be straightened by the ropes and tackle on the ship (R.D. Tonkin 89).

"Before the tree was cut, it was examined by the eye as to straightness, etc., and the side selected for the face (concave side) was marked." (Mitchell 21) All trees selected to be raft sticks were marked in this manner. Why they did this will be evident when we get to constructing the different rafts.

Preparing a bed for the tree was the next step. To fell the tree the master spar maker selected a spot where the tree was to fall by driving a stake two to three inches into the ground, so that when the tree fell it would drive the stake all the way into the ground. The position where the tree came to final rest, or its bed, was selected to protect the tree from breaking. How the spar haulers got it out of the bed to the landing was not the concern of the master spar maker. Often a number of small trees were cut down over the bed to soften the tree's fall and snow was also a great help in felling a big tree (Mitchell 23). A 15 to 20 inch diameter tree or log was placed across the path the tree would fall in, about 20 feet from the stump. The butt of the falling tree would strike the log placed across this path. This acted as a fulcrum and saved breakage at the top. There was no danger of a break at or near the butt. The cutter tried to throw the tree into heaviest hemlock or hardwood timber to ease it down. Breaking down this smaller timber eased the tall pine to the ground. Trees that were cut to make spars were cut close to the ground so that as much straight trunk as possible was available to make the spar (Huntley 404). This method was also used to fell square timbers and round logs to prevent them from breaking. All the felling was done with axes as late at the early 1880s (McGovern, *Rafting Trips*). Later the tree was notched with an axe and then sawed down from the backside. If the tree broke during felling it was sawed into logs 26 inches long and split into shingles to be loaded on top of the raft and taken to market.

Manufacturing a Stick into a Spar

Once the tree was on the ground the top and any branches were removed. Then the men moved it to a spot where it could be jacked around until the face (the marked concave side) was up. The chopped end was sawed off and a carpenter's level was used to mark off a horizontal tenon on both ends. With a saw they cut down through the spar about eighteen inches from the end and chopped away the wood to the end of the spar to make one side of the tenon. This was done at both ends of the spar, and then the spar was jacked around until its face was down, and the carpenter's level was used again to mark off the other sides of the tenons on both ends. The excess wood was removed in the same way. Then two four inch holes were bored down through the tenon on the butt end and one four inch hole through the tenon on the top end (Frank phone conservation). After the bark was removed, the 12 feet at the butt end was hewn into an octagon shape so that this 12 feet had the same diameter

(Huntley 404). Axe marks were not allowed on the spar. Reducing the spar to an octagon shape made it easier to fit into the raft, and if the spars were shipped overseas, the butt end was further reduced to 16 sides to save shipboard space. This done, the spar was ready to be hauled or skidded to the landing. When all 20 spars were made, the master spar maker's job was complete and he moved on to another site.

Manufacturing a Stick into a Square Timber

The head hewer was to the square timber as the master spar maker was to the spar. His job was to make the sticks into square timbers to fit into the raft. After the tree was cut down and the length measured, he would determine what length platform the stick would go into. The top was cut off, and the stick was moved to a location where it could be made into a square timber. The stick was turned with a cant hook or hoist jack so that the face or concave side was perpendicular to the ground.

The hewer then determined how much should be taken off to square up the timber. The timbers were not squared entirely, but left with unfinished corners called the "wane." Wanes were two to a maximum of four inches wide. An axeman would stand on the stick and notch the face plumb to the ground about every three feet, or closer if needed. The hewer made sure the axeman's scores were all the same depth so the timber would not show axe marks after it had been hewn. These notches were cut in even, and then the spaces between the notches were split off with a broad axe, which had a blade from ten to thirteen inches long. The resulting chips were called juggles. This process continued on the face side of the stick until all the spaces between the notches had been split off. The juggles were taken off the back or convex side in the same manner.

Then the stick was turned upon its back, or face up, and was made level, and one of the men would stand on the face with his feet spread apart, and in that manner would test when the stick was level (Mitchell 21). Some hewers turned the face down (McGovern, *Rafting Trips*).

The hewer judged how much would be taken off and then a tracing line was stretched on both sides of the face at that point. A trace line was a chalked line held tight along a log and snapped, leaving a white line to chop along (sometimes wood ashes were used instead of chalk). The line had to be snapped in the same plane as the hewer was going to chop or the line was useless.

The sides were scored plumb with the ground and just short of the tracing line before the juggles were split off. The hewer, like the axeman who chopped down the tree, was very meticulous about his chopping. When he was finished, it was impossible to see where one juggle stopped and the next started, for the full length of the timber showed no axe marks. Today some of their work graces fireplace mantels and open beam constructed homes.

The maker always put a keel mark across the stick at its middle so that the inspector could see the point at which the measuring was done. This was called scaling or determining the board feet in a stick.

There was some timber made called bill timber that was squared up twelve inches or nearly so without any wanes. This was made from selected trees, as nearly as possible the right size. It was a very wasteful method, but the timber was for special uses and brought a better price. It was not re-sawed.

A broad axe, with which the hewing was done, had a short handle, crooked out so that the hewer's hand would not come too close to the stick. There were both right and left handed hewers, and the left handed ones used an axe with the crook in the handle, just the reverse of the right handed one.

In the earlier days timber was so plentiful that only the better part of the tree was used, and the longest length cut was never over 60 feet. A 60 foot stick would be all that was made out of one tree, even if the tree were free from limbs and large enough and straight much farther up. This was soon changed and the whole tree fit for use was made into timber. Very often 100 feet of a tree would be used, but this would be made into two sticks. The first timber was made from 30 to 60 feet long, but later from 20 feet to 90 feet, and a very little above that length. Sometimes three sticks would be made from one tree (Mitchell 22). Pine timber was not usually made before the middle of September, as before that time the sap would stain black.

Timber makers paid little respect to hours, but began as soon as they could see and worked as long as they could see, and did their walking to and from the job before daylight and after dark. Timber makers worked in small crews, very seldom above five or six men. A large camp of timber makers was not known. Timber makers could make from 100 to 150 cubic feet per man per day. Very few accidents happened (Mitchell 21–22). The square timbers, like the spars, would lay in the woods until a snow made it possible to haul or skid them to their landing.

Building a Hauling or Skidding Road

Hauling or skidding roads were usually prepared during the summer or early fall months when there was no snow and the ground wasn't frozen. The road was built as straight as possible with long sweeping turns because men would be dragging spars up to 100 feet long with four to seven teams of horses. Cross poles eight to twelve inches in diameter were cut the width of the road and fastened six to ten feet apart over rough places, with sharp stones to carry the trailing end of the spar over these areas. A deep snow would help to protect the spars, but the haulers couldn't count on having that much snow. When snow was light, hauling was often done at night after the snow had frozen (R.D. Tonkin 222).

Along the road on downhill slopes where the spars could outrun the hauling teams, snubbing posts were planted in the ground when tree trunks weren't available. Snubbing posts were located on alternating sides of the road about 75 feet apart when using two 100-foot snubbing lines (R.D. Tonkin 99). Some spar haulers used 325 foot snubbing lines and probably placed the snubbing posts 300 feet apart (Mitchell 25).

Hauling or Skidding Spars

Hauling or skidding spars was quite difficult as a result of their great weight and length, and required good men with considerable experience to do it successfully. The spars first had to be moved onto a skidding road from the point where they lay. This often required the use of a block and tackle.

Spars had to be hauled on sleds made especially for the purpose. These sleds were made very heavy and strong, and longer than a sled for hauling timber, but not much wider since ordinary lumber roads were used. Eight horses were the usual number for hauling spars. The sled had a cross piece, called a bolster, for supporting the spar and this was rounded out in the middle about eight inches deep to help keep the spar in position on the sled. The spar was chained loosely in position on the bolster, so that it could roll without rocking the sled about too much, and was hauled by passing a chain through the hole in the end of the spar which was called the eye. This latter chain was fastened to the tongue of the sled by means of a staple and a wooden key, in order that the chain could be loosened at any time. This method was probably first adopted to permit the easy loosening of the spar from the sled in case of an accident.

All spars had to be snubbed when going down the hills, and this was done by means of two long ropes tied into the eye at the rear end (top) of the spar. Each rope in turn was placed around tree stumps or snubbing posts several times, forming a brake, the intensity of which depended upon the tightness with which the snubber held the free end of the rope. By the time one rope had been paid out, the snubber with the second rope had already made another hitch with his rope and took up the snubbing, while the first man hitched his rope to another stump farther down the hill, and so on, until the bottom of the hill was reached. Unfortunately, with the unevenness of narrow and crooked roads, some accidents and upsets were bound to happen. These problems had to be overcome by the tact of the haulers, who always carried along a double set of block and tackle.

A man rode each of the three leading teams and the man who guided the back team stood on the side of the sled. When the sled would sometimes be raised going over a knoll and was inclined to turn over toward the driver, he would have to jump over to the other side of the sled to save himself and to prevent the sled from overturning. In snubbing, in addition to the two men mentioned above who did the actual hitching, a third man was employed as a helper and in turn helped each man to carry his rope forward and make a new hitch. In order to give the men time to make these hitches, the teams were driven slowly, and men and teams soon became accustomed to the process.

The great majority of spars were not hauled a long distance. But Leavy, Mitchell and Company hauled spars off of Curry Run over a divide of western waters (Eastern Continental Divide) from six to nine miles and for one raft (20 spars), 11 miles. They hauled six rafts (120 spars) from what was then known as the green woods over the Penfield Road into Clearfield, a distance of eight to 11 miles. Coming down Moose Creek Road, 84 continuous hitches (snubs) were used, with 325 foot ropes (about five and one half miles). This hauling was done at both points with but one accident, which was caused by a rope breaking and one horse was made useless.

While eight horses usually made up a team, as many as 14 were used in hauling up some of the heavy grades (Mitchell 24–25). The smallest spars were hauled first, in order that the horses and men could learn to work together. This had the advantage of using the lightest loads to build coordination, but the disadvantage was that with each load hauled, the snubbing lines got a little bit weaker and the heaviest spars were hauled when the snubbing lines were at their weakest (R.D. Tonkin 92). R.D. Tonkin tells of one such snubbing line snapping, driving the spar into the five horse teams and men, pushing them down the hill and up over the spars piled at the landing. One horse was put out of its misery and the other horses never got over the accident (100).

Along the Sinnemahoning Creek the men cut the white pine trees between the dark of the moon in September and the dark of the moon in the following April, in order to prolong the wood's life and to prevent it from weather staining (Huntley 259). Weather staining was caused by too much sap in the wood when cut, which would turn the wood black.

For the winter of 1873–74, Huntley moved his spar camp to Short Bend Run on the First Fork of the Sinnemahoning, where he put in 50 spars. Short Bend Run was apparently below Walton, or where the East Fork joins the First Fork of the Sinnemahoning. The road out of Short Bend had some steep places, and one of the teamsters wanted to snub the spar down the road. The foreman was in a hurry, so he had the sled's runners wrapped with chains and the spar wrapped with a chain to slow the spar's run down the road. The teamsters objected, saying it was too dangerous for the horses.

The foreman said he had the road dirted (spread dirt over the snow to slow the spar down), and insisted that it was safe. The foreman gave the word to start and two teams of horses began pulling the spar down the road. The chain around the spar didn't create enough drag and the spar started to overtake the sled and horses. The horses moved faster trying to outrun the spar, but as the spar passed over the dirted road, the spar was stopped very suddenly, breaking the chain around the spar. The spar shot forward hitting one of the horses and breaking its back. The horse had to be killed. Horses usually got hurt when snubbing ropes broke, but this appeared to be poor judgment on the part of the foreman (Huntley 297–8).

The next year (1874–1875) Huntley moved up the creek to Jimmerson Fork (not on today's maps) on the East Fork of the Sinnemahoning. He also got a contract with F. G. and G. Churchman of Wilmington, Delaware, to deliver one hundred spars to Marietta for twenty five hundred dollars ($25.00 a spar). This was a much better price than saw logs were bringing and the best price for spars.

These spars were coming off the top of the mountain and because he had a horse killed the year before, Huntley ordered a manilla rope from Philadelphia, which was two and one fourth inches thick and 1,200 feet long. One post was placed at the top of the hill and several hitches were wrapped around the post, then the short end was tied to the spar, which was snubbed down the mountain. For the second spar, the short end was tied to it and snubbed down the mountain, pulling the long end up the hill. In this manner they snubbed 111 spars safely down into the valley (Huntley 330).

Landings or Rafting Grounds

The law compelled owners of the shores of streams to allow timber to be piled on their land until rafts were made up from it and floated away. The places used for timber in this way were generally called rafting grounds, and where many rafts were put in, it was very profitable to the owner of the land so used, as they were allowed to charge a reasonable amount, generally not more than $10.00 a raft, but sometimes higher according to the demand for room. Most of the large rafting grounds were near the junction of a stream with the river (Mitchell 26).

Oars or Sweeps

Each raft (spar, square timber and round log) had an oar placed at the forward and rear ends, and these oars were used for guiding the raft only. They consisted of a long stem pivoted on the end of the raft, with a blade on the water end. The stem projected back over the raft where, when the raft was in motion, it was raised high so as to lower the blade into the water. When in this position it was pushed to the opposite side of the raft by the oarsmen, where it was lowered, thus raising the blade out of the water. In this position it was carried back to the other side of the raft where it was again raised, and the same process gone through repeatedly.

The oar stems were usually 50 feet long and the blades 16 feet long. The blade, about two and one half inches thick at the back end or top, was placed into a mortise in the stem for about three and one half feet. The other end of the blade was about one and one quarter inches thick and 16 inches to 20 inches wide. The blades, pinned into the stem by one and one half inch round pins with a slight knob at one end, ran diagonally through the stem and wedged at the other end, so as to hold the blade very securely in the stem. The oar stems, usually about nine inches in diameter at the balancing point, narrowed down to about seven inches at the oar blade end. The other end of the stem narrowed down to about three inches with a hand hold shaved on the end. The completed oar was balanced on what was known as a head block, usually about 12 inches high, and pinned securely to the raft. The oar, when balanced, would be about 35 feet on the raft, with the remainder out over the water. A two inch hole went through the oar stem into the head block and a pin, usually made of oak, was driven through.

There were some scientific principles in the construction of an oar to give it the greatest efficiency, but much ignorance was practiced in their construction, consequently making the labor of guiding the raft much harder than it otherwise would have been, had the oar been properly constructed (Mitchell 30–1).

Rafting-in a Spar Raft

Once the spars and other requirements were at the landing, the raftsmen had to wait until the "ice went out" (broke up and flowed downstream) before they could start rafting-in. If the raftsmen built their rafts on top of the ice, the ice would take their rafts along when it went out, so when the ice went out great excitement occurred along the river at the landings. The raftsmen worked from first light to dark and through the weekends to build their rafts, so they could ride the spring freshets down the river before the rafting flood receded. They only had about two to three weeks before the water went down and they would have to wait for the next freshet, which may not come for another year.

Each spar had a face marked on it on the concave side while the tree was standing in the woods and once felled, tenons were cut at both ends perpendicular to the face side. One 90 foot spar contained about 304 cubic feet of green white pine that weighed almost 5.5 tons, and a ten spar half raft weighed almost 55 tons. Therefore, the rafts had to be built in the water, with the raftsmen wading in the ice cold water to lash the spars into the raft.

We don't know which end of the raft the raftsmen put upstream while rafting in a spar raft, but if the raft were going to have spars that were too short to fasten both ends into the raft (bobbers), then they probably constructed their raft with the butt ends upstream. They always lashed the butt end into the raft, because it was the heaviest end, and with the butt end upstream the current would help hold the spar in the raft.

They notched a lash pole several inches in from the end and rolled the first spar into the water, top end downstream. The spar was twisted so that the face was up and the convex side down in the water (belly down), with the tenons on both ends horizontal with the water's surface. This insured that the spar would lay straight in the water. (This is the information that proved difficult to find; O. Lynn Frank explained with a personal note and drawings.)

Then whiths were used to lash the spar to the lash pole by wrapping through one eye in the butt tenon and around the hickory lash pole about three or more times. (A whith was the green end of new growth hickory limbs about 10 to 12 feet long. The whiths were as strong as steel cables, and when soaked in the river water, held very tight.) Next a stake was driven down through the eye, compressing the whiths and holding the spar secure to the lash pole. The whiths, used to lash the end spar, were wrapped into the notch on the lash pole to prevent the whiths from slipping off the end of the lash poles. This pulled the lash pole down tight against the tenon.

Builders pushed the first spar out away from the shore to make room for the next spar. A second spar, with a rope tied to its butt end, was rolled into

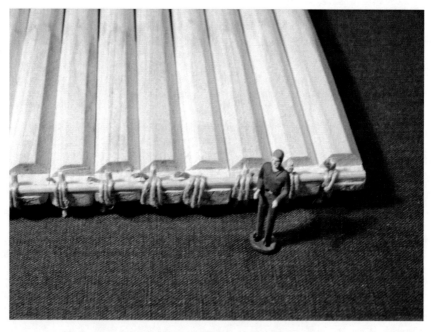

Butt end of a model pup spar raft. The left eyes on the butt ends of each spar were lashed to the lash pole with the whiths. The right eye was used to lash one pup raft to another when the raft had gone down the river far enough.

Top end of a model spar raft, with headblock and sweep or oar. Notice the bobber (a short spar), the fourth spar in from the right side of the raft. The model is 1:48 scale or one inch equals four feet.

the water, butt end upstream. Then the second spar was floated downstream past the first spar and pulled up into the raft. This method prevented the man lashing the spars into the raft from having to wade out into the deeper water. Remember there was a rafting flood and the water could be three to four feet deeper than normal. A pole was put down through one eye and the spar was rolled "belly down" in the water. The spar's butt end was lashed to the lash pole using the same eye as used by the first spar.

This was repeated until all ten spars were lashed onto the lash pole. Before the last spar was lashed down tight, the ten spars were drawn together firmly to give the raft the smallest width. With all spars belly down, the ten spars would take up the minimum width. Only trees with a slight bend in one direction were used for spars. Then the lash pole was notched to hold the end spar in place and the whith fastened. The top ends of the spars were fastened to a lash pole in the same way if the spar was long enough, using the one eye in the top end of the spar. Chutes were only 28 to 30 feet wide and there were 14 dams in the headwaters of the West Branch and seven more dams from Lock Haven to Port Deposit, Maryland (Mitchell 14).

The second spar half raft was made the same way, except at the butt end the opposite eye was used to lash the spar to the lash pole. Once down the river far enough to lash both spar half rafts together at the butt ends, one open eye on one half raft would be opposite another open eye on the other half raft. Whiths were wrapped through both opposing eyes, and a peg driven down through one eye hole, fastening the two half rafts together. Each spar half raft was fitted with a head block and oar for each end before they could "tie loose." A spar raft was 186 feet long, 28 feet wide and weighed about 110 tons.

Rafting-in a Square Timber Raft

The square timber stick had been marked with face up on the concaved side of the tree in the woods before felling and then chopped square with one side marked as the face. "A [square timber] raft was made up of a number of platforms, each platform consisting of from 16 to 20 sticks side by side, firmly held together by lash poles placed across their ends and fastened to them. The number of sticks used for a platform depended upon their size, but no more were used than enough to make the platform 27 feet wide" (Mitchell 27). The lash poles, which were usually made of hickory or white oak, sometimes of iron wood, were about 2½ inches thick at the small end, and 4 to 5 inches through at the large end (Mitchell 28).

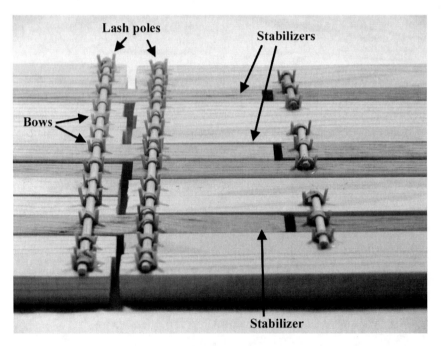

Coupling of a model square timber raft.

This picture, taken at Clearfield, Pennsylvania, in 1889, shows several square timber pup rafts or half rafts. The pup rafts were between 130 and 180 feet long and 26 feet wide. Below Clearfield the raftsmen coupled two pup rafts together end-to-end to make a raft about 300 feet long. Once through the dangerous Buttermilk Falls at the village of Cataract, two square timber rafts were coupled together side-by-side to form a fleet, about 52 feet wide and 300 feet long, weighing about 400 tons. These rafts were controlled with sweeps (courtesy Clearfield County Historical Society, Clearfield, Pennsylvania).

If the raftsmen wanted to make a raft 300 feet long with five platforms of 40, 50, 60, 70 and 80 foot long sticks, they started with the raft's last platform of 40 feet. The last platform in a square timber raft was usually the shortest one. They would first take three sticks from the 40 foot pile and put them with the 50 foot pile, and take three sticks from the 50 foot pile and move them to the 40 foot pile.

To start the builders would roll the first 40 foot sticks into the river. Using cant hooks, they would turn the stick face up (belly down) and attach the end of a lash pole to it. To attach the lash pole to the first stick a notch was made over the lash pole so a bow could fit into the notch. Then four 1¼ inch holes were bored into the stick, two on each side of the lash pole. Then two bows were laid over the lash pole and the ends were put down into the bored holes. Bows were made from only young white oak which was split about a ¼ inch thick and from 1 to 1¼ inch wide and about 20 inches long. The outside bow was fitted into the notch in the lash pole. Nine-inches-long 1¼ inch white ash square wooden pins were then driven into the holes that contained the ends of the bow until they held down the lash pole securely. The outside bow went into the notch on the lash pole, so it would prevent the bow from slipping off the lash pole.

A rope was fastened to the upstream end of a second 40 foot stick and it was rolled into the water and floated down past the first stick. Then the first stick was pushed out from the shore and the second stick was pulled up into the raft and turned face up, where it was fastened to the lash pole with two bows in the same manner as the first, except no notch was used. The third stick was 50 feet long and it was inserted into the raft in the same manner. Forty foot long sticks were added to the raft until they got to the middle of the raft, where another 50 foot stick was added. The 40 foot sticks were added until they had three sticks to complete the raft. Here they put in the last 50 foot stick and then the last two 40 foot sticks, making up the outer edge of the raft. All these sticks were double bowed.

Then all sticks in the platform were drawn together tightly to make sure the platform was less than 28 feet wide and the last bow was fitted into a notch in the lash pole to prevent slipping. A wedge was also driven into the small end of the lash pole in order to expand it and make it practically impossible for it to slip from the bows at that end. Then the downstream end was fastened using another lash pole. The two outside sticks received two bows each and the lash pole was notched to insure the bows wouldn't slip off the ends. The internal stick only received one bow each. This made one complete platform. The three sticks protruding ten feet ahead of the 40 foot platform were called by three names: couplers, stiffeners or stabilizers. Their functions will be discussed later.

The next platform to be rafted-in was the 60 foot platform and it would be constructed downstream of the 40 foot platform. The first 60 foot stick was tied with a rope, rolled into the water and floated down past the 40 foot platform and lashed to a lash pole just like the first 40 foot stick. It received two bows. The 60 foot platform was built 6 to 8 inches downstream from the 40 foot platform. The second stick was put into the 60 foot platform the same way, but only one bow was used. The third 60 foot stick was brought into the raft the same way, but the 50 foot stabilizer from the rear platform prevented the stick from being pulled the last ten feet. The stick was held a few inches from the stabilizer. The fourth stick was put into the raft like the first two sticks. Then the third stick was lashed into the raft by putting a short lash pole across the second, third and fourth sticks near the end of the third stick. One bow was used on each stick with a short lash pole being notched over the second and fourth sticks.

Then the long lash pole at the rear on the 60 foot raft was lashed down with two bows to the stabilizer from the rear (40 foot) raft. The raftsmen finished rafting-in, using the same procedures with the center and other side stabilizer. The bows on the three stabilizers acted as couplers. Going over a falls (riffles) or through a chute the bows on the stabilizer served as a hinge, giving the raft the flexibility needed. Also, the stabilizers sticking ten feet into the forward platform stiffened or stabilized the raft in rough water.

The 70 foot platform was added just like the 60 foot platform, but when they added the 80 foot platform, the stabilizers were not bowed down. The last platform was 50 feet and when they got to the stabilizers, they pulled in 40 foot sticks. This gave the raft's front an even look. The stabilizers between the 80 and 50 foot platforms were double bowed. Head blocks and sweeps were added to the raft's front end, the rear of the 80 foot platform, the front of the 70 foot platform and the rear of the raft. The head block made for the front end of the 70 foot platform was special. A squared timber was pegged down across the front ends of the three stabilizers and the sweep was mounted over the middle stabilizer.

When the raftsmen "tied loose," the 80 foot platform slipped free of the 70 foot platform and this became the front half raft. And the 40, 60 and 70 foot platforms became the rear half raft.

Downstream when the raftsmen wanted to couple the two half rafts together, they would slip the stabilizers from the 70 foot platform into the 80 foot platform and double bow the stabilizers into the 80 platform.

A square timber fleet was about 56 feet wide, 300 feet long and weighed about 560 tons. This made the fleet as long as a football field, from goal line to goal line, and about one third the width of the playing field.

Double Bowing

In both the front and rear ends of the rafts two bows were put in each stick, which was called "double bowed." This was also the practice in the two outside sticks on each side of the raft and in all stiffeners. When a raft was put together in this way, it was very strong. Early rafts were usually made about 220 to 250 feet long and up to 27 feet wide. Generally the rear platform was ten feet shorter than the front platform.

The length of timber sticks in the early days usually were from 30 to 60 feet, and a little later from 20 to 90 feet, and occasionally 100 foot sticks were made, but it is doubtful if a hundred foot platform ever went down the river. Mitchell says he once saw part of a platform made up of one hundred foot sticks (30–31).

On the Little Ditch, the part of river above Clearfield, usually only half rafts were run, commonly called "half lengths" or "pups." These were generally coupled together end to end at Lumber City Dam, Curwensville Dam and Clearfield, but some were run further down river before coupling. Once below Buttermilk Falls, 33 miles below Clearfield, two rafts were lashed side by side into what was called a fleet and run through the mountains to Lock Haven with a crew of 5. There was a pilot, in charge of the fleet, a steersman in charge of the rear oar and a crew of three.

Landing and Snubbing Rafts

An 80 foot rope, one and one quarter inches thick, was most commonly used for snubbing rafts in the earlier days when rafts were not made so large. But later an extra rope was usually taken along for safety.

To land a raft one man (a snubber) jumped ashore with the rope and ran down the stream until he found the first suitable tree, around which he would place the rope and take a hitch (a couple of wraps) with all possible haste, leaving the snubber with as much rope to play out as possible, but the raft was seldom stopped with one hitch (wrap). If the rope ran out on the snubber he was 80 to 100 feet behind the raft and would have to run down the shoreline to another tree and wait for the snubbing line to be thrown back to him. While the snubber was running down the shoreline the crew on the raft would pull the snubbing line aboard and get ready to toss the line to the snubber ashore. This took very quick, strenuous work, and often when one man would become tired, after making a couple of unsuccessful hitches, a fresh man would be sent from the raft to help. It was frequently the case that the first man sent out would become so exhausted from his extreme exertions that he could hardly scramble back onto the raft. There were a few cases where the landing was unsuccessful and the man sent out to do the snubbing was unable to get back and was left behind.

At some places landing posts were placed for the purpose of snubbing. These were very beneficial and made the landing much easier. At Lock Haven large piers or abutments were built out from the shore and posts built in them for landing purposes. In large landings where numbers of rafts were already landed, the snubbing was done by hitching to the other rafts, by running the ropes under the lash poles between the timber sticks. This was a very good way to land and often those already landed would help those coming in to the landing to tie fast. In the latter days of rafting much of the snubbing was done on the running rafts, and ropes were used as long as two hundred feet. One man was sent ashore with the end of the rope and took a firm hitch on a tree, post or raft, and the man on the raft would snub on a post driven into a three inch auger hole in one of the sticks of the raft. This post was usually about a foot long above the raft, made of hickory, and about five inches at the top. This made the landing much easier and safer, and it was particularly beneficial where two rafts were tied together in a fleet. It was considered safer on high water to uncouple the rafts in a fleet for the purpose of making an easier landing (Mitchell 32–3).

Rafting Shanties

Most raftsmen lived in shanties on rafts while going down the river. Shanties were usually 12 by 16 feet, and two to four feet high on the sides and had a comb roof. Sheet iron stoves were used for heating and cooking. Many raftsmen lived well. Ham was the principal meat and in the springtime eggs were plentiful and cheap. There was no place that ham smelled so good as while being cooked in a raftsman's shanty. In a large landing where a great number of rafts were tied up; the shanties gave the appearance of a village. Shanties were not built on all rafts, and you would hear, "Had it a shanty on it?" or "Was it a shanty raft?" (Mitchell 33).

Rafting-in a Round Log Raft

Rafting-in a round log raft was done the same as a square timber raft, with the exception that the sticks ware not squared, but were put into the raft face up and belly down to give the raft a minimum width to get through the smaller chutes.

Round log raft at Clearfield, Pennsylvania (courtesy Clearfield County Historical Society, Clearfield, Pennsylvania).

Log Slide Construction

Log slides were a means of getting the sawlogs down from the top of a mountain or hill or from deep in the forest to a stream bank for flushing when the log drive began. Many slides were over 10 miles long.

Building a slide through virgin forest was like building a road 16 foot wide. It was the job of the buck swamper to survey the land and determine where the slide and towpath would go. The towpath was where the horse team would walk while pulling the logs in the slide. Slides were planned to take advantage of gravity where available, and the towpath was off to one side where the horses were safe if the logs decided to continue down the slide on their own. The buck swamper marked both sides of the right of way and all trees within the right of way were cut. The pine was cut into 16, 14 or 12 foot lengths and set aside for taking out. The hemlock and hardwoods were left to be used in building the slide.

Slides were made from small hemlock with stump diameters of 14 to 20 inches. Hemlock was used because it brought a very low price. Often hemlock was peeled of its bark and the bark was used for tanning and the logs were left to rot in the woods. Slide timbers were cut in 10 foot lengths of 20, 30 or 40 feet. The slide was braced every 10 feet with cross members to prevent it from vibrating or trembling when logs slid over it. If the slide moved it would break the ice on the slide, causing a spot which was difficult to pull logs over. Cross members were made of short logs.

To make the slide ridge a man with a peavey or cant hook turned the slide logs, lining them up so that a 1½ inch auger could be drilled down through the slide timber into the cross member and pinned down with a white oak pin. To start building the slide, 2 slide timbers were chosen, one 10 feet longer than the other, and they were pinned down to the end cross member. When the builders got to the end of the shorter timber, a third timber was pinned to the same cross member, while the longer slide timber extended 10 feet beyond the shorter timber. In this manner one timber always spanned the cross member, making the joint between timbers more rigid and less likely to have ice break off the slide when in use.

Once the slide was in, two round logs ran its length. Then the broad axe hewers chopped away the inside of each log, making a V trough the length of the slide. To make the V, each side log was scored much like when making square timbers. Then axe men scored the logs about every 3 to 5 feet apart. The juggles were cut on an angle to form the V, not vertical like the square timber. The broad axe hewers chopped off the juggles, making a smooth trough. There are left and right handed broad axes with a blade 13 inches long and ground on one side, giving a flat surface to make a smooth cut on the other. A good hewer's work looked like the log had been run through a planer. He left no marks where one chop started and where the next chop had been made.

Before using the slide it was iced with a wooden barrel with skids fitted to the barrel and handles like a plow. The skids fit into the V notch and the barrel was hooked to the rear end of a log, while a horse team pulled the log and barrel along in the slide. Two ½ inch holes in the barrel top (now the rear end) sprayed water on the slide logs. This was usually done in December when it was below freezing. Repeated applications of water kept the slide working throughout the winter.

To use the slide several logs were loaded into it, a log grabber was hooked to the last log and a horse team pulled from the towpath. If gravity started moving the logs, the grabber was quickly disconnected and the logs were let go. Slides that had long downhill runs could be heard miles away when logs ran down the slide, knocking together like a giant bowling alley.

When the slide was frozen the men worked from dawn to dusk, but when the afternoons became too warm and the ice on the slide melted, log sliding was halted until after dark when the weather got cold enough to freeze it again. Then the water barrel came out to ice the slide again, and the men and horse teams would work through the night and next morning until the ice on the slide started to melt. Then the men and horses were rested until sundown, when they worked through that night. When the slide was used at night, logs were not stacked neatly at the landing, but just dumped there in a pile. This type of piling was called "rough and tumble landing" and required more space and more work when breaking the landing.

West Branch logs were branded as they were put into the landing, whereas John DuBois required his logs to be branded before they were put into the slide (R.D. Tonkin 169–191).

Glossary

This section on rafting terms is compiled from John H. Chatham (105–111) and M.J. Colcord (112–113) in French, R. Dudley Tonkin (267–271) and terms used in other sources for this work. Chatham lived in McElhattan, a village five miles downstream from Lock Haven. He was a poet, naturalist and a teacher who worked as a raftsman from Lock Haven to Columbia. He started in 1862 when he was fifteen and worked for twelve years, or until 1873, making four trips a year. M.J. Colcord, of Coudersport, editor and a former pilot, worked along the Sinnemahoning Creek about the same time that Chatham ran rafts to Columbia. R. Dudley Tonkin knew the upper reaches of the West Branch of the Susquehanna River. Together these men gave us a waterman's lexicon. The only disagreement I find in these three sources is in the use of the words "raftsman" or "raftman" and "raftsmen" or "raftmen."

Chatham said raftsmen was not the term used by the men engaged in the business of rafting. They were raftmen, and one was a raftman, the same as a boatman was a boatman, not a boatsman. In the earlier days, back from the river, where they traveled on foot to their respective homes, they were called "watermen." Raftsmen was always used above Lock Haven. Watermen was the only term used to describe arksmen and raftsmen in New York State. Chatham said they were all up-river men above Lock Haven, whether they came off the river at Clearfield or the Sinnemahoning, Moshannon or any of the creeks that emptied into the river or even its branches.

There were many peculiar terms in rafting parlance that are not known to the generation of today, and nearly forgotten by those of us who followed the river in the heyday of lumbering and rafting.

Algerian— A lumber thief. He usually went out at night and found stranded logs, sawed off the ends that were branded, put his own brand on the log, then pushed it out into the water. When it got to the boom and sawmill, he was given credit for the log. This was done mostly by families with connections to the judge, who made them pay for the log, if caught. If not caught, they collected the money for the stolen log (Huntley 354).

Bait— Loggers' term for food.

Batteau (or bateau)— French type of wooden boat used in log driving; it was poled.

Before the sun sets— At once between two days; night.

Big auger— Owner or high official in camp.

Bill raft— Raft timber made to certain sizes.

Black and white— A written agreement.

Boil up— Wash clothes; exterminate grey backs (body lice).

Boom— Cross member of the rigging of a vessel, i.e., yard arms to carry sails.

Boom— A system of long timbers fastened to timber cribs, filled with stone, to stop and hold logs.

Boom rats— Men and boys sorting logs out of a boom.

Boom scale— Footage of logs measured out of a boom.

Boot corks— Spikes in loggers' boots, like the bottom of golfers' shoes with calks.

Bows— Bows were made out of white oak, split after quartering and splitting the heart out of the blocks. After being hearted, they were split open from the center until the last split could be done with the hands, after starting it at the end with an axe. The last split was manipulated by the hand so that it did not split off at the side, and was done by pressing on the stronger piece in a bowed manner, letting the weaker one run in, and, if too much, then the other side was bent, thus making it come out at the other end of uniform thickness, which was about one-fourth of an inch.

Bowsprit— An octagon stick of timber extending forward from the bow of a vessel.

Broad axe— An axe with a 10- or 13-inch blade used in making square timber.

Bunks— Beds.

Called for time— Asked for statement of account when a logger is going out or leaving the job so he can get paid.

Chute— An opening with a timbered floor and side walls to carry water over or through a dam, with gates or splash boards to hold or release water.

Cubic-foot, per foot or ft.— Unit of measurement for raft square timber, equals 12 board feet.

Double trip— Running a half raft a certain distance, tying up and walking upstream to the other half, and running it to or below the first, to where the stream is large enough to carry the two half rafts coupled end to end as a full river raft.

Down Easter— Anyone born northeast of the Susquehanna River.

Driving camps— Stations and buildings along a stream to take care of an outfit in lieu of arks.

Driving hook— A lightweight peavey, i.e., with stock about two inches in diameter at the first iron clips.

Early morning latcher— A leather shoe with a metal fastener in lieu of shoestrings.

Face— The concaved side of a tree. This side was marked on the tree while it was still standing in the woods; when building a raft the stick was put into the raft face up or belly down.

Fleet— A fleet consisted of two rafts lashed side by side, and had therefore four oars. Rafts were run double after coming through the Lock Haven chute and were not necessarily separated until they got to Shamokin, which was a single chute, the same as at Lock Haven. From there on they were run double to Marietta. From Marietta to tidewater they were all run single.

Float— Several rafts (about four) piled one on top of the other to move from Port Deposit, Maryland, to Baltimore or Philadelphia. A chain was wrapped around the rafts and a steamboat towed them to market.

Floaters— Men engaged in towing and moving timber on bays, in canals, or on the ocean.

Gimlet— An officious, conceited man in camp.

Grey backs— Body lice. These bugs were the curse of bedroom arks and lumbering camp bedrooms.

Grouser— A stout skid inserted between the ends of timber sticks, to help stop the raft by skidding on the bottom of the stream.

Grouser hole— The grouser hole was made in a raft by putting in a shorter stick than the others in the platform by dropping the stick that butted against it and letting it project at the other end. The hole generally was from eighteen inches to two feet upward. The grouser was a large skid, ten or twelve feet in length, and all one man could handle alone, placed in the hole and shoved to the bottom, where it bit on the gravelly bottom and helped to retard the progress of the raft.

Grub— A white oak sapling cut with the bulge of the roots on. Used in board rafts, grubs were often made from ironwood saplings, when the white oak was not available, shaved down to fit auger holes, two inches, two and one-half inches or three inches, in the binding boards of a platform.

Halyards— Halyards were large hickory whiths twisted out of poles, and were in use in stopping rafts which were made smaller than in the days of ropes. They would be thrown out on the shores where the ends were grabbed, stood upon and dragged along. With the aid of the grouser the rafts were stopped.

Hat floated— Man that was in water over his head.

Headblock— The headblock consisted of a pine or oak timber used to support the oar or sweep. One was used at each end of every raft.

Hearth— The hearth consisted of five or six boards or slabs laid on the timber on the most level spot and about eight or ten inches of mud and sand were placed over them. When completed the fireplace was about five feet square. Hearths were built on rafts without shanties.

Hole in the water— Man to fall in. A spot where the water is over a man's head.

Hung, or hung up— Stopped.

Inspector— Name applied to men inspecting and measuring rafts at the market places.

Juggle— A 3 to 5 foot section chopped away by a hewer to make a log smooth.

Key log— The one log often holding the jam. If this log is released the whole jam will go out.

Landing— A place along a stream where spars, timbers or saw logs were stored until the spring freshets, when they could be moved downstream to market.

Lashpole— A pole placed cross-wise of a timber raft near the ends of the platforms, fastened with bows and pins.

Lead of the water— The area in a body of water where the current is the strongest.

Little ditch— Headwater of the West Branch of the Susquehanna River. The river above Clearfield, Pennsylvania.

Lobby hog— The combination doorman, porter, bellhop, chambermaid, laundry worker, lamp tender, and fireman in a logging camp.

Log brands— Identification marks or stamps on each end of a log, made with an eight to ten pound hammer.

Log drivers— Men who kept the logs moving in a stream and followed to release and start all stranded logs.

Log driving— Moving logs by water.

Log jam— A stoppage of the log drive in a stream.

Logging camp— A cabin or set of cabins to take care of men, teams, and equipment while cutting logs.

Manufacture— The process of making a tree into a spar, timber or saw log.

Muley saw— A water-powered up-and-down saw.

Oar blade— A plank about sixteen feet long and twenty inches wide, sawed thin at one end.

Oar stem— Body of a small tree, about forty-five feet long, tapering from two inches at the round hand hold to six inches at the outer end, which was mortised to hold the thick end of the blade.

Old salt— Deep sea sailor.

Old timer— Old logger or log driver.

Paper— Bankable or negotiable notes.

Paying the coat tail— Treating. The first trip a lad went down the river and through Conewago Falls, he was to treat all hands. If not, someone would cut one of his coat-tails. Raftmen wore frock coats.

Pilot— Commander of the raft or ark; manages the head oar and directs the work of the steersman.

Pin— One and one-half inch square ash piece of wood, nine inches long, driven into auger hole where bow has been placed, to tighten and hold same to lash pole.

Platform— One length of timber or boards. In timber it ran from twenty-five feet in length to eighty or ninety, according to the lengths of the trees cut. These lengths were looked after in the woods by the hewer, who saw to it that he did not make more than a platform, or enough for three or four platforms, all of the same length.

Pumped water out of him— Resuscitated a log driver.

Pup— A creek raft, built and run in creeks where there were too many turns for a large raft, or where the obstructions were too great for large timbers. They were run out to the larger streams, butted together at the end and lashed, thus making a full-length raft, with two useless oars in the center, hanging over and riding each other's raft. These sometimes were rigged up on the side of the raft and used to pull "headway" in the wind. This was resorted to only on special occasions. A "pair of pups" made up a full-raft. A raft was one lot of timber put into the usual form of rafting and equipped with oars, fore and aft.

Pushing Hands— Men working an oar on a raft, not the pilot or steersman.

Rafting-in— Building a raft.

Rainbow— To spring a peavey handle by lifting, i.e., evidence of energy applied.

Rear— The upstream end of a log drive, consisting of the boatman and his batteau with a pike pole and peavey man on each side of the stream; their duties are to follow the drivers and keep all slow moving logs in the stream flow. These four men are the highest paid within the outfit.

River raft— A raft 250 to 300 feet long.

Robber stick— Scale rule used by a man under-scaling logs, a dishonest scaler.

Rope—One and a fourth inch rope, fifty to seventy-five feet long, used to tie up rafts.

Run—To float a raft downstream.

Satchel stick—A slender stick over a logger's shoulder used to carry his belongings.

Saw log—A log usually sixteen feet long that was sawed into boards. They came in all lengths such as twelve, fourteen and twenty feet long, and usually were driven down the river on the spring freshets to the sawmill's boom.

Scoring—chopping notches into a log so a hewer can cut away the juggles between the scores to make a log smooth.

Scribner rule—A system of top diameter and length measurements to determine the average board foot content of a log, as used during the pine era on the Susquehanna.

Set—Go to work on a log job.

Shingle logs—Short or defective logs.

Skidding—Moving timber or logs a short distance.

Snub—A turn with the rope (tied to a lashpole) around a tree, stump or post on shore, one turn or two thrown around the rope, with all the slack possible taken up, hopefully to stop a raft.

Snubbing posts—Snubbing posts were of two kinds. One type was along the landing places, put in by the landlords and anchored with a pin through an auger hole at the bottom to prevent them from being pulled out. They were anchored posts. The other was a post with a square bottom fitted into a mortised timber stick on the raft and were much in use after raftmen began to use two hundred feet of rope or "line." The old ropes were only from seventy-five to eighty feet in length, and could not be used to as great an advantage as the longer ropes.

Spar—A white pine stick that was about ninety feet long or longer and had at least an eighteen inch diameter at the top. These spars were used to rig sailing ships.

Spindle—The tenon on the end of a spar. Used along the Sinnemahoning Creek.

Splash—Water released from a dam to create an artificial flood to drive arks, rafts or logs down the river.

Square timber—A stick that was made square after felling. The stick was not squared, but nearly squared, because it was allowed to have "wanes" on each corner. Wanes were two to four inches wide.

Stagged pants—Pants with eight or ten inches cut off the legs to keep a logger from tripping.

Steersman— Managed the rear oar; second in command of the raft.

Stick— A tree made into a spar, square timber or round log that would be part of a raft.

Stomach robber— A poor camp cook.

Stove— Used in either tense to designate disaster when a vessel hit obstructions; staved.

Thumbing— A drinking game played on rafts while running down river. A bottle of whiskey was placed alongside something on the raft, so that the contents were just one drink above the top of the object measured by. Some raftmen were quite expert in finding the proper height to leave a good, liberal supply above the thumb. Lower levels were continually needed as the game progressed.

Thundergust mill— A water-powered mill that could only run after a rain shower.

Tie loose— Unfasten the rope or halyard that holds a raft in place.

Tied on— Go to work on the drive.

Timber brand— Initials or characters made on the top of raft timber with a hammer, to denote ownership.

Top loading— When a raft was completed, whatever number of sticks were left over were rolled onto the raft or floated alongside of it. A rope was tied to the lashpole, the other end slipped under the timber stick and a skid rammed under the stick, and the stick held in place by the rope with two or three men holding it. The man with the skid pried it with his "purchase" on the edge of the raft, lifted it out of the water enough that the man on the rope could roll it in the rope and thus place it on the raft. Skids reaching nearly across the raft were laid and the timber on the skids apportioned, thus making the weight of the raft uniform on the entire platform. If it was a board raft or scantling raft, the lumber was simply piled on top, with skid bottoms sometimes.

Turn in— Go to bed in camp.

Turn out— Up in the morning, individual.

Turn out— Orders of camp boss, at lobby door, to go to work.

Wane— Round of a timber stick. In measuring, the wane on one side of the upper surface is not counted. The portion that lacks filling the square of the stick.

Whiskey boats— Whiskey boats were simply skiffs used through the entire length of the river by what we might call "whiskey runners." Operatives of these skiffs found a good eddy where they could sit in their boats without mooring them, and each boat was provisioned with whiskey, bread, pies, cakes and eggs. If the operative was onto his job, he carried these provisions; if he wasn't, he only carried the whiskey. Sober men would buy a tiny cup of whiskey, place it on the raft and drink at leisure; drunks bought their whiskey by the coffee pot full.

White water— Churning, foaming water below dams, falls, rocks, or obstructions.

Whiths— Green hickory branches off the ends of limbs, new growth. Used to lash spar rafts together.

Widow maker— Broken branches or limbs suspended over workmen, creating a hazard.

Works Cited

Adams, Joseph. *Account of Huntingdon County*. Philadelphia: Historical Society of Pennsylvania, 1853.

Africa, J. Simpson. *History of Huntingdon and Blair Counties, Pennsylvania*. Philadelphia: Louis H. Everts, 1883.

Ames, Alfred. *From the Stump to Ship* (video). Orono, Maine: University of Maine at Orono, 1985.

Beck, John S. "Lumber Rafting on Big Pine Creek." *The Journal of the Lycoming Historical Society*, Vol. 1, No. 6, November 1957.

Biddlecombe, George. *The Art of Rigging*. New York: Dover, 1848.

Brubaker, Jack. *Down the Susquehanna to the Chesapeake*, University Park: Pennsylvania State University Press, 2002.

Caldwell's Atlas of Clearfield County, 1878.

Campbell, Thomas. "Gertrude of Wyoming." *Voices from 19th-century America, 1809*. Web 31 March 2009. www.merrycoz.org/adults.htm.

Carey, Mathew, and J. Bioren. *Laws of the Commonwealth of Pennsylvania*, 6 vols. Philadelphia: J. Bioren, 1803.

Carmer, Carl. *The Susquehanna*. Rinehart, 1955.

Carr, Kurt W., Douglas C. McLearen, James Herbstritt, and Andrea Johnson. "The Pennsylvania Dugout Canoe Project." *Pennsylvania Heritage*, Fall 2006.

Carrol, Charles F. *Wooden Ships and American Forest*, date unknown.

Casler, Walter C. *Tionesta Valley*, book number 8 in the series *Logging Railroad Era of Lumbering in Pennsylvania*. Published by the author, 1973.

Chase, Emily. "Gateway to First Industrial Center." *Clearfield Progress*, July 18, 1955.

Conrad, Bertha. *Excerpts from Bertha Conrad's Diary and Two Photographs of the Women*. Donated to the Clearfield Historical Society by the Hiller Family of Houtzdale, April 1893.

Cox, Thomas R. "The Diary of William Langdon for 1855: A Pennsylvania Lumberman Raftsman's Year." *Journal of Forest History*, July 1982.

Cramer, Hiram M., and Thomas R. Cox (ed.). "Harvesting the Hemlock: The Reminiscences of a Pennsylvania Wood-Hick." *Western Pennsylvania Historical Magazine* Vol. 67, No. 21, date unknown.

Dallas, A. J. *Laws of the Commonwealth of Pennsylvania*, Vols. I and III, 1795 and 1797.

Down the Susquehanna: A Merry Lot of Ladies and Gentlemen from Up the River Take a Pleasure Trip. Raftsman's Journal, Clearfield, April 1893.

Dunaway, Wayland Fuller. *A History of Pennsylvania*. New York: Prentice Hall, 1946.

Dunkelberger, George. *The Story of Snyder County*. Selinsgrove, Pa.: Snyder County Historical Society, 1948.

Ellis, Franklin, and Austin N. Hungerford. *History of that Part of the Susquehanna and Juniata Valleys, Embraced in the Counties of Mifflin, Juniata, Perry, Union and Snyder, in the Commonwealth of Pennsylvania*, in two volumes, Philadelphia: Peck & Richards, 1886.

Evans, Oliver. *The Young Millwright and Miller's Guide*. Philadelphia, by author, 1795.

Fahr, Marian. "A View from Karthaus." *Clearfield Progress*, undated.

Fox, William F. *History of the Lumber Industry in the State of New York*. New York: Harbor Hill, 1901.

Frank, O. Lynn. *The Early Settlement and Water Transportation Era, Rafting, Canals, and Log Drives in Pennsylvania.* Clearfield, published by the author, 2002.

_____. *80 Miles of Wilderness Adventure.* Clearfield, published by the author, 1970.

_____. *History of Timber Rafting and the Settlement, Log Drives, and Rafting Points on the West Branch of the Susquehanna River* (slide presentation) Clearfield, 1999.

_____. *Left Bank, Right Bank: The Reenactment Raft* (video). Penn State University, 1976.

French, John C., et al. *Rafting Days in Pennsylvania.* Altoona: Times-Tribune, 1922. Contents:

"Pennsylvania's Forest Needs are Urgent Now," by J. Herbert Walker.

"Rafting Tales Give Glimpse of Lumbering Days of Years Ago," by John C. French.

"Susquehanna Rafting Surpasses Other Streams," by John H. Chatham.

"Rafting Days on the Susquehanna's North Branch," by John C. French.

"Rafting Days Across the Atlantic Ocean," by John C. French.

"Rivermen Were a Carefree Lot," by John C. French.

"Allegheny River Rafting Days and Rafting Tales," by John C. French.

"Forest Lore of Rafting Days on the Delaware," by John C. French.

"Clarion River was Famous Rafting Stream of Keystone," by John C. French.

"Bubbles on Water Good Sign of Rafting Time," by M. J. Colcord.

"Running Arks on the Famous Karoondinha," by A. D. Karstetter.

"Glossary of Rafting Terms."

"Appearance and Customs of Early Raftmen," by John H. Chatham.

"11,233 Board Feet a Day," by anonymous.

Frysinger, George. "Water Street in Arking Days." *The Sentinel,* Lewistown, Pa., March 28 and April 22, 1931.

"George Washington and Jefferson National Forest." *The Historic Iron and Charcoaling Industries in Virginia's Shenandoah Valley,* 18 August 2006. Web 31 March 2009. www.fs.fed.us/r8/gwj/cultural/pig_iron/index.shtml.

Gilliland, Harry T. *History of Karthaus Township and Vicinity from 1815,* paper from the Harold D. Woolridge collection, undated, early 1920s.

Glaze, Olive Aucker. "Rafting on the Susquehanna River." *Snyder County Historical Society Bulletin,* Vol. 2, No. 5, 1943. Presented before the society, December 17, 1943.

Gould, Jay. *History of Delaware County, New York.* Roxbury, N.Y.: Keeny and Gould, 1856.

Hall, Asaph B. *Rafts on the River. The Chemung Historical Journal,* Elmira, New York, Vol. 22, No. 4, June 1977.

Hall, Elizabeth Lowman. "Lowman's Love Letters." *The Chemung Historical Journal,* Elmira, New York, Vol. 22, No. 4, June 1977.

Hanlon, Howard A. *The Ball-Hooter.* New York: Prospect Books, 1960.

Hollingsworth, Levi. *Correspondence, Hollingsworth Papers 1789–1827,* Historical Society of Pennsylvania, Philadelphia.

Host, Mel (reproduced photographs) and Smith, Elmer L. (compiler and editor). *Logging in the Pennsylvania North Woods,* Lebanon, Pa.: Applied Arts Publishers, 1969.

Humes, James C. "The Susquehanna Boom: A History of Logging and Rafting on the West Branch of the Susquehanna River." *Now and Then: A Quarterly Magazine of Muncy Historical Society,* October 1962.

Hunter, Brooks. "Wheat, War, and the American Economy During the Age of Revolution." *The William and Mary Quarterly,* July 2005.

Huntley, George William, Jr. *A Story of the Sinnemahone.* Williamsport Printing and Binding, 1936.

Kahler, Clark. "Lumbering Days." *Journal of the Lycoming Historical Society,* Vol. 2, No. 3, Summer 1961.

Kelly, Richard. "Rafters or, Dancing Over the Columbia Dam," *Lancaster News,* June 21, 1872.

Kelso, Fred. *Port Deposit Collections: Trade and Commerce.* Pamphlet, 1952.

Kephart, Cyrus Bishop. "The Biography of Bishop Cyrus Kephart," 12 pages in James Mitchell, *Lumbering and Rafting.*

King, Samuel A. "A Log Drive to Williamsport in 1868." *Quarterly Journal of the Pennsylvania Historical Association,* Vol. 29, No. 2, April 1962.

_____. *Twenty-five Oral Histories of Men Who Worked in the Lumbering and Rafting Industry,* unpublished, Clearfield, Pa., 1963–4. Contents:

Beck, Coss, age 90, of Mt. Pleasant, Elk County, Pa. May 16, 1964.

Berkey, Charles, age 87, of Penfield, Pa. March 26, 1964.

Byers, Billy, age 90, of Mahaffey, Pa. April 22, 1964.

Cathcard, Jess C., age 82, of Olanta, Pa. April 17, 1964.

Connors, Levi "Bud," age 88, of Glen Campbell, Pa. April 4, 1964.

Crittenden, Arthur T., age 86, of Coudersport, Pa. June 14, 1964.

Dickey, Bill, age 91, Hepburnia, Pa., with Jim Rafferty, age 85, April 1, 1964.

Dunlap, Luther V., age 84, and wife, of Olanta, Pa. May 29, 1964.

Foster, Joe, age 90, of Red Hill, Weedville, Pa. May 1, 1964.

Himes, Ruban La Verne, age 87, of Brookville, Pa. April 27, 1964.

Johns, Bert, age 78, of DuBois, Pa. May 4, 1963.

Keenan, Mike C., age 79, of DuBois, Pa., with Earl Mix. May 11, 1964.

Kepler, William W., age 84, of Sinnemahoning, Pa. May 27, 1964.

Klingensmith, Albert "Bees," age 84, of Callensburg, Pa. April 28, 1964.

Koozer, Alfred, age 84, of Clearfield, Pa. June 10, 1964.

Mason, Mr. and Mrs. John W., age unknown, of Sterling Run, Pa. June 11, 1964.

Menzie, Freeman, age 71, of DuBois, Pa. June 12, 1964.

Miller, Clarence J., age 88, of Sterling Run, Pa. June 11, 1964.

Ober, R.C., age 73, Wyside, Sinnemahoning, Pa. undated.

Rafferty, James, age 84, of Grampian, Pa. March 22, 1964.

Ranson, "Granpa" Edwin, age 92, of Falls Creek, Pa. September 9, 1962, and May 4, 1963.

Shawkey, Oscar, age 87, of Sigel, Pa. July 10, 1963.

Whitcomb, Harry of Dents Run, Pa. April 20 and May 28, 1964.

Wingert, John, age 95, of Luthersburg, Pa. April 14, 1964.

Wrigley, Maurice, age 81, of Clearfield, Pa. June 10, 1964.

Kline, Benjamin F., Jr. *Dinkes, Dams and Saw Dust,* book number 12 in the series *Logging Railroad Era of Lumbering in Pennsylvania,* published by the author, 1975.

_____. *Pitch Pine and Prop Timber: The Logging Railroads of South-Central Pennsylvania,* published by the author, 1971.

_____. *"Wild Catting" on the Mountain: The History of the Witmer and Steel Lumber Company,* book number 2 in the series *Logging Railroad Era of Lumbering in Pennsylvania,* published by the author, 1970.

Kuhlmann, Charles B. *The Development of the Flour Milling Industry in the United States.* Boston and New York: Houghton and Mifflin, 1929.

Laepple, G. Wayne. "The Last Raft." Sunbury *Daily Item,* June 17, 2004.

Langdon, William. *The Diary of William Langdon 1855.* Harrisburg: Pennsylvania State Archives, unpublished.

Larson, Agnes M. *History of the White Pine Industry in Minnesota.* University of Minnesota Press, 1949.

Lever, Darcy. *The Young Sea Officer's Sheet Anchor; or a Key to Leading of Rigging and to Practical Seamanship.* Dover Publications, 1998, originally published 1819.

Linn, John Blair. *Annals of Buffalo Valley, Pennsylvania 1755–1855.* Harrisburg, Pa.: Lane S. Hart, 1877.

Livingood, James Weston. *The Philadelphia–Baltimore Trade Rivalry 1780–1860*. Harrisburg: Pennsylvania Historical and Museum Commission, 1947.

Magee, D. F. "Rafting on the Susquehanna." *Lancaster County Historical Society*, Vol. 24, No. 9, 1920, pp. 193–202.

McCullough, Robert, and Walter Leuba. *The Pennsylvania Main Line Canal*. York, Pa.: American Canal and Transportation Center, 1973.

McGovern, William J. "Rafting on the West Branch: A Fateful Trip Recalled." *Clearfield Times*, 1938.

_____. "A Rafting Trip on the West Branch One Hundred Twenty Years Ago." *Clearfield Times*, 1938.

_____. "Rafting Trips on the West Branch." *Clearfield Times*, 1938.

McGrain, John W. *Grist Mills in Baltimore County*. Typescript, Maryland Historical Society, 1980.

McIlnay, Dennis P. *Juniata, River of Sorrows: One Man's Journey Into a River's Tragic Past*. Hollidaysburg, Pa.: Seven Oaks Press, 2003.

Meginness, John F. *History of Lycoming County*. Chicago, 1892.

Meyer, Henry, *Genealogy of the Meyer Family*. Cleveland, Ohio: Lauer and Mattill, 1890.

Miller, Alice. *History of Cecil County Maryland*. Date unknown.

Missimer, Hortense D. "Rafting on the Old Susquehanna." *Journal of the Lancaster County Historical Society*, Vol. 95, No. 2, Spring 1993.

Mitchell, James. *Lumbering and Rafting*. self-published, 1922.

Namowitz, Samuel N., and Nancy E. Spaulding. *Earth Science*. Lexington, Mass.: D.C. Heath, 1985.

Near, Irvin W. *A History of Steuben County, New York and Its People*, Vol. 1. Chicago: Lewis, 1911.

Noll, W. C., W. M. Gamble, J. B. Smyth, and M. Y. Shuster. *Historical Renovo*. Published by the Committee on Printing and Advertising, Renovo, 1908.

Officer, Lawrence H. "Dollar-Pound Exchange Rate from 1791," *Measuring Worth*, 2008. Web 1 April 2009. www.measuringworth.org/datasets/exchangepound/result.php#.

Palmer, Tim. *Rivers of Pennsylvania*. Keystone Books, Pennsylvania State University Press, 1980.

Pike, Robert E. *Tall Trees, Tough Men*. New York: W. W. Norton, 2000.

Pippin, Bill. *Wood Hick, Pigs-Ears and Murphy: The Historical Story of Galeton, Pennsylvania and Surrounding Area*. State College, Pa.: Jostens, 1976.

"Rafting in Olden Times." *Public Press*, Northumberland, Pa., Feb. 17, 1893.

Ringwalt, John Luther. *Development of Transportation Systems in the United States*. Philadelphia, 1888.

Row, S. B. *Clearfield County: Or, Reminiscences of the Past*, 1859. State College, Pa.: Commercial Printing, reprinted 2000.

Rung, Albert M. *Rung's Chronicles of Pennsylvania History*. Huntingdon Daily News 1949–1951.

_____. *Rung's Chronicles of Pennsylvania History, Vol. 2*. Reprint of 200 columns, Huntingdon Daily News, 1951–1957.

Russell, Charles Edward. *A-Rafting on the Mississippi*. New York: Century, 1928.

Scott, George A. *Clearfield, Today and Tomorrow: Railroads of the Area*. Self-published. Undated.

_____. "Lumbering Industry of the 1800s...." *Clearfield Progress*, Clearfield, Pa., July 31, 1987, p. 4.

_____. "Rafting and Logging are Legendary on the Susquehanna in Clearfield." *Clearfield Progress*, Clearfield, Pa., June 13, 1991, p. 22.

Seaver, James E. *A Narrative of the Life of Mrs. Mary Jemison*. North Haven, Conn.: Linnet, 1990.

Seeley, Ralph. *Great Buffalo Swamp: A Trail Guide and Historical Record for the Quehanna Plateau and the Moshannon State Forest*. Karthaus, Pa.: Quehanna Area Trails Club HCI, 1887.

Shank, Ellsworth B. "Navigation of the Lower Susquehanna River." *Harford Historical Bulletin* No. 30, Harford County, Maryland, Fall 1986.

Shank, William H. *The Amazing Pennsylvania Canals.* York, Pa.: American and Transportation Center, 1960.

Sharrer, George Terry. *Flour Milling and the Growth of Baltimore, 1783–1830.* Ph.D. diss., University of Maryland, 1975.

Sherrill, Richard James. "The Tidewater Canal: Harford County's Contribution to 'The Canal Era.'" *Harford Historical Bulletin* No. 58, Harford County, Maryland, Fall 1993.

Shively, J. G. "Navigation on Penns Creek." *Millmont Times,* Union County, Pa, 1963.

_____. *The Lumber Industry in Northumberland County.* Northumberland County Historical Society, 1955. Presented before the society March 11, 1955.

_____. *The Pennsylvania Canal.* Northumberland County Historical Society, 1968. Presented before the society October 9, 1968.

"Stories from PA History: Chapter Four, The Pennsylvania Turnpike-Story Details." *ExplorePAHistory.com.* undated. Web February 25, 2005. www.matrix.msu.edu/~expa/expa/story.php?storyId=10&chapter=5.

Stranahan, Susan Q. *Susquehanna, River of Dreams.* Baltimore, Md.: Johns Hopkins University Press, 1993.

Strong, Schuyler S. *A Voyage Down the Susquehanna River: Spring 1838.* From eleven articles in the Bath, New York, *Plaindealer* of March to May 1887.

Swetnam, George. "On The Trail of Cherry Tree Joe." *Lycoming College and the Pennsylvania Folklore Society,* Vol. 7, No. 1, Spring 1962.

Taber, Thomas T. III. *Ghost Lumbering Towns of Central Pennsylvania.* Book number 3 in the series *Logging Railroad Era of Lumbering in Pennsylvania,* published by the author, 1970.

_____. *The Goodyears, an Empire in Hemlock.* Book number 5 in the series *Logging Railroad Era of Lumbering in Pennsylvania,* published by the author, 1971.

_____. *Sunset Along Susquehanna Waters.* Book number 4 in the series *Logging Railroad Era of Lumbering in Pennsylvania,* published by the author, 1972.

_____. *Williamsport Lumbering Capital.* Published by the author, 1995.

Theiss, Lewis Edwin. "Lumbering and Rafting on the West Branch." Northumberland County Historical Society, 1999. Presented before the society August 9, 1950.

Tonkin, Joseph Dudley. *The Last Raft.* Published by the author in Harrisburg, 1940.

Tonkin, R. Dudley. *My Partner, the River: The White Pine Story on the Susquehanna.* University of Pittsburgh Press, 1958.

W.S.W. "A Letter from Marietta." *Raftsman's Journal,* Clearfield, Pa., May 27, 1857.

Wackerman, A. E, W. D. Hagenstien, and A. S. Michell. *Harvesting Timber Crops.* New York: McGraw-Hill, 1966.

Weatherford, Jack Mclver. *The History of Money.* New York: Crown, 1997.

Welsh, Peter Corbell. *The Brandywine Mills 1742–1815.* University of Delaware, 1956.

Whitford, Noble E. *History of the Canal System of the State of New York, Together with Brief Histories of the Canals of the United States and Canada, Vol. I. Supplement to the Annual Report of the State Engineer and Surveyor of the State of New York.* Albany, N.Y.: Brandow, 1906. Web 30 March 2009. www.history.rochester.edu/canal/bib/whitford/1906/contents.html.

William Penn Museum. *Video of the Last Raft, 1938.* Harrisburg, Pa.

Wood, Richard G. *A History of Lumbering in Maine, 1828–1861.* Orono, Maine: University of Maine at Orono, 1971.

Yates, Thomas. *Charts of the Susquehanna River,* 1850 and 1852.

Index

An act declaring the Penns Creek a public highway to the mouth of Sinking Creek (Spring Mills), Pennsylvania 1792 31

An act declaring the river Canisteo (New York State) a public highway, NY 1800 44

An act declaring the river Susquehanna, and other streams therein mentioned, public highways, for improving the navigation of the said river and streams, and preserving the fish in same, Pennsylvania 1771 11, 12, 30, 33

An act declaring the river Susquehanna and several of its tributaries common or public highways, Pennsylvania 1799 (a reiteration of the act of 1771) 24

An act to allow the improvement of creeks and rivulets, Pennsylvania 1871 170, 171

An act to authorize Alan Hamaker to re-build a mill-dam over Swatara, at the place lately occupied for that purpose, Pennsylvania 1793 32

An act to authorize Simon Snyder, and the heirs of Anthony Selin, deceased, to erect a dam on Penn's Creek, in the county of Northumberland, under the limitations and provisions therein pre-scribed, Pennsylvania 1793 32

An act to band import of staples from Pennsylvania, Maryland 1704 9

Act to prevent the exportation of bread and flour not merchantable, and for re-pealing, at a certain time, all the laws heretofore made for that purpose, Pennsylvania 1781 13

Act to prevent the exportation of bread and flour not merchantable, Pennsylvania 1700 9

Act to require inspection of bread and flour not merchantable for exportation, Pennsylvania 1724–25 9

Algerian 156

Allegheny River 188, 189, 191

ark 20–24, 26, 27, 30–41, 43–58, 60, 67, 80, 83–85, 92, 97, 98, 110, 116, 154, 156, 162–164, 166, 188, 193–195, 198; con-struction 20, 31, 39, 40, 80, 163, 193

Baltimore 9, 11, 13–16, 17–20, 23–25, 27, 31, 33–35, 37, 39, 41, 43–50, 53–55, 73, 96, 97, 195

baseball 179, 181, 182

bateaux 162, 166

Bloom, Abe 182

brands (logs) 151, 155, 162–165, 168

broad axe 124, 151, 157, 202, 203, 216

Buttermilk Falls, North Branch 64, 65, 82

Buttermilk Falls, West Branch 50, 51, 110, 120, 127, 128, 139, 142, 163, 213

Campbell, Ambrose 160, 173, 175, 185

Campbell's Rock 66

canal feeder dams: Chemung 43–45, 55; Columbia 80, 82, 83, 80, 82–84, 100, 103, 117; Green's 89–91, 116, 120; Lock Haven 49–51, 55; Muncy 56, 100, 116, 120; Nanticoke 66–68, 81, 82; Shamokin 34, 55, 56, 68, 69, 81–83, 84–86, 116, 120, 125, 126

canals 26, 47, 48, 50, 54, 55, 75, 84, 125, 170

Cherry Tree Joe 123, 134–137, 139, 140

Childs, Len 185

chutes 12, 32–34, 54–56, 62, 66, 67, 69, 80, 84, 85, 89–92, 103, 110, 115, 116, 121, 125, 126, 138, 142, 147, 154, 166, 198, 212

Clearfield 49, 51, 110–114, 117, 123, 128, 132–134, 137, 139, 141–143, 153, 155, 159, 163, 168, 171, 172

Columbia (town) 21, 22, 24, 46, 47, 49, 51 54, 55, 70, 72, 74, 77, 82, 84, 92, 95, 97, 100, 101, 103, 104, 107, 117, 126, 132, 136

Conestoga wagons 7, 8, 15, 17, 20–25

Conewago Falls 14, 34, 35, 47, 57, 71, 72, 82, 84, 92, 94, 96, 116

Cryder, Michael 17, 25

Dent, Miles 165, 184

DuBois, John 151–153, 156, 158, 159, 161, 162, 164–169, 172

Durham boats 7, 17, 19, 30–32, 68

Gallows Harbor 123, 141, 142, 149

Gowdy, Big Bob 185–187